RICHARD PAUL HUDSON

CYBERTWISTS
HACKING AND CYBERATTACKS EXPLAINED

Published by Richard Paul Hudson, Am Steinbruch 3,
83565 Tegernau, Federal Republic of Germany

Production and printing: On-Demand Publishing LLC, 100 Enterprise Way, Suite A200, Scotts Valley, CA 95066, United States
and Amazon Media EU S.à r.l., 5 Rue Plaetis, L-2338, Luxembourg

Set in Cardo by David Perry, Lato by Łukasz Dziedzic
and Anonymous Pro by Mark Simonson

Cover design: Lisa Schötz and André Ihme
Cover background image: Copyright madmaxer/123RF Stock Photo

Interior sketches: André Ihme

Author photograph: Ralph Hawranke

ISBN: 1981885706

ISBN-13: 978-1981885701

CONTENTS

PREFACE

Hardly a month goes by without hacking and cyberattacks making it to the daily news headlines. Data is stolen from multinational corporations and published on the internet; nation states accuse one other of cyberespionage; and a single ransomware worm suddenly halts the daily business of millions of individuals, businesses and governments across the globe. News bulletins are not the right place to explain these events in detail. The technical background is inevitably glossed over, leaving current-affairs audiences with no more than a nebulous notion that it must somehow be possible to make computer systems behave differently from how their designers intended. The unspoken implication behind the lack of clarification is that cyberattacks must be so complicated that only experts have any real hope of grasping how they work.

At the other end of the spectrum are those whose lives revolve around computer security: criminal and government-sponsored hackers on the one hand and the information technology professionals tasked with protecting systems from those hackers on the other. These groups speak their own language, and in many cases they revel in it. They are also the intended audience of most books that set out to explain hacking and cyberattacks. Typically, whenever a book goes into any technical detail at all, it ends up covering so much ground that the reader who works his way through to the end will have already begun to amass some of the skills of the information security professional or active hacker.

Cybertwists aims to fill some of the vast middle ground between these two poles. It was written on the premise that it is very much possible to explain a cyberattack so that the reader gets a solid idea of what is going on, but without covering the minutiae of what the hacker types into his computer. A relatively high-level approach makes more sense anyway. The precise details of a hack are often only relevant to specific and short-lived technologies or systems, while the underlying principles have an essentially timeless application.

Although somebody is certainly likely to do a better job of protecting his own systems once he understands how the main types of cyberattack work, the aim of this book is not training in the practice of computer security. *Cybertwists* is not an instruction manual. It is rather rooted in the tradition of popular science treatises familiar from fields like biology, physics and astronomy. Focussing as much on hacks that are the preserve of secret services and governments as on crimes committed by private individuals, it seeks to provide an overview of an area of knowledge that is both increasingly relevant to society and inherently interesting. There is something genuinely fascinating about many aspects of hacking theory and practice, especially when they are considered in their political and historical contexts.

Cybertwists is intended both for the general reader and for the information technology professional looking for an introduction to the security field. The fact that the book has more than one target audience has sometimes posed dilemmas as to how much knowledge to assume, which words to clarify and which concepts to take as given. Apologies are offered to anybody who feels that the starting points for some of the discussions are unnecessarily basic, but consistent and uncompromising priority has been given to the needs of the reader with no prior knowledge of computing. Anyone can skip over an explanation he does not require, while leaving a basic term or idea unexplained risks leaving a section of readers behind.

On the one hand, *Cybertwists* contains conceptual descriptions of cyberattacks and the technology they target. Although the depictions stick to everyday language, they still go into sufficient detail to provide a real understanding of how things work. On the other hand, the narrative covers notable hacking events that have hit the headlines. The book is a continuous monograph, intended to be read from cover to cover, in which the current affairs items illustrate the technical concepts. However, it is also designed to allow readers to focus on one or other of the two aspects. The computer professional who is looking for a summary of how Tor and Bitcoin work can consult the relevant sections in isolation. At the same time, somebody who is more interested in the accounts of specific hacks may well choose to skip some of the more technical descriptions and should nonetheless remain able to enjoy the anecdotes that follow them.

The book is divided into five chapters, each of which views the world of cybersecurity from a different angle. Chapter I, *Secrets*, describes the various encryption methods used to obscure information as well as techniques that have been applied to reveal what other people had tried to hide. Chapter II, *Programs*, considers cyberattacks that are based around computer software. It looks both at malware, which is software specifically designed to perform cyberattacks, and at the exploitation of unintended loopholes in existing, legitimate programs. Chapter III, *Identities*, explains the various ways in which systems verify who their users are. It examines the limits and weaknesses of available authentication technology and how these can enable attackers to pose as other people.

Chapter IV, *Messages*, starts by describing hacks that are based around the internet communications infrastructure. It then goes on to discuss both the methods that some internet users employ in an attempt to hide their locations and the counter-techniques used by law enforcement authorities to unmask those users. It also explains blockchain and Bitcoin. Finally, Chapter V, *Objects*, is concerned with the interplay of the cyberworld with the concrete world. This encompasses physical hacks that can be carried out on computers in the vicinity, as well as physical damage caused by cyberattacks within the Internet of Things and in the context of cyberwar.

The discussion is mainly descriptive and objective. In the later chapters, however, some passages take on a more prescriptive tinge. This is not without reason. While it is possible to treat hacked game consoles and viral tweets from the vantage point of the disimpassioned and sometimes amused observer, it would not be right to describe the worst abuses of internet untraceability or to weigh up the risk that nuclear weapons might fall victim to cyberattacks without proposing some solutions at the same time.

Warning to the reader

Any book that sets out to describe cyberattacks and hacking inevitably involves the discussion of illegal and unethical behaviour. This has a purely illustrative purpose. The author has gone to his utmost care to avoid including any information or ideas that are not generally known or available elsewhere and that might inadvertently assist criminals or terrorists. In no way does he condone or encourage any of the illicit techniques that this book describes. They may make for captivating reading, but that does not make it morally right to carry them out.

Because *Cybertwists* is not a manual, it is unlikely to furnish you with the skills necessary to mount a successful hacking attack anyway. However, it could conceivably provide you with just enough information to try and to get caught in the process. Readers are strongly advised that hacking and attempted hacking are serious offences in most jurisdictions. You should expect them to have severe consequences under both criminal and civil law. However trivial some of the techniques described in this book may seem, performing them for real can still land you with a long prison sentence. If you do fancy trying out any of the methods under discussion, there are several websites that have been set up for the sole purpose of enabling hackers to hone their skills legally. Over and above that, stop reading right now unless you are confident in your ability to keep your fingers under control. You have been warned!

Notes on language

Cybertwists is intended for an international audience, while the author is a native speaker of British English. Publishing a separate U.S. version of the book would have eliminated the risk of irritating American readers used to their own variety of the language, but it would also have warped the author's voice. In the worst-case scenario, a U.S. version would have ended up consisting of nondescript turns of phrase characteristic of nowhere and served up with American spelling. Instead, this single edition essentially uses the UK standard, but care has been taken to avoid some of the more arcane examples of Britspeak. American readers may well still be surprised by some expressions—hopefully pleasantly so—but it is sincerely hoped that they will nonetheless always remain able to follow the discussion.

Anyone writing English non-fiction and making use of examples and thought experiments is faced with the problem of choosing between two sets of third-person pronouns, based on *he* and *she*, that specify that the referent is male or female respectively. Some authors choose the inclusive but clumsy *he or she* to express the irrelevance of sexual characteristics to their discussion. Although it goes without saying that gender is utterly unimportant in a cyberworld where participants are identified by their actions alone and it is sometimes not even clear whether a human being or a computer program is at work, I generally stick to *he*, *him* and *his* throughout for brevity's sake.

When an example has two participants, however, one is normally introduced as male and the other one as female. Although the gender of the hypothetical actors is consistently totally extraneous to whatever is being illustrated, the distinction allows each one to be clearly and concisely identified in the text that follows. A sentence like *Peter called Sue and she told him he had a problem* conveys a wealth of information that could not be expressed anywhere near as succinctly in a language that does not maintain the gender distinction.

Note on online references

All online references were retrieved on 2nd January 2018.

Thanks

On learning that a member of their staff was planning to write a book in his spare time, many consultancies would probably tell him to focus on his day job. This was not the case with my employer, msg systems. They offered me not only support and encouragement but also access to the expertise of various colleagues. Especial acknowledgements go to Ralf Engelschall for an initial ten-minute chat that altered the strategic course of the undertaking; to Lisa Schötz for the cover design; and to André Ihme for the interior illustrations.

My family has had to put up with my effective absence on numerous evenings. I am immensely grateful to my wife, Christine, and to my father, Paul, for providing a fresh angle on multiple facets of the project. This book would not be what it has become without the two of you. Thanks also to Mandy Balthasar, Bernd Endras, Carol Gutzeit, Mark Lubkowitz and Danijel Husak for the invaluable comments and suggestions you provided.

RICHARD PAUL HUDSON

CYBERTWISTS
HACKING AND CYBERATTACKS EXPLAINED

I. SECRETS

The internet is an open system. A message is routed from its sender to its recipient via an unpredictable path on which its contents will be visible to various other people if they only care to look. If there were no way around this inherent transparency, the internet would be essentially useless for anything other than disseminating news and public information. That it has been able to revolutionise the world of business is thanks to the existence of effective means of transmitting messages as secret code. These fulfil the dual purpose of keeping what somebody is saying safe from eavesdroppers and of demonstrating who is talking. If the two of us have agreed a secret code that only we know and you send me a message using our shared code, I know that the message must really originate from you.

This first chapter takes a look at the different ways in which information is converted into secret code and back: at encryption and decryption. Of the five chapter subjects, encryption is probably the one that is least likely to spring to most people's minds when they think about cyberattacks and hacking. Nevertheless, it is clearly the right place to start. Appreciating the details of how information is kept confidential is not only interesting in its own right. It is also a prerequisite for understanding the four chapters that follow, which are peppered with references to encryption.

This initial chapter also stands apart from the rest of the book in that it covers a much more extensive span of time. The other aspects of cybersecurity that we shall look at come on to the radar of history at around the turn of the millennium, or at the earliest a few years before that. Sending messages so they remain secret, on the other hand, is an endeavour that is probably scarcely younger than communication itself. Human beings have always looked for ways to talk in private. And, even today, encryption rarely requires any specific technology. The most modern and secure of encryption procedures could theoretically be carried out using a pen and paper, even if, in practice, the calculations are too involved to be achievable without a computer.

The discussion begins with a look at a range of simple and mostly ineffective encryption techniques that have been employed in the past. During the Second World War in particular, several nations made their first serious attempts to encode messages securely and ultimately failed for various instructive reasons. The resulting knowledge of what not to do has informed the standard encryption procedures that are used today. These are covered later in the chapter along with the political issues around their use and the allegations that the U.S. National Security Agency (NSA) has attempted to subvert them.

The Caesar cipher and the Sicilian Mafia

One organisation that modern knowledge and technology seems to have largely passed by is the Sicilian Mafia. Traditionally, Mafiosi communicate using cryptic handwritten messages called pizzini. The mid-2000s saw a wave of high-profile Mafia arrests of which the most notable was the capture of kingpin Bernardo Provenzano in April 2006 after more than forty years on the run.[1] One of the main reasons he was caught was that the Mafiosi had tried to disguise within their pizzini information such as names using a technique called the Caesar cipher that was actually trivial to decode.[2]

The Caesar cipher, thus named because it was invented by the ancient Roman military, consists of replacing each letter in a text with its corresponding number—*A* with *1*, *B* with *2*, *C* with *3*, and so on—and then adding to each number that results a secret number or key. If the secret number is *5*, *A* will become *6*, *B* will become *7*, *C* will become *8*, and so on. The Sicilian Mafia used the resulting numbers directly as their code. The Romans, on the other hand, converted the numbers back into their corresponding letters, so that *6* became *F*, *7* became *G*, *8* became *H*, and so on. Had the Latin alphabet had 26 letters like the modern English alphabet, *27* would have become *AA*.[3]

In ancient Rome, whoever received the code would first convert each letter in it into its corresponding number; in modern Sicily, he would already have the numbers. With either variant, the idea is that he has already received the key from the sender on some previous occasion. He can then subtract the key from each number in the code and change each resulting number to its corresponding letter to retrieve the original message.

The flaw in this method is that somebody else who knows or suspects that a secret code is a Caesar cipher can easily reveal the original text without having to know the key in advance. If the lowest number in a secret code is 35 and the highest number is 60, and we know the original message is written in English with an alphabet of 26 letters, it follows that the key must be *34*, because any lower key would cause the first letter *A* to be encoded as a number less than 35 and any higher key would cause the last letter *Z* to be encoded as a number greater than 60.

Even when a shorter message does not contain all the available letters in the alphabet and the difference between the lowest and the highest numbers in the corresponding code is less than 26, there will still only be a handful of possible values for the key. Somebody trying to decode the message can simply try these possible values out one by one and will know he has the right value when he ends up with a text that makes sense rather than with a meaningless string of letters. Interestingly, whether by design or by chance, the Sicilian Mafia's messages were encoded with the same key—*3*—that Julius Caesar is known to have employed some two thousand years earlier![4]

Recording the enciphered text

Provenzano and his accomplices may have speculated that anyone finding their code would not be able to decode it with such techniques because the way it was written would prevent it from being recognized as a Caesar cipher in the first place. Firstly, they recorded it as numbers rather than the letters of ancient times. Secondly, the key value *3* allowed an encoded message to be written as a continuous chain of numbers even though the individual code numbers that made up the sequence were partly single-digit and partly double-digit.

The first letter *A* becomes *4* and the second letter *B* becomes *5*: there are no letters that correspond to the single-digit numbers *1*, *2* and *3*. At the same time, the last letter *Z* becomes *29*: there are no letters that correspond to double-digit numbers whose first digit is *3*, *4*, *5*, *6*, *7*, *8* or *9*. This means that even if the message is written without spaces between one encoded letter and the next, whoever is decoding it has a foolproof way of knowing whether each new number he encounters should be interpreted as a single-digit number or as the first digit of a double-digit number.

This allowed a word like *GITALLI* to be written in code as *1012234151512*.[5] The Mafia probably presumed such a contiguous string of numbers would be completely impenetrable to anyone not knowing what it was. In fact, it betrays an obvious pattern that almost jumps out of the page: there is a strong tendency for each second digit to be either 1 or 2. This quickly leads to the suspicion that the code is made up of smaller units of which at least some are double-digit, and from there it is only a small step to identifying and decoding the Caesar cipher. In any case, the Caesar cipher is so notorious that it is one of the first possibilities any codebreaker would consider.

The 'Ndrangheta and the San Luca code

More recently in January 2014, the Italian police managed to decode messages they had captured a year earlier that had been written by the Sicilian Mafia's Calabrian cousins, the 'Ndrangheta.[6] The San Luca code dates from the late nineteenth century and was developed as a way of writing down secret information that had previously been passed on by word of mouth. The confiscated material documented quasi-religious initiation rites for budding Mafiosi as well as a myth outlining how the Mafia originally came into being.

The code consisted of replacing each letter of the alphabet with a secret symbol. Because the 'Ndrangheta wrote messages with a space after each word, the code could be broken much like a Sudoku puzzle. Like other languages, Italian has a limited number of words made up of one or two letters. This means that there is only a handful of letters that could correspond to a symbol that appears within an encoded one-letter or two-letter word. Once the codebreakers had cracked the first few symbols by analysing the shortest words in the text, they were able to make educated guesses as to what some of the longer words were because they then knew some of the letters that made them up. As they deciphered each word, they decoded more symbols. They continued with the same technique until they had revealed the whole alphabet.

Even in the event that the San Luca messages had been written as contiguous text without spaces between the words, the police would still have been able to decode them. A computer could be programmed to try out all possible combinations of symbol-to-letter correspondences. The program would recognise a potential hit when the string of letters that resulted from applying a combination to an encoded message contained known Italian words as opposed to gobbledegook. If the computer had too little material to reach a definitive answer on its own, it would be able to find a hopefully small number of candidate solutions that a native speaker of Italian would then have to work through to determine which one made sense.

A technique called statistical frequency analysis would give this process of trial and error a considerable head start. In any language, some letters occur much more often than others. For example, any reasonably long English text will contain many more instances of the letter *E* than it does of the letter *X*. How often a given symbol appeared in an encoded San Luca message compared to the other symbols could be used to determine whether the symbol in question was likely to represent a letter that occurs frequently or infrequently in Italian. With shorter messages, this knowledge would enable a computer trying out all possible correspondences to start with the ones that were most likely to be right. And with a sufficiently enormous amount of encoded text, it could be used to crack the code all on its own: if the statistical sample were large enough, the relative frequencies of the symbols would be arranged in an order that would exactly match the relative frequencies of letters observed for the Italian language in general.

Although the two Mafia groups have supplied us with examples of encodings that were particularly trivial to crack, codemakers underestimating the ingenuity, tenacity and intuition of codebreakers is a recurring theme in the history of encryption. Human intelligence seems to be better suited to the goal-oriented challenge of finding patterns than to the open-ended task of hiding them.

Running keys

A running key cipher takes the basic idea behind the Caesar cipher to the next level of complexity. If you distribute copies of a book—for example, this one—to a group of people who you want to be able to encode and decode messages, they can use the individual letters in the book to derive separate Caesar cipher keys for the individual letters in each message. This book begins with the word *HARDLY*, so the first letter in each message would be encrypted using the letter *H*, which is the eighth letter of the alphabet. If a message began with the letter *B*, the *B* would be replaced by the letter eight places after it in the alphabet, which is *J*. The person decoding the message would know to use the letter *H* from the book to decode the letter *J* by going back eight letters to yield the original *B*.

The third letter in this book is *R*, which is the eighteenth letter of the alphabet. If the third letter in the message to be encrypted were *U*, we would not be able to advance eighteen positions from it without reaching the end of the alphabet first. We would then cycle back round to the beginning of the alphabet again and take *A* as following *Z*. The encrypted version of the letter would be *M*. Again, the recipient of the encoded message would know from the *R* from the book to go back eighteen places from the encrypted *M*, cycling round in the opposite direction from *A* to *Z* to retrieve the original *R*.

A running key cipher is much more challenging to crack than a Caesar cipher. Nevertheless, if a single book has been used repeatedly to encode different messages, frequency analysis can be applied to determine probable values for each letter within the book and then to decode the messages. For example, if *Cybertwists* were used as a key source over and over again, the relative frequencies with which the first letters in the encrypted messages occurred would parallel the relative frequencies with which letters occur at the beginning of English texts, but the values would all be shifted eight letters to the right, which would identify the first letter in the book as an *H*.

Such purely frequency-based analysis requires a very large number of encrypted messages to crack an entire running key cipher. However, running key ciphers can be revealed on the basis of a surprisingly limited amount of input when frequency analysis is used in conjunction with other, more complicated analysis techniques. In any language, there are strong patterns around which letters of the alphabet tend to follow which other letters of the alphabet. There are also specific words like *the* that can reasonably be expected to occur often in any text. Such knowledge can be applied to several messages that are known to have been encrypted using the same key to work out probable letters at various points within that key.

Eventually, part of a longer word—say *NFORMATI*—will become visible either in one of the messages or in the key itself. Completing that word within the text that contains it will then allow more of each of the other texts to be decoded, hopefully exposing parts of other words there. The analysis will probably involve a good measure of trial and error, but a computer brings speed to the process as well as the ability to compile definitive lists of all words within a language that contain whatever strings of letters have already been found.

And even if this book were only used as a key on a single occasion, a skilled analyst examining the encoded message would still have a good chance of deciphering at least parts of it. Ascertaining that the key is itself based on English text would not be particularly difficult. Because the relative frequencies of letters in both the book and the original message would be uneven, the relative frequencies of letters in the encrypted message would themselves form a telltale signature. For example, because the letter *E* (the fifth letter of the alphabet) occurs very frequently in English, the letter *J* (the tenth letter of the alphabet) would occur fairly frequently in the encrypted messages. It would result whenever an *E* in the original message that had been encrypted happened to coincide with an *E* in the book that had been used as a key.

Once the analyst had worked out that the encrypted message had been generated from two parallel texts, he could make a tentative stab at deciphering it. The methods he would apply are similar to those that he would have been able to use with more confidence of success if he had been able to access several messages that he knew to have been encoded with the same key. Although a single text would give him little chance of working out the whole sequence, recovering snippets of the message might still turn out to be valuable. And, perhaps more significantly, recovering sections of the book could conceivably lead the sleuth to it via an online search. He would then have the entire key and would be in a position to decode the entire message.

One-time pads and the Venona project

This sort of analysis can be made impossible by deriving the key from a random sequence of letters rather than from a pre-existing text. When a stream of gobbledygook is put to work to encrypt a single message and then never used again, it is known as a one-time pad. A one-time pad has the distinction of being the only encryption method that is theoretically totally unbreakable. It may seem surprising that encoding secrets without using a computer retains any relevance in the twenty-first century, but this queen of encryption methods requires no complex mathematics and can be easily performed by hand.

However, the one-time pad does not represent a practical answer to most problems that encryption might realistically be required to solve. For every secret message that is to be sent, a new random sequence of letters has to be generated and distributed to its intended users without being intercepted by anybody else. The logistical hurdles these requirements entail are identical to those that motivate using encryption in the first place. If you can send the one-time pad safely without encryption, why not just send the message safely without encryption? In most situations, a one-time pad merely shifts the challenges of secure transmission from one document to another: from the secret message to the one-time pad.

On the other hand, this can be exactly what is called for if the conditions for secure and trusted communication exist at one point in time but cannot be guaranteed at some future point in time. In 1963, following the Cuban missile crisis, the United States and the Soviet Union set up an emergency hotline between their respective leaders that was based on one-time pads.[7] Each country generated pads and passed them to the second country via diplomatic channels. This allowed the superpowers to build up a basis for communication slowly and during a period of low tension that would be ready for use if the situation heated up in the future.

As soon as a one-time pad is used more than once, it loses its status as an unbreakable encryption method. The Soviet Union based their confidential communications during World War II on one-time pads. However, because the unit generating the random pads was unable to meet the demand for them quickly enough, pads ended up being recycled. The authorities tried to reduce the resulting risk by making sure the same pad was never reused in similar places or situations, but this measure proved insufficient to stop American analysts, who had obtained a large quantity of encoded messages, from taking advantage of the situation. That they were able to crack messages that had been sent with reused keys is what one would expect. On the other hand, what seems genuinely remarkable given the vast amount of data they were analysing is that that they were able to detect the reuse in the first place and to identify which groups of messages it applied to.

The project to analyse the Soviet messages was called Venona and work on it continued right up until October 1980: once an adversary is in possession of encrypted messages, he has all the time in the world to try and decipher them.[8] The messages that were successfully decoded made up but a fraction of the total, but they still contained a considerable amount of pivotal intelligence information. Venona led to the definitive exposure of double agent Klaus Fuchs, who was responsible for passing the Soviets top-secret U.S. information about hydrogen bomb design.[9]

The Enigma machine

On the opposing side in the Second World War, the Germans encrypted and decrypted messages using Enigma machines. These created keys as they went along, which avoided the practical problems that resulted from using one-time pads. The machines were invented during the First World War[10] and were available for commercial use in the 1920s before being commandeered by the German military.[11] The sender typed his message letter by letter into a keyboard. Each time a letter was pressed, a lamp lit up on the machine and displayed the encoded version of that letter. The encoded message was then sent by

Morse code. If the receiver had an Enigma machine that he had set up identically to the sender's, he could type the encoded message into his machine and read the original message off its lamps.

This was before electronics had come into general use. Enigma machines worked with a combination of mechanics and simple electrics. Electric current flowed through a number of linked components. Each component substituted whatever letter it received for another letter that it then passed on to the next component in the chain. The most important components were rotor wheels. Each rotor wheel had twenty-six equally spaced notches and was placed into a perpendicular slot in the machine where it made contact with twenty-six connections arranged in a circle to its right and another twenty-six connections arranged in a circle to its left.

There were several types of rotor wheel that were distinguished from one another by their internal wiring. The wires in each type linked the connections on their right to the connections on their left in a different, randomly chosen way that determined which letter was substituted for which when current was passed through the rotor. One rotor might have replaced *A* with *D*, *B* with *M* and *C* with *T*, while another rotor might have replaced *A* with *U*, *B* with *N* and *C* with *P*. An Enigma machine had three or more slots into which different rotors were placed. The rightmost rotor might have replaced *A* with *D*, then the middle rotor *D* with *Q*, and then the leftmost rotor *Q* with *F*.

Each time a key was pressed and a letter had been encoded, the rotors were incremented much like the units, tens and hundreds columns of the mechanical counters that were used in the pre-digital age to track how far a vehicle had been driven.

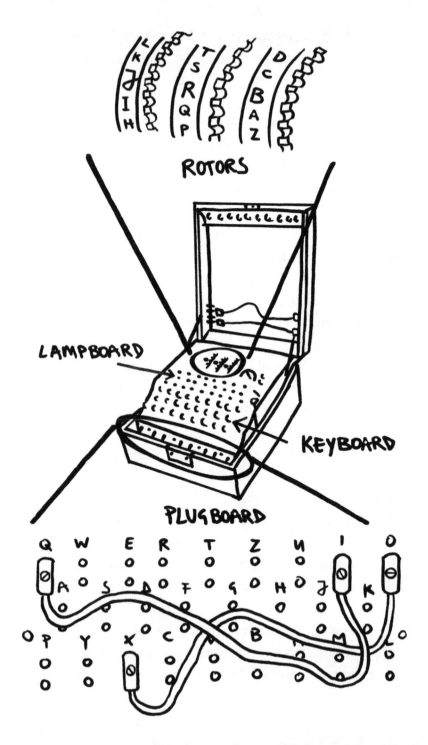

ROTORS

LAMPBOARD

KEYBOARD

PLUGBOARD

The rightmost rotor would move by one position after each key press. Each time the rightmost rotor had turned through a whole circle, the middle rotor would move by one position, and each time the middle rotor had turned through a whole circle, the leftmost rotor would move by one position.

Choosing three letters out of the twenty-six at random as examples, a rightmost rotor that had replaced *K* with *C*, *P* with *X* and *T* with *H* before being moved by one position would now replace *J* with *B*, *O* with *W* and *S* with *G*. The advancement of the rotors had the effect that each letter position within a message was encrypted using a completely different set of correspondences between the original alphabet and the encoded alphabet.

To make the system yet more complicated and difficult to crack, the rotors were used in conjunction with a plugboard. The plugboard had a socket for each letter of the alphabet and leads could be plugged into it to link letters in a pairwise fashion. For example, *D* and *M* might be linked by a lead. This would cause *D* to be replaced by *M* and *M* to be replaced by *D* when current passed through the plugboard. Normally, ten pairs of letters were connected in this way, while the other six letters were left unconnected.

When a user typed a letter into the keyboard, the current flowed from the key he had pressed to the plugboard. If the letter was connected on the plugboard, it was replaced by its pair. Otherwise, it remained unchanged. The current then flowed through the rotors one after the other, a new substitution occurring each time. It then passed through a reflector. Like the plugboard, a reflector connected letters in a pairwise fashion. However, important differences were that a reflector did not leave any letters unchanged and that its wiring was fixed rather than being set up by the person using the machine, although there were different types of reflector that paired up the alphabet in different ways. The letter the reflector returned was then passed backwards through the three rotors in reverse order before finally the plugboard was traversed a second time. The encoded version of the letter then lit up on the lampboard.

Coupled with the fact that the plugboard and the reflector both linked pairs of letters, the symmetrical nature of this setup—plugboard, then rotors, then reflector, then rotors again, then plugboard again—was what allowed two people to communicate using Enigma without any difference in the way the encrypting and the decrypting machines were configured or used. It meant that the Enigma machine as a whole itself encoded letters in a pairwise fashion. If pressing the letter K with the machine set up in a certain way and its rotors in a certain position caused the W lamp to light up, pressing the letter W with the same setup and rotor positions would cause the K lamp to light up. The electric current would take the same path in both cases, just in opposite directions.

Information about how to set up groups of Enigma machines so they could encode and decode one another's messages was distributed to military personnel in advance using paper codebooks. It included which rotor and reflector types to use, which rotors to place into which slots and which pairs of letters to link on the plugboard. Unlike a Russian one-time pad, which had to be the same length as the message (or as the unfortunate reality had it, messages) it was encoding, an Enigma setup took up a mere line in a table. Each setup was normally valid for a day, so that configurations for a whole month could be captured on a single sheet of paper.

In order to make use of the full range of substitution alphabets the Enigma machine could generate, the rotors had to be set to different starting positions each time a new message was sent. If the same initial positions had been used for a large number of messages sent on a single day, the resulting cipher could have been decoded using the frequency analysis techniques discussed earlier in this chapter. For example, all original messages that began with the letter *E* would then have resulted in encrypted messages that themselves began with the same letter, and it could then have been determined that, for the first position within each message, this letter must encode *E* based on how often it was observed to occur relative to the other encoded letters.

The twenty-six positions into which each rotor could be placed were marked using an alphabet wheel that circled the rotor. This showed the twenty-six letters of the alphabet in alphabetical order. When a rotor had been slotted into the machine, one of these letters was visible in a window at the front. The three letters that were displayed on the sending machine before a message was typed into it showed how the rotors on the receiving machine would have to be set up to decode that message. It is important to understand that the alphabet wheel was merely a convenient way of labelling the different positions a rotor could be in. Which letter showed at the front of a rotor had nothing to do with the substitutions it would perform when current was passed through it.

Because the sender of a message set the initial rotor positions randomly for each new message, they had to be somehow transmitted to the recipient. Different procedures were used to achieve this at different points during the war and by different armed forces. However, the most common one was based on the concept that one set of three initial rotor positions, which was transmitted in unencrypted form, was used to configure the machine to encrypt a second triad of letters that then formed the initial rotor positions for the actual message. The idea was that somebody who eavesdropped on the first set of positions would remain unable to decrypt the second set because he would not know the other settings that were valid for that day.

The sender would choose three letters at random and set his rotors accordingly. These three letters, say *TDH*, formed what were known as the indicator. He would then choose the initial rotor positions for the actual message, say *WOF*, and type them into the machine to obtain the encrypted version, say *LSG*. Before sending the actual message, he would transmit the indicator *TDH* and the encrypted initial rotor positions *LSG*. The recipient would set the rotors on his machine to the indicator *TDH* and type in the encrypted initial rotor positions *LSG*. The lampboard would display the chosen initial rotor positions *WOF*. The recipient could then set his rotors to these positions and begin decrypting the message that followed.

To make things more complex and to reduce the amount of information the indicator and the encrypted initial rotor positions would give to an eavesdropper, the wiring component within each rotor was built so that it could itself be turned through a circle with twenty-six positions. The position of the wiring component was shown by a single dot on the rotor that aligned with one of the letters on the alphabet wheel. Moving the wiring component changed which letter on the alphabet wheel referred to which of the twenty-six groups of letter substitutions of which the rotor was capable.

In the example above, a rotor that had replaced *K* with *C*, *P* with *X* and *T* with *H* was moved by one position so that it replaced *J* with *B*, *O* with *W* and *S* with *G*. Perhaps the wiring component had been set with its dot aligned to *R* and the rotor was advanced from the *L* position to the *M* position. The same effect could have been achieved by leaving the rotor in the *L* position but moving its wiring component one notch in the opposite direction from *R* to *Q*. Together with the types of rotor to use, the slots to place them in and the plugboard settings, the positions of the wiring components within each rotor made up part of the pre-distributed setup information that was valid for a day at a time.

The Bletchley Park project

It was inconceivable for most Germans using the Enigma system that anyone would be able to glean anything from the encrypted information without access to the codebooks. That so many of the messages were in fact successfully decoded by the western Allies was a tremendous intellectual achievement that played a decisive role in their eventual victory. The Bletchley Park project to decipher the Enigma messages has since attained the status of national legend in several countries that were involved: the United Kingdom; Poland; France; and the United States.[12]

The mathematicians and linguists working at Bletchley Park used a variety of analysis techniques to crack the Enigma code, many of which are well beyond the scope of this book. Different situations called for different combinations of methods. For example, while most Enigma machines had three rotor slots, some machines used later in the war had more, and the German navy used a more complex means of transmitting initial rotor positions than the one described above. Much of the decoding work relied on mechanical analysis machines called bombes that were developed at Bletchley Park specifically for the task. Whether or not it is apposite to regard the bombes as the first computers depends largely on how a computer is defined.

The overall design of the Enigma system had already been in the public domain before the war. On occasion, military operations led to the physical capture of Enigma machines that could then be examined to gain crucial information like the internal wirings of previously unseen rotor types.[13] The seizure of a codebook would reveal helpful facts about operating procedures, and if nobody noticed it had been lost it could even allow a couple of days' messages to be read without any work on the part of the Bletchley Park teams.[14] In general, however, details that seeped in from outside played much less of an important role than patterns that were discerned within the messages themselves. That these so often allowed the original content to be retrieved resulted from a combination of flaws both in the basic design of the machines and in how the Germans used them.

The most important weakness of the system was that no letter could ever be encrypted to itself because the machine could only be configured to substitute the letters of the alphabet in a pairwise fashion. On one famous occasion, this feature was used to derive the wiring for a previously unknown rotor type when somebody sent a test message that consisted exclusively of the letter *L* repeated over and over again. The person at Bletchley Park examining the encoded version of the message noticed that it did not contain the letter *L* anywhere and had a hunch as to what had happened.[15] And in everyday decoding work, the same shortcoming could be exploited to discover which position within an encrypted text encoded a specific stretch of original text. How did this work?

The Bletchley Park team frequently knew or strongly suspected that an encoded message would include certain phrases, because military communication is highly formulaic. The German for *Nothing to report* was often transmitted day in, day out, and, even when there was something to report, it was frequently couched in standardised language. Identifying which individual was sending a message could further increase the predictability of its contents. This was sometimes possible if the sender transmitted Morse code with a distinctive rhythm, as well as by virtue of the fact that the preamble to each message contained an unencrypted call sign that identified which station was sending the message and which station was intended to receive it.

Recurring stretches of text like *Nothing to report* were called cribs. An analyst who thought that a given crib formed part of a message but did not know exactly where in the encoded message it lay hidden could often work out its position using the fact that no letter could be encrypted to itself: all candidate positions within the encoded message could be excluded where at least one encoded letter had the same value as its unencoded counterpart from the crib. For example, the word *ENIGMA* could not possibly be positioned at any point in an encrypted message where the first encoded letter was an *E*, the second encoded letter an *N*, the third encoded letter an *I*, the fourth encoded letter a *G*, the fifth encoded letter an *M* or the sixth encoded letter an *A*. By process of elimination, this technique would ideally identify a single position in a given encrypted message at which a string of letters began that was expected to encode the crib.

Postulated correspondences between cribs and encoded letters were used to set up the bombe machines. Although there are a huge number of possible permutations in which the various components of an Enigma machine can be configured, a bombe was capable of proving that most of them could not have possibly led to all the correspondences between cribs and codes that had been observed on a given day. Once the vast majority of the candidate setups for a day's messages had been discounted as impossible, the remaining configurations could be tried out one by one by hand until the analysts hit on the one that was seen to work in that it yielded a sensible German message.

The repetitive nature of the messages meant that they typically contained cribs in sufficient quantity to allow each day's codebook settings to be determined. However, the Allies were not always prepared to leave this to chance. When they were planning a particularly important military operation and needed to be sure of their ability to read enemy communication on the day it began, they would sometimes lay mines purely so that the positions of the mines would appear in messages transmitted shortly afterwards and could then serve as cribs.[16]

The rotors interacted with one another in a way that was supposed to make the system more secure but that actually had the opposite effect. When a numerical counter with units, tens and hundreds columns is incremented, only the units column advances most of the time. When the units column moves from nine to zero, this causes the tens column to advance as well; and when the tens column itself moves from nine to zero, the hundreds column advances. The rotors that were slotted into an Enigma machine were interconnected according to a similar principle. A middle or leftmost rotor advanced when the rotor to its right was moved to a specific letter on its alphabet wheel. However, for each rotor type it was a different letter that caused the rotor to its left to advance. This was designed to make the machine more complicated and harder to crack, but it actually helped analysts to determine which rotors had been placed into which slots by observing statistical patterns in encoded texts that betrayed when the middle and leftmost rotors had moved.

The German military was concerned that Enigma might be used with a small selection of simple, easily memorable setups that the enemy would quickly be able to recover. To force codebook authors to vary how the machines were configured, it was stipulated that a rotor should never be allowed to remain in the same slot on the machine on two subsequent days, nor should a letter ever be wired to its immediate neighbour in the alphabet on the plugboard. These decisions actually handed unintended advantages to the Allies by reducing the number of permutations the bombes had to consider in their process of elimination on any given day.

At the same time, the fear was absolutely founded that personnel under pressure would cut corners and fail to use the full range of possible setups effectively. Just like the Russians with their one-time pads, the office responsible for generating codebooks would sometimes reuse settings from previous months, which was a godsend to the analysts at Bletchley Park once they realised what was happening.[17]

More generally, the military personnel responsible for transmitting messages often had little or no understanding of the rationale behind the operating principles that they were supposed to be following to keep the system secure. They had precise instructions detailing how to use the Enigma machines, and if they had followed them exactly the Allies would not have been able to listen in quite as often. As it was, they started to cut corners because doing so made life easier. And because they had no way of knowing that their sloppiness was allowing others to eavesdrop, bad practice became ingrained as an unchecked habit.

The security of the system relied on the initial rotor positions for each message being chosen randomly. In reality, though, certain message transmitters—who we have seen were sometimes identifiable based on the rhythm of their Morse code—tended to use trivial settings like *AAA* or *BBB* or settings based on names or obscenities. Knowing the probable initial rotor positions for a message made the task of determining the other machine settings easier. And as the other settings were valid for all messages sent by a particular group within the armed forces on a particular day, a small number of messages that had been encoded sloppily could end up allowing the Bletchley Park teams to decode a much larger number of messages whose transmitters had observed the rules down to the last detail.

Before the first message of each day could be transmitted, the wiring component within each rotor had to be set to the value specified in the codebook. One of the most useful insights at Bletchley Park was that the easiest way of moving the dot on the wiring component to align with a given letter on the alphabet wheel was to move both the letter and the dot to the front of the machine so that the letter would be visible through the rotor window: the physical act of setting a rotor's wiring component tended to entail moving the rotor itself to a corresponding and predictable position.[18]

The operating instructions stated that the rotors should then be moved to random positions to use for the indicator of the first message. However, this step was often skipped or performed perfunctorily, perhaps advancing one or two rotors by one or two notches. It may have been that message transmitters reasoned that the indicator was not really that important because it was not used to encrypt the actual message, but merely to communicate how to set up the machine.

In fact, because the indicators were sent unencrypted, clusters of indicator values that were observed in the messages sent first thing in the morning immediately after the wiring components had been set to their new positions for the day greatly aided the Bletchley Park teams in the task of finding out those wiring component positions. If twenty initial messages were sent on a given day and the indicator value for the rightmost rotor was *D* for two of them, *E* for three of them and *F* for two of them, with the remaining values distributed randomly throughout the alphabet, it was likely that the wiring component for that rotor had been set to a position around the letter *E*.

It took until 1974 for the Bletchley Park story to enter the public domain.[19] The techniques that had been developed and applied to decipher messages had shown that the mere complexity of an encryption system was no guarantee it could not be cracked until a sufficient number of codebreakers had tried and failed. They had also demonstrated that even a theoretically secure method could only be relied upon if people were forced to use it as designed. These insights played a crucial role in informing the first modern encryption methods, which were developed and standardised shortly afterwards.[20]

Block-based encryption methods

Nowadays, keys are generated randomly by a computer to prevent the sort of problems seen with Enigma when operators were left to make up components of their own keys. And, unlike Enigma, modern mechanisms distinguish between encryption and decryption. The computer sending a message uses a key to create a list of actions to transform the original version into the encrypted version, and the recipient machine uses the same key to derive a list of opposite actions that are performed in reverse order on the encrypted version to get back to the original version.

Today's techniques operate at the level of individual bits, or ones and zeroes, rather than on letters in a text. Every file or message stored or transmitted by a computer is ultimately represented as a long string of bits. A computer has a different way of representing in bits each of the types of object it processes: texts, pictures, films and so on. For example, one way in which a computer can store a text involves it using 16 bits to represent each letter, so that *1000101001011011* might denote one letter, and *0010011000111100* some other letter. An important advantage of encryption techniques that work with strings of bits is that they can be used regardless of whether it is a document, a photograph or some other type of file that is being encoded.

A typical encryption method starts by splitting into blocks of a predefined length the string of bits that is to be encoded.[21] Each block might consist of 128 bits, corresponding to eight letters in the above representation. The bits that make up each block are then subjected to a long series of changes that mangle them up. Identical actions are carried out in parallel on all blocks that are being encrypted. Some alteration steps switch ones for zeroes and zeroes for ones at various positions within each block. For example, considering only the first ten bits within each block for brevity, the values of the bits at the third, fifth, eighth and ninth positions might be switched, leaving the bits at the first, second, fourth, sixth, seventh and tenth positions unchanged.

Other alteration steps work by splitting the stream of bits that make up each block up into sub-sequences and replacing each old sub-sequence with a new sub-sequence, either according to a dictionary or by means of mathematical operations that depend on the values of other sub-sequences within the block. Operating on sub-sequences rather than merely on individual bits means that a modification may or may not happen to switch the bit value at a given position within a given block, because a new sub-sequence will normally share some of its bit values with the old sub-sequence whose place it takes. Still other alteration steps swap around the positions of sub-sequences or individual bits within each block.

Each encryption method uses its own specific sequence of individual alteration steps. Within at least some of the steps any given method prescribes, the precise operations that are performed will depend on the key. The key is itself a string of bits that is typically the same length or somewhat longer than each of the blocks being encrypted, and the encryption method uses it to work out the details of alterations it is to apply. In an oversimplified example that is helpful to illustrate the point, if the key length and the block length are both 128 bits, the encryption method might start by looking to see which of the 128 positions within the key have a bit with the value *1* rather than the value *0*. It might then switch the values of the bits at all of the corresponding positions within each block in the data to be encrypted.

An encryption method is secure if knowing the details of how it works cannot be used to decrypt a message it was used to encode unless you have the right key. Techniques in current use can achieve this security with relatively short keys. A typical modern encryption method uses a complex chain of bit-mangling steps particularised by a key that is between 128 and 256 bits long. Compare this to a one-time pad, which uses a very simple message transformation in conjunction with a key that is the same length as the information to be encoded.

Initialization vectors

The fact that each block is several times longer than the individual letters that were encoded using the Enigma system is one of many features that make modern techniques more secure and harder to crack. At the same time, there is one important way in which block-based encryption in its simplest form is less secure than Enigma. While Enigma generated a new substitution alphabet for each letter, nowadays all blocks are encrypted in the same way, and however thoroughly the bits within each block are mangled up, this can lead to problems if there are two or more blocks that are identical.

For example, a high-resolution image of a sketch of a castle on a white background will contain a large number of identical blocks that represent empty space. If all these blocks are encrypted using the same encryption method and the same key, their encoded versions will all be exactly the same. Someone examining the resulting data, despite not being able to decode it, could surmise that these identical blocks probably represent empty space. He could create a picture where the identical blocks are white and all the other blocks are black. The picture would be blotchy and without details but would still show the unmistakable outline of a castle.

Most real-life applications of block-based encryption guard against this weakness as follows. The original version of each block is subjected to a change step based on the encrypted version of the previous block and only then encrypted itself. The original second block will be subjected to a change step based on the encrypted first block before it is itself encrypted. This change step will ensure that the encrypted second block is distinct from the encrypted first block, which also means that the encrypted second block will produce a new and different change step when it is in turn applied to the original third block. The procedure ensures that even if three adjacent original blocks are encoded that are identical, the encrypted version of each one will still be different from its neighbours.

At the beginning of the process, when the first block in the string of bits is to be encrypted, there is obviously no encrypted previous block to use. Instead, the details of the change step that is applied to the original version of the first block are determined by a randomly generated string of bits called an initialization vector. Using initialization vectors means that even if the same message is encrypted twice, the two encoded versions that result will be completely different from each other. The initialization vector is transmitted or stored at the start of the encrypted message, but it itself remains unencrypted. In this it corresponds to the indicator of the Enigma system.

Encrypting streams of information

Tackling information block for block is fine when you are working on a single computer, but it is often a bad idea when audio or video data is being transmitted across a network. With block-based encryption, reproducing a film or song smoothly would be challenging because the receiving computer would have to wait for the end of each block before it could decrypt and play it.

A stream cipher is a sequence of bits that is used like a one-time pad—consisting of bits rather than letters—to encrypt and decrypt information in a continuous fashion. A common way of generating a stream cipher is to use a block-based encryption method but to apply it to the randomly chosen initialization vector instead of to the information being encrypted. The sender and the recipient of a message agree on an initialization vector, which they can communicate openly. With their shared key, both parties encrypt this initialization vector to derive the first block of the stream cipher. This encrypted information is then encrypted again to derive the second block, which is then encrypted again to derive the third block, and so on until the resulting stream cipher is the same length as the information the sender wants to transmit to the recipient. The sender then uses a very simple mathematical operation to combine the stream cipher with the message, deriving the encrypted message bit by bit as he sends it to the recipient, who can then decrypt it at the other end using the same simple mathematical operation.

Practically all wireless routers communicate with laptops and phones using a protocol called Wi-Fi Protected Access 2 (WPA2) that encrypts information using stream ciphers.[22] In October 2017, Belgian researchers revealed that an attacker could trick a wireless router into using a stream cipher a second time by pretending not to have received the first message the router had used it to encrypt.[23] Because the stunt could be repeated over and over again, the router could be persuaded to reuse the same cipher on multiple occasions. Just as with one-time pads, it is bad news if a stream cipher is ever used more than once, and wireless networks were left vulnerable to eavesdropping. In a way that recalls the cribs at Bletchley Park, the weakness relied on a hacker being able to engineer a situation where a message was sent whose content he could predict: comparing its original and the encrypted versions revealed the stream cipher, which he could then go on to use to decrypt subsequent messages.

Private and public keys

The type of encryption we have been discussing up to now is referred to as symmetric. This is because the steps used to encode a message are carried out in reverse order to decode it again, with the same key describing both operations. This key has to be somehow distributed to everyone who is going to use it to communicate. Enigma codebooks and Russian one-time pads were issued in advance in paper form. However, this is hardly workable within the huge and anonymous system that is the internet.

Most internet business of any consequence would actually not be possible at all were it not for a second means of encoding data developed in the 1970s that is known as asymmetric encryption.[24] Understanding it is a crucial prerequisite to much of the discussion in Chapters II, III, IV and V. Because it can be difficult to grasp and has no genuine counterpart in the physical world, I shall illustrate it with a counterfactual thought experiment.

Picture a door with a lock and its normal key, which we will call the weak key. Now imagine a second key with extra teeth. We will call this second key the strong key. In the physical world, locking the door with the strong key would mean the strong key would be required to unlock it again, because the weak key would not be able to operate the additional parts of the lock mechanism. If the door had been locked with the weak key, on the other hand, either the weak key or the strong key would be able to open it again.

To understand asymmetric encryption, it is necessary to throw overboard all your preconceptions about how real doors work and to imagine a physically impossible lock system with a strong and weak key where the access rules are as follows: in any cycle of the door being locked and unlocked, the weak key can be used to perform at most one of the two actions. This means that if the weak key was used to lock the door, it cannot be used to unlock it again: the strong key is required for that. If, however, the door was locked using the strong key, either strong or weak key can be used to unlock it again.

If I am the owner of a room secured with this door and possess both keys, there are two ways I can use them. In both cases I keep the strong key for myself and give copies of the weak key to one or more friends. I can lock an object in the room and any one of my friends who is able to use his weak key to open the door knows that it must have been me who put the object in there, because I am the only person who has the strong key. Alternatively, any one of my friends can use his weak key to lock an object in the room in the sure knowledge that I with my strong key am the only person who will be able to retrieve it; nobody else's weak key will be able to reopen the door.

Asymmetric encryption methods use mathematics to create virtual relationships that correspond to the one between the door owner and his friends. The operations that are performed on the data as it is encoded and decoded go beyond what we can cover here, but, just as with symmetric encryption, they are determined by series of bits that make up keys. I generate a random private key, which I keep secret, and a corresponding public key, which I disseminate to everyone I wish to communicate with. A message encoded with the private key can only be decoded with the public key, and a message encoded with the public key can only be decoded with the private key.

Enigma used a single, identical procedure for both encryption and decryption; modern symmetric encryption uses the same key to derive distinct procedures for encryption and decryption where each is the mirror image of the other; and now asymmetric encryption uses different keys for encoding and decoding.

In some types of asymmetric encryption, the public key is mathematically derivable from the private key.[25] In other types, although strictly speaking the two keys are equal partners that are generated simultaneously, the superior status of the private key is still reflected by the fact that the structure used to store it contains the public key as well.[26] In both cases, then, anyone who has the private key effectively has the public key at the same time and can encrypt and decrypt messages as he likes. This makes the private key like the strong key to the door in the above analogy, and the public key like the weak key.

Just as with the door, the system can be used in two opposing directions. As we shall see in Chapter III, I can sign a message with the private key, allowing anyone with the public key to verify that the message did indeed originate from me. Or, alternatively, someone can encrypt a message using my public key and send it to me in the knowledge that only I will be able to read it, because decoding it requires my private key.

The NSA and Perfect Forward Secrecy

Two computers could theoretically hold a private conversation over the internet by each encoding messages with the other's public key. However, because asymmetric encryption is much slower than symmetric encryption, two computers do not normally exchange large amounts of data using public and private keys. Instead, they employ them at the beginning of a conversation to agree on a symmetric key, which is then used to communicate everything that follows.

When you access a website, you use a browser like Internet Explorer, Firefox, Chrome or Microsoft Edge to contact the web server that is in charge of maintaining and supplying the website's content. The web server will typically have a private/public key pair, but your browser will not. Until quite recently, the standard procedure was for your browser to generate a random symmetric key, encrypt it with the web server's public key and send it to the web server. The web server would then decrypt the symmetric key with its private key. That way, your browser and the web server would have agreed on a symmetric key that they both knew but that anyone eavesdropping on the conversation would not have been able to read.

The security of this procedure had already been questioned by experts.[27] What made the rest of the world sit up and take notice were the secrets disclosed by the former U.S. intelligence officer Edward Snowden in 2013. These included the revelation that the NSA was storing huge amounts of encrypted internet traffic that it was not initially able to decode.[28] In the event that it should become desirable at some point in the future to decrypt conversations that had involved a particular website, the plan was to hack into that website's server and gain access to its private key. The private key would then enable the NSA to decode the symmetric keys that had been used on the various occasions the site had been accessed and allow the organisation to read the rest of each conversation that had ensued.

Since this strategy has become common knowledge, more and more websites are protecting their customers and users against such attacks with a technique called the Diffie-Hellman exchange.[29] Two computers that are negotiating a new symmetric key agree on some numbers. Each one then generates a huge random number that it keeps to itself, and each one performs a certain type of calculation involving its secret random number and the mutually agreed numbers. The two machines then exchange the results of their calculations. A nifty piece of mathematics enables them to use this information in such a way that they end up with a common symmetric key. Somewhat counterintuitively, the method ensures that, even if an eavesdropper captured all the information sent between the computers in both directions—the mutually agreed numbers and the results of the calculations—he would still be unable to reconstruct the key whose creation it facilitated.

When the technique is used to encrypt a conversation between a browser and a web server, the common key is discarded at the end of each communication session without being stored anywhere, so that an organisation like the NSA will be unable to gain access to it at some point in the future. This quality is known as Perfect Forward Secrecy.

The Diffie-Hellman exchange would theoretically allow a browser and a web server to agree on a secret symmetric key without using private and public keys at all. However, the browser would then have no way of knowing whether it was really the web server that it was talking to. An attacker intercepting the traffic could negotiate one key with the browser and a second key with the web server. He could decrypt and then re-encrypt the messages as they travelled in each direction. This would put him in a position to read or even alter the ensuing conversation, a technique known as man-in-the-middle.

Avoiding this requires a symmetric key that is created in such a way that the people talking can identify each other and is at the same time resistant to being decoded at some point in the future. This is achieved by marrying asymmetric encryption with Diffie-Hellman, which is actually relatively easy to do because the mathematical techniques involved in the two cases are closely related.[30] This still leaves the issue of how the browser knows that the web server's public key really originated from the web server rather than itself being generated by a man-in-the-middle. We shall look at some solutions to this problem in Chapter III.

Steganography and the Al-Qaeda porn video

Combining the various types of encryption enables people to identify one another and to exchange messages that are indecipherable to eavesdroppers. In many situations, however, communicating parties also wish to conceal the fact that a message exists in the first place. Most people have been faced with the dilemma that they have to be sure they will not forget their credit card personal identification number (PIN) but that they have been warned against writing it down anywhere. A common solution is to disguise it somewhere in one's household. The number *2839*, for example, could be captured as *Outstanding grocery bill: $28.39* written on a piece of paper stuck to the refrigerator with a magnet, or as *Bedside cabinet: 28cm x 39cm* noted in the back of an interior design book. Anyone who has instinctively used such techniques has taken his first steps in the practice of message concealment, or steganography. In the context of the internet, steganography typically refers to techniques for hiding messages in files where they would not normally be expected, like pictures or videos.

One of the simplest steganographic techniques allows a piece of text or other information to be concealed in a photograph as follows. Each pixel of a digitised image is stored as three numbers that specify the amounts of red, blue and green that make up its colour: in one common standard, the possible values for each of the numbers range from 0 to 255. Each bit in the message to be hidden is assigned to a pixel in the photograph: remember that any data, encrypted or otherwise, is ultimately representable as a string of bits. If a bit from the message is a zero and the red value for the corresponding pixel in the photograph is an odd number, the red value is altered down to the next lower even number. If, on the other hand, the bit from the message is a one and the red value for the pixel is an even number, the red value is altered up to the next higher odd number.

Somebody who wishes to retrieve the message reconstructs the string of bits that make it up by examining the red value for each pixel in the photograph. Each pixel that has an even red value represents a zero in the message, while each pixel that has an odd red value represents a one in the message. However, because the distinctions in hue caused by such tiny changes in redness are much too subtle to be discernible by the human eye, nobody viewing the photograph would guess that it actually contained a secret message.

On the other hand, someone who suspects a secret message might be lurking in the photograph will be able to find where it is concealed without too much difficulty, because genuine colour tones do not change backwards and forwards from one pixel to the next. It is important to understand that any steganographic method is only designed to make messages inconspicuous and not to prevent them from being found by somebody who knows where to look for them. This holds even for other, more complex concealment techniques.

In May 2011 in Berlin, a memory card was confiscated from alleged Al-Qaeda member Maqsood Lodin.[31] It was found to contain a folder named *SexyTanja*. The folder was protected by a simple password mechanism that was trivial to circumvent. It contained a pornographic film called *KickAss* which turned out to be a goldmine for the intelligence services fighting the terror network. Hidden within it were no fewer than 141 unencrypted files with names such as *Future Works* and *Report on Operations*. The investigators had found top-secret documents giving them a direct insight into the strategy and tactics of Al-Qaeda's inner command circle.

The Navajo code talkers and Bernardo Provenzano again

Standard encryption and steganography involve encoding or concealing messages using methods that are independent of the content the messages contain. This is normally the only viable option, especially in an internet situation where the communicating parties may have never met in person. However, altering the meaning, rather than the form, of a message according to a pre-agreed code can also play an important role in keeping information secret.

During the Second World War, the U.S. military employed speakers of the Navajo language as a means of transmitting confidential messages.[32] Scarcely known beyond the Navajo Nation at the time, the language offered a ready-made means of communicating secrets. Essentially, its fiendishly complex grammar formed the encryption method, while the correspondences between its vocabulary and English acted as a very long key. Because of the completely fixed nature of this key, signals experts within the U.S. army were initially somewhat sceptical of the whole idea.

In the event, however, it was an additional and largely coincidental feature of the Navajo messages that prevented the Japanese from deciphering them. Because the Navajo language did not contain equivalents for many of the military terms under discussion, the Navajo code talkers pre-agreed a 211-word code that consisted of circumlocutions for them. The Navajo for *between waters* meant *Britain*, the Navajo for *iron hat* meant *Germany*, and the Navajo for *chicken hawk* meant *dive bomber*. It is striking that, despite their tiny number, it was these specially invented words that played the decisive role in keeping the Navajo messages impenetrable. They meant that even when the Japanese captured and tortured a native speaker of Navajo who was not a code talker, he was unable to make any sense of the messages.[33]

In more recent years, one person who seems to have been successful in outwitting law enforcement authorities with a meaning-based encoding scheme is none other than Bernardo Provenzano. Following his capture and arrest in 2006, he spent hours each day marking the Bible in his cell with cryptic signs and references that bore a close resemblance to annotations found in the Bible he had had with him when he was caught. Eventually, in 2008, the prison authorities cut off all contact between Provenzano and the outside world because they suspected he was using a code based on Bible annotations to run his criminal empire from behind bars.[34]

The Federal Bureau of Investigation (FBI) tried to crack the Bible code, but as far as we know they could not.[35] We might presume this is because it was founded at least partially on pre-agreed meanings taken from the fabric of the Mafia subculture. On this occasion at least, Provenzano seems to have been successful in keeping his messages secret.

Encryption standards

The Enigma system had been developed by a small group of inventors who believed the messages it encoded to be practically undecipherable. They turned out to be anything but when a much larger group of analysts applied themselves to cracking them. Solving a puzzle is so much more motivating than creating one!

The modern encryption methods that most businesses rely on are open standards that can be scrutinised by all the mathematical brains in the world who care to look. Because they are designed so that understanding how they work is of no help in deciphering a message unless you know the right key, the fact that their inner operations are common knowledge makes them no less secure. On the contrary, opening them up for all and sundry to analyse before they enter general use greatly reduces the chance that ways to attack them will be discovered when it is too late.

The organisation that evaluates and standardises the encryption techniques that are generally employed in global commerce, and probably by most governments as well, is a U.S.

government agency called the National Institute of Standards and Technology (NIST). Although a few countries, notably China[36], Japan[37] and South Korea[38], have released their own encryption methods for private-sector use, in practice the U.S. standards are used almost everywhere. In Germany, the Federal Office for Information Security regularly issues businesses based in the country with detailed encryption guidelines that invariably prescribe a selection of the NIST standards.[39]

The San Luca story earlier in this chapter showed how an encryption method whose inner workings are understood can be hacked by simply testing all possible keys until one is found that decrypts a code to give sensible text rather than nonsense. The standard NIST methods are no more immune to this sort of brute-force attack than less sophisticated encryption techniques, but the problem is addressed by allowing a sufficiently large number of possible keys that trying them all out one by one would take an impracticably long time.

However, the power and speed of computer hardware is constantly increasing. One common estimation is that it doubles every two years.[40] A brute-force attack that is infeasible now could come within the reach of attackers in only a few years' time. The 2017 version of the German commercial encryption guidelines states unequivocally that many of the techniques it describes may only be used until the end of 2022. This means that systems intended to operate past this point have to allow for the eventuality that, in the future, the encryption methods with which they were originally designed to run might have to be replaced with new ones. Making this possible is a sensible precaution anyway, because an unexpected mathematical breakthrough could crack a previously secure encryption method at any time.

Quantum computing

Independently of computing power and mathematical research, many currently standard encryption methods are set to become obsolete thanks to a brand-new technology. Quantum computing takes place at the sub-atomic scale and is still at the experimental stage. It aims to take advantage of some frankly mind-blowing properties of the particles that form the building blocks of matter and light and works in a completely different way from classical electronics-based computing.

In a classical computer, a bit is set to either zero or one at any given moment in time. A program might be written to add two whole numbers between zero and fifteen. Storing a number between zero and fifteen requires four bits, because there are sixteen permutations of four digits where each digit is either a zero or a one: *0000*; *0001*; *0011*; and so on. This means that storing both numbers would require eight bits in total. The values of the eight bits at the point in time when the program carried out the addition would determine the result.

Contrary to everything common sense tells us, a bit in a quantum computer, which is called a qubit, can have both values—zero and one—simultaneously. A quantum program might take eight qubits as its input. Because each qubit has two values at once, eight qubits together have 256 concurrent values (two to the power of eight). The quantum program would effectively perform 256 calculations at the same time.

Unfortunately, though, the fact that each qubit in a quantum computation has both possible values at once does not mean that the results of a huge number of mathematical calculations can all be obtained using a single quantum computation. Rather than saying that each qubit has *both* values, it would perhaps be more accurate to say that each qubit has *either* value with a given probability. As long as a computation is taking place, each qubit really is set to zero and to one at the same time. However, as soon as each of the qubits that makes up the result of the computation is read, the act of observing the qubit makes it stick in one of these two values. Retrieving the result of a quantum computation yields the result of only one of the many calculations that were performed, and none of the other results then remains accessible.

You may well ask what the use of the answer to a mathematical calculation is if there is no way of choosing the question. The crucial point is that some of the operations used in quantum computing can skew the probability with which each qubit has one or the other value. Such operations can be cleverly combined to increase close to the point of certainty the likelihood that the result retrieved from a computation will be the answer to a specific question chosen by the programmer.

It may be a helpful thought experiment to compare the eight-qubit quantum computer with its classical counterpart and imagine it adding in parallel each of the members of a complete range of whole numbers between zero and fifteen to each of the members of a second, identical range of numbers. However, this analogy misrepresents the way quantum computing works. In quantum computing, it is not just the storage of information that is revolutionary. The simplest building blocks that a classical computer uses when it runs a program are based on interactions between flows of electric current. A quantum computer, on the other hand, makes individual physical particles interact with one another in ways that are totally unlike anything in our everyday experience. While it is certainly possible to write a quantum program to add two numbers, the steps that would be used to do so are completely different from the ones somebody programming a classical computer would have at their disposal.

In short, a quantum program is not just lots of classical programs operating in parallel. Because quantum computing and classical computing operate in totally dissimilar fashions, they tend to be good at different things. A quantum computer would not be an appropriate tool to solve the simple arithmetic at which classical computers excel, while the new mechanisms it offers can be exploited to achieve quick fixes for some mathematical problems that classical computers can only solve using brute-force methods. In many cases, these are the very mathematical problems on which today's encryption standards are based.

It turns out that a quantum procedure called Grover's algorithm will make cracking contemporary symmetric encryption methods easier, but that the advantage can be counterbalanced by doubling the number of bits used in each key to increase the number of possible values.[41] On the other hand, a second quantum technique called Shor's algorithm will pose a much more serious problem for the asymmetric methods that use private and public keys, as well as for the closely related Diffie–Hellman exchange.[42] For asymmetric encryption, quantum computing will provide easy solutions to the mathematical problems on which today's established standards are based. In the right circumstances, currently used private/public encryption methods will no longer serve their purpose because a quantum computer will allow its owner to find out other people's private keys.

Although practical research has certainly confirmed the theory behind quantum computing[43], none of the experimental quantum computers built so far has been able to use more than a very small number of qubits, nor have they worked well enough to be able to solve any mathematical problems more rapidly than the fastest classical computers. Nonetheless, it is probably only a matter of time until the remaining engineering problems are satisfactorily solved and the technology becomes mature enough for practical use.

New methods of encryption and decryption are expected to emerge that can only be carried out using quantum technology. For the time being, however, the race is on to standardise quantum-resistant asymmetric encryption techniques.[44] These can be performed on classical computers just like the methods that are in widespread use today. At the same time, they rely on mathematical problems that a quantum computer cannot solve in a trivial fashion, which provides assurance that the encodings they provide will not be open to analysis by quantum computers at some point in the future.

Bullrun

We have seen that encryption techniques tend to become easier to crack over time as a side effect of the march of technology. In 2013, Edward Snowden revealed the existence of a secret NSA programme known as Bullrun that showed that they have also been subject to deliberate attempts to weaken their integrity.[45] The aim of Bullrun was to undermine the effectiveness of commonly used encryption methods, and the tactics employed included attempts to subvert NIST standards.

The New York Times has alleged that, over several years in the mid-2000s, the NSA had manipulated the authorship process of a NIST standard that specified a supposedly secure method of generating random numbers called *Dual_EC_DRBG*.[46]

Encryption methods rely on the randomness of their keys. The NSA is claimed to have had a secret way of predicting the sequences of numbers that *Dual_EC_DRBG* would produce, which would have enabled the U.S. authorities to recreate encryption keys that had been generated using the method.

In the event, the NSA's attempt to introduce an ineffective technique had already attracted negative attention well before the Snowden revelations. Question marks over the mathematics the standard was based on were raised even before it was adopted in June 2006[47], and November 2007 saw the first suggestion that the flawed method had been deliberately planted by the U.S. security services.[48] On the one hand, this is a tremendous vindication of the theory that open standards lead to secure encryption. On the other hand, it is telling that the broken standard continued to be available in a number of important software products well after it had been conclusively demonstrated to be ineffective. In one of them it was even the default option, which meant anyone who was not up on encryption would be likely to end up using it.[49]

The Bullrun documentation that is in the public domain claims that the NSA has the capacity to defeat a great deal of the encryption in common use on the internet. Exactly what this entails remains a secret, partly because Snowden did not have access to all the information himself and partly because the NSA has persuaded journalists not to reveal all the details for reasons of national security.[50]

Although it is certainly possible that the NSA has discovered secret mathematical means of cracking some encryption methods, this is most likely to be the case for techniques that are no longer state-of-the-art. Because of their open nature, most of the world retains its trust in the best of the NIST standards even in the light of the revelation that there have been active attempts at sabotage. It would be genuinely astounding if the NSA were so far ahead of the curve that they had managed to defeat methods that mathematicians working in the public domain still regard as watertight.

In the light of the *Dual_EC_DRBG* story, it seems probable that most of the Bullrun capabilities instead result from sabotaging common software as it is being produced so that it uses outdated encryption methods. Building software that works well is hard, and, as we shall see in the next chapter, building software that works well securely is harder still. With many developers already operating at the limits of their ability and understanding, getting a hidden flaw deliberately introduced into a system is probably not all that difficult. One can imagine that a combination of misinformation and a quiet word in the right place at the right time is often sufficient to ensure that software is released that ends up encoding its information inadequately.

Secret encryption methods

If NSA employees are attempting to undermine publicly known encryption methods, it is understandable that they have developed alternative techniques for their own use. The organisation maintains a Suite A of encryption methods that are kept secret.[51] It regards Suite A as the more secure option and employs it for especially sensitive information.

That it uses the standard NIST methods known to everyone else at all is a consequence of the fact that Suite A encryption can only be used for communication between organisations that can be trusted to keep the hardware and software with which it is carried out safe from prying eyes. At the same time, because the advice that encryption methods should always be subject to open review is repeated like a mantra by many experts, it is surprising that the U.S. security services choose to ignore the principle for their most important messages.

An attacker with access to a computer using a Suite A method could analyse it to discover what it was doing, but he would still have to crack the procedure mathematically to be able to decode encrypted information without the right key, and with any technique worth its salt this should certainly be the hard part. After all, private individuals all around the world have tried to attack the well-known NIST methods, and nobody has succeeded, otherwise the methods would have been removed from the canon.

Even if the NSA does have an unmatched team of world-class experts, it remains possible that one or more of the Suite A methods has a weakness none of them has noticed. It seems extraordinary that they seem to value secrecy about how the techniques work over the additional assurance that would result from free reviews. Perhaps the Suite A methods are actually extensions of publicly known methods rather than genuinely distinct techniques.

Government restrictions on encryption

The Bullrun program came into being to try and prevent people from talking out of earshot of the NSA. Governments' bids to achieve the same end have not always been quite so surreptitious. In 2015, the then British Prime Minister David Cameron expressed his disquiet over messages between internet users being encrypted in such a way that their content could no longer be read by security services.[52] Cameron pledged to ban applications that persisted in offering customers such secrecy. "In our country, do we want to allow a means of communication between people, which even in extremis, with a signed warrant from the home secretary personally, that we cannot read?", he pleaded.

The former British Prime Minister is far from alone in his views. In February 2016, a similar argument flared up in the United States between the FBI and Apple.[53] And numerous governments have placed legal restrictions on encryption. Perhaps the most memorable constraints apply in North Korea. When asked, the government of the Democratic People's Republic of Korea (DPRK) refused to divulge exactly what restrictions applied to the use of encryption in their country.[54] Complying with an anti-secrecy law that is itself secret must prove something of a challenge!

Furthermore, the United States of America used to place limits on the export of encryption products, which is again hard to marry up with the fact that the mathematical procedures the encryption constitutes had been published and were openly accessible around the world. Until the late 1990s, the country regarded software products that made use of effective methods of encryption as weapons.[55] They were subject to similar controls as military design documents.

Social media sites are indeed increasingly using encryption in a way that is fully resistant to government eavesdropping. The messaging application WhatsApp generates a private key on your phone and does not copy it anywhere else.[56] When two phones need to exchange messages, asymmetric encryption is used in conjunction with the Diffie–Hellman exchange to generate a symmetric key as described earlier in this chapter. This guarantees that you are the only person in the world who can read what is communicated; even the WhatsApp administrators have no way of decoding it.

On the one hand, the wish to deny terrorists a safe way of talking to one other is understandable. On the other hand, encryption is not technology restricted to large internet firms, but mathematics. Trying to outlaw encryption is a bit like trying to prohibit multiplication or division. Banning effective encryption from mass-produced items like smartphones and the standard apps that run on them would obviously raise the bar for criminals wanting to use it. However, anyone with the right knowledge who can program a computer can easily use well-known encryption mechanisms to encode messages in such a way that an eavesdropper cannot read them.

Terrorists would soon be using the black-market products that would inevitably follow hard on the heels of any legislation enacted to ban encryption. These products would generate encoded messages that could be copied letter for letter into a WhatsApp that would no longer need to perform any encryption itself. Meanwhile the general public, left without a secure way of exchanging information, would become easy prey to internet criminality.

Legislation restricting the use of encryption typically focusses on the creation, distribution and use of software capable of performing it. Laws forbidding the transmission of encrypted messages are essentially unenforceable unless they prohibit nonsense at the same time, because there is no way of distinguishing information encrypted using a block-based method from a random string of ones and zeroes. This mathematical fact obviously does nothing to guarantee that somebody who sends such a message will not receive unwelcome attention from the authorities, especially under a repressive regime.

Even jurisdictions where encryption is generally permitted often have special provisions for when there is circumstantial evidence that a string of bits makes up an encrypted message that was sent in the context of a crime. The police can typically obtain a warrant requiring the surrender of the relevant key. Somebody who wishes to conceal his real activities even in the face of such a warrant could employ deniable encryption.[57] This allows two or more messages to be encoded using different keys and the results to be merged into a single encrypted message. The essential property of a deniable encryption method is that even if somebody has observed one original message being successfully retrieved from an encrypted message using one key, he has no way of knowing whether the encrypted message is hiding any further original messages and, if so, how many.

To some extent, it is the relative maturity of encryption that has placed it so firmly in the crosshairs of secret services and politicians. Luckily for them, however, the other technologies that make up the internet have not yet had the chance to become anywhere near as robust. This means that governments have no need to make encryption techniques illegal in order to carry out surveillance within today's internet. However a message is transmitted, there are at least two places where it has to exist in its original, unencoded form: the computer or phone where it is written and the computer or phone where it is read. And as we will see in the chapters to come, gaining covert access to these machines is well within the reach of nation states.

II. PROGRAMS

Most computers are general-purpose. Even though different models are good at different things, the vast majority of machines could potentially take on a diverse range of roles. The tasks that almost all computers perform are defined by software programs that are temporarily loaded into their memory from hard drives, memory sticks or the internet. In this chapter, we examine the central role that programs play in cyberattacks and hacking. On the one hand, we begin by looking at software that a hacker writes for the specific purpose of getting computers to do what he wants. On the other hand, many legitimate programs harbour unintended faults. We go on to describe how an attacker can exploit these faults to gain illicit access to the computers where the programs are running.

Malware: viruses and worms

Software that has been created specifically to make computers behave differently from how their owners would wish is called malware. The traditional but by no means the only way in which malware authors spread it is by programming it to copy itself from machine to machine without the need for human involvement. Such self-replicating malware is sub-classified into worms and viruses. Like any other software programs, malware is made up of code instructions that computers carry out when they run it, but while a worm is a complete program in its own right, a virus is a string of instructions that attaches itself to existing programs and changes what they do. The name is born of the analogy with biological viruses, which are strings of DNA that alter the behaviour of infected cells.

One of the first malware threats was a virus called Form that spread in the early 1990s via the floppy disks that were commonly used in those days to share programs and information between computers.[58] How did Form work? When a computer is switched on, there has to be a place defined from where it is to retrieve its very first code instructions. On a laptop or desktop computer, this is generally a specially defined part of the hard drive called the boot sector, whose contents typically specify a position elsewhere on the hard drive from which the computer is to load and run an operating system like Windows or Linux. An operating system is a special type of program that has the onerous task of managing the flows of information between a computer's processor (brain), its memory and the various gadgets connected to it. The operating system needs to be up and running on most computers before you can get them to do anything else.

Floppy disks had boot sectors just like hard drives. If you started your computer with a floppy disk in your drive and that floppy disk had something stored in its boot sector, a typical computer back then would take its initial boot instructions from the floppy disk rather than from the hard drive. This was necessary to enable you to install a different operating system from the one your computer had originally come with.

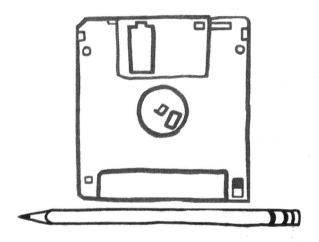

The normal, hard-drive-based boot sector of a computer infected with Form contained additional instructions. When the computer was switched on and loaded its operating system, the extra code meant the virus was activated as well. If a floppy disk was then read from or written to on that computer, the computer would silently infect the boot sector of the floppy disk, and if the floppy disk happen to be transferred to some other computer at a later point in time, the code in the floppy-disk boot sector would order that computer to adulterate the instructions within its own hard-drive boot sector with the virus. Thus was formed a self-perpetuating cycle of contagion.

The symptoms of Form—what the virus did other than simply reproducing—were tame by today's standards. The main effect was that typing on the keyboard produced a clicking sound on the 18th day of each month. However, as is often the case for modern malware, poor programming practices meant Form would sometimes cause more serious problems that its creators had not envisaged. If a hard drive was not structured in the exact way Form expected, the changes the virus made to it were liable to render it permanently unreadable.

Evolutionary theory and antivirus software

Although many of the most serious virtual plagues have actually been caused by worms, it was the idea of the computer virus that captured the popular imagination when malware was first written and disseminated. The meme fell on fertile ground. With bacterial disease largely conquered by antibiotics, biological viruses would have remained the main communicable health threat in the late-twentieth-century developed world even without the addition of a deadly newcomer, the Human Immunodeficiency Virus (HIV), whose untreatability dominated the collective consciousness at the time when computer viruses rose to prominence.

The parallels between computer and biological viruses are manifold. Former Soviet army officer Ken Alibek oversaw a large biological warfare program in Russia before emigrating to the USA in 1992. He has claimed that researchers under his command mixed smallpox and ebola genes to generate a terrifying chimera dubbed ebolapox.[59] There is no way of verifying his assertions. However, whether or not they are really true, it does seem quite possible that a deadly virus could be created by grafting together parts of existing ones. Creating a viable biological weapon from scratch by writing novel genetic code, on the other hand, is well beyond the capabilities of contemporary bioengineering.

The situation is comparable for computer viruses. Cutting and pasting existing malware is an attractive option for attackers without the skills to write it themselves. A computer virus generally consists on the one hand of a fairly complex part that is responsible for infection and replication and on the other hand of a relatively simple payload that determines what the virus does: in the case of Form, the original payload caused the clicking noise on the 18th of each month. It was easy for new attackers to graft their own payloads on to Form's infection and replication base. This led to variants of Form appearing that caused the clicking noise to occur all the time or on different specific days of the month.

Really malicious criminals could have modified Form to do serious damage like reformatting the hard drive. Maybe some did. However, it is not just chance that the variants that were widely observed were more benign. Just as in the biological world, a computer virus that destroys its host is unable to spread effectively and soon dies out. Natural selection also explains why the viruses that survive are those that infect whatever operating systems are extensively used by the general public at any given time: DOS in the 1990s; Windows for most of the time since then; and more recently the mobile operating systems Android and iOS.

Linux is a lesser-used operating system that has not been plagued by malware like its more widespread counterparts. It does have some technical features that make it intrinsically more resistant to malware attacks than its main competitor, Windows. In reality, though, the more pertinent reason why there is not much Linux malware around is probably that the relative dearth of vulnerable host machines prompts cybercriminals to focus their efforts elsewhere.

Computers are protected from malware using antivirus software, which despite its name also covers worms and other threats. Traditionally, antivirus software has detected infections by searching the computers it guards for tell-tale stretches of code. An antivirus program can diagnose a specific virus or worm because it knows the sequences of instructions that make it up. It checks that they do not appear within programs that the computer is about to run or within files stored on its hard drive or other disks.

In an attempt to mimic the way in which many biological viruses trick the immune system with constant mutations, some malware authors have tried to evade discovery by anti-virus software by writing so-called polymorphic malware that alters its own code every time it is copied from one computer to another.[60] However, this is one instance where the analogy between the realms of DNA and program instructions fails to hold up. The virus that has you in bed with the flu reproduces billions of times within your body, so that it does not matter if a significant proportion of the individual viruses that come into being are not viable. For malware, on the other hand, each reproductive cycle normally entails jumping across to a new host machine. This means someone designing a piece of polymorphic malware cannot permit it to change its code in a genuinely random fashion, because it would then fail to infect many if not most potential victims.

In the virtual world, uncontrolled mutations would drive a species to a swift extinction. However cleverly it metamorphoses, a virus that is designed to spread from one computer to another, send an E-mail or wipe the hard drive always has to retain instructions for spreading from one computer to another, sending an E-mail or wiping the hard drive. Removing these instructions would stop the virus from functioning. The fundamental need for changes to occur in a behaviour-preserving way is the malware author's Achilles' heel. It enables the antivirus-software author to employ mathematical and statistical techniques that do a good job of detecting polymorphic viruses despite their shapeshifting attempts.

A traditional antivirus product has to maintain a list of all the code signatures of viruses and worms that might threaten the computer it is protecting. It requires periodic updates from the company that wrote it to keep its charge immunised against newly emergent variants. The major drawback with trying to find malware by looking for the instructions that make it up is the window of opportunity that will always remain between when a new strain is released into the wild and when antivirus software companies detect it and distribute its signature.

In an attempt to defend their customers against previously unseen malware, antivirus companies are increasingly focussing on what malware does rather than exclusively on the program instructions that make it up.[61] Returning to the biological analogy, they focus on the actual organism rather than on its genetic code. If it looks like malware, sounds like malware and smells like malware, it probably is malware.

Both antivirus software and many modern operating systems might classify a program as suspicious if it tried to change certain operating-system files or make contact with random computers over the internet without involving the user. These are typical illicit behaviours that most genuine programs would have no reason to exhibit. The offending program is then stopped in its tracks and the user is asked whether he really wants his computer to perform the action in question.

An older virus like Form did not need to employ any special tricks to get its malicious code run: it just did whatever it wanted. Today, CDs and thumb drives are used in a similar fashion to the floppy disks of yesteryear to install operating systems, but viruses like Form no longer pose the same sort of direct threat because computers check with their owners before booting from anywhere other than their own hard drives. To get around such safety mechanisms, modern malware has had to adopt various strategies to outwit the computers it infects and their users.

Spying with rootkits

A very simple way in which some attackers have sneaked malware on to computers is to get somebody to install it just like any other software. For malware that is designed for a particular machine or group of machines, this is typically the preferred option if it is feasible. In Chapter V, we shall cover the alternative. We shall look at an example of a worm that copied itself around but whose payload only came to life when it happened to infect its intended targets. However, as we shall see, it is better for malware not to self-replicate unless it really needs to: there is always the risk of it being discovered and analysed on some machine that has no relevance to its purpose.

In 2005, it was discovered that computers responsible for routing phone calls within the network of telecommunications provider Vodafone in Greece had been hijacked with a modified version of their proprietary operating system.[62] Calls to and from around one hundred phones belonging to senior officials including the Prime Minister were having copies of their soundtracks routed to wiretappers. Given the considerable complexity of the software, it is presumed to have been developed by a foreign secret service, and because its code contained no instructions to spread from computer to computer, it seems probable that the spies recruited a telecommunications employee to install it.

If you wish to determine which programs are stored and running on a computer, or if you want to see who has performed what actions on it in the past, you use its operating system. This means that compromising the operating system gives a hacker the capacity to hide his activities. The Greek Vodafone malware was a classic example of a rootkit: a concealed piece of operating-system-level software. The additional program that enabled spies to eavesdrop on politicians did not appear on standard file listings. It only came to light because it contained an unintentional bug that prevented other functions on the computer from working properly. The engineers investigating the error eventually uncovered what was going on.

Ransomware: Love Letter and CryptoLocker

When a hacker is trying to get a program running on a large number of unspecified machines, recruiting people to sneak around and install it is not an option. However, tricking genuine users into installing it themselves often is. In 2000, this strategy was employed on a large scale for the first time by the authors of the Love Letter worm.[63]

Love Letter was spread using E-mails that had the title *ILOVEYOU* and that appeared to contain a love letter as an attachment. It took advantage of the fact that, in some circumstances, Microsoft Windows displayed files according to what they claimed to be rather than what they really were. What seemed to be a document to be opened and read was actually the worm: a program that was reactivated whenever E-mail recipients clicked on it. It then performed various acts of vandalism including overwriting documents and pictures on the infected computer with copies of itself. It would also send an E-mail to all the contacts in the computer owner's address book.

The combination of a romantic declaration from a recognised contact person and a cunningly disguised attachment proved irresistible to millions of people. Just as in a biological epidemic in which each new victim of a disease passes it on to several contacts, the number of computers infected by the worm continued to increase exponentially for as long as multiple recipients of each address book mailshot clicked on the file.

A piece of malware that poses as something innocuous is called a trojan after the Trojan Horse of Greek legend. While the Trojans were tricked into carrying a wooden horse full of enemy soldiers into their city, users are persuaded to run software that is designed to cause harm to their computers. The Love Letter trojan was the event that elevated malware from the status of a geek's joke and exposed it as a serious threat to the corporate world.

In more recent years, businesses have come to view malware more seriously still as it has developed into a major source of underworld income. Once associated with bored teenagers typing away in their bedrooms, hacking is increasingly the preserve of sophisticated organised crime gangs. Across the globe, internet criminality, much of it involving malware, is now claimed to be more lucrative than drug dealing.[64]

In late 2013, a Russian-written trojan called CryptoLocker was spread as an E-mail attachment taking advantage of the same Windows weakness as Love Letter: it was able to masquerade as a document file although it was really a program that was executed when the user clicked on it.[65] Unlike Love Letter, however, it did not self-replicate using the address book on each target machine. Instead, its authors had it sent to lists of E-mail addresses that had been cobbled together from various sources.

The CryptoLocker trojan is an example of ransomware. When it was run on a machine, it encrypted many of the files on it so they were no longer usable. It did this using the asymmetric encryption described in Chapter I. The trojan started by contacting the central server that was responsible for managing CryptoLocker attacks. The server generated a new private/public key pair and recorded the private key together with details of the newly infected computer. The corresponding public key was sent back to the trojan and used to encipher the files on the victim machine.

A message then appeared on the screen explaining that the centrally stored private key could be used to decrypt the files again in exchange for an online payment in bitcoin, which we will cover in Chapter IV. At the same time, the user was warned that if no money had been received by a specified deadline, the key would be deleted from the server. Because CryptoLocker used an unbreakable encryption method, the unfortunate owner of a computer it had ravaged had to choose between paying the $400 ransom or losing everything he had stored on it. Ransomware abuses insecure software to get secure encryption carried out on its victim machines, leveraging the relative immaturity of the one technology versus the other.

I know of an occasion when a senior IT consultant had the misfortune to download CryptoLocker as he browsed his mails from within a large corporation where he was working. (He shall remain nameless, but I would like to stress that he was in no way associated with my own employer, msg systems.) The effects were somewhat more wide-ranging than for somebody using a home PC because the trojan did not restrict itself to encrypting what was on the computer he was working from. It went on to scramble large numbers of the corporation's files that were located on shared drives to which he had access. Luckily, however, the damage was limited by the fact that the corporation had backed everything up. This enabled its employees to restore the files without having to pay the ransom.

It is estimated that the CryptoLocker operators managed to extort around $3m from their victims.[66] Nonetheless, the story has a happy ending. This is one occasion where the security community eventually managed to stop the attackers in their tracks. In May 2014, law-enforcement agencies and private-sector experts collaborating in an international effort called Operation Tovar succeeded in taking down the server infrastructure behind CryptoLocker.[67] This prevented any new infections. Better still, the counter-attackers discovered the stash of private keys that provided the means of recovering garbled files.

A few months later, two firms who had worked on the project launched a website that made use of these private keys to enable CryptoLocker victims to decrypt their information for free.[68] You just had to upload any one of your encrypted files to the companies' server, which would try and decode it using each of the salvaged keys in turn. The decryption would only yield a valid file in a recognised format when the server chanced upon the key that fit your machine. You then received instructions describing how to use this key to decode everything else.

HummingBad and botnets

Some trojans make no secret of the fact that they are programs to be run. Instead, they entice you to install them by posing as useful or fun applications. In 2016, it was discovered that malware called HummingBad had used this tactic to infect millions of phones running the Android operating system.[69] The official Google Play Store checks that the apps it makes available do not contain obvious malware, but there are alternative stores where no such verification takes place. This makes sneaking malware on to phones as easy as creating an app that is attractive enough that people will take the risk of downloading it from a dodgy source.

HummingBad's authors seem to have been working together with Chinese online advertising producers who were paid according to how often people accessed their content. It made a phone silently click on Chinese advertisements in the background, unbeknown to its owner. This slowed your phone down. It could also cost you a considerable amount of money if your payment plan depended on how much data you downloaded. More worryingly still, HummingBad achieved its goal by handing over complete control of your phone to its authors. Together, the totality of phones infected with HummingBad formed what is known as a botnet: a mass of machines dominated using malware. There was nothing to stop its masters from finding additional ways to abuse their power. They could have stolen their victims' personal data or directed the phones they controlled to take part in criminal activity.

Drive-by downloads and key loggers

Love Letter and CryptoLocker tricked people into running them by posing as documents to be read, while HummingBad duped its victims into installing it by posing as an authentic app. Some malware authors are more devious still in that they manage to infect your computer without you realising you have downloaded a file at all. One way of achieving this is to sneak the malware into the content that is sent to your browser as you access the internet. When you have the misfortune to fall victim to such an attack, you think your browser is just displaying a normal website. In fact, however, it is silently installing malware on to your computer at the same time.

A browser is supposed to make these drive-by downloads impossible by always asking its user for explicit consent before allowing a website it is displaying to make any changes to the computer on which it is running. However, releases of the main browsers have sometimes contained unintentional design faults that have enabled attackers to get around this requirement. We will go into more detail about such faults later in this chapter.

Drive-by download was one of the main means used to spread Zeus, a trojan first observed in 2007.[70] Zeus infects computers running Microsoft Windows and is capable of sending its authors what you type into your browser. Depending on what you do on the internet, this might include the name and password for your online E-mail account or the passcode for your internet banking.

In an attempt to harden its website against such so-called key loggers, your bank may well allow or require you to enter your internet banking passcode by using your mouse to click on pictures of keyboard buttons displayed on the screen. Any malware will then find it considerably more difficult to get hold of the information than if you had typed it in normally. However, if a malicious piece of software can observe mouse clicks as well as key presses and its author knows where on the screen the specific website being used displays each key, it could still discern which letters and numbers are being entered. Some banking websites try and thwart this more advanced type of attack as well by displaying their virtual keypads at a slightly different position on the screen each time.

The original botnet that Zeus created was used for a variety of criminal purposes above and beyond basic key logging. And just as the Form virus was modified to generate clicks on different days of the month, the Zeus code was copied and altered to produce variants that handed over control of your browser to new botnets managed by different people. As it so happened, the computers trapped within one of these copycat botnets, Gameover ZeuS, had been exploited by the authors of CryptoLocker as the principal vehicle to send victims of the trojan the E-mails that contained it; the same Operation Tovar that captured the CryptoLocker private key database also took down the entire Gameover ZeuS botnet.[71]

The fuzzy line between malware and useful software

Hardly any software you install or use on your computer gives you a full technical account of all the changes it makes to your system. Most people are not interested in such details, nor would they understand them if they were. This leads to a situation where many applications you use on your machine are able to get away with performing actions that are probably more in their authors' interest than yours, which can sometimes blur the distinction between bona fide software on the one hand and malware on the other.

There have been various occasions when applications have been released that their authors claimed were legitimate but that behaved in a way that eventually led the computing community to classify them as malware. In October 2005, security expert Mark Russinovich published information about a piece of software called Extended Copy Protection (XCP) that was being distributed using audio CDs produced by Sony BMG.[72] It was a Windows program that was published as standard on the CDs alongside the sound information you would normally expect to find on them and that was billed as a giveaway that enabled you to play your music on your PC.

The software was made to look like a simple media player, but it was actually a rootkit that hid itself deep within the Windows operating system. Its true aim was to prevent the machine from being used to make illegal copies of CDs. However, because it was poorly programmed, it also caused computers to run slowly and crash frequently and left them vulnerable to more destructive types of malware.

And in 2014, computer manufacturer Lenovo began installing software written by a company called Superfish on some of its machines before they were sold.[73] Superfish examined the information that flowed to and from the web browser on the computer where it was active. It also altered web content, adding advertisements that were judged to be relevant to whoever was accessing the internet.

What Superfish did is an example of the man-in-the-middle technique we discussed in the previous chapter. When somebody used their browser to view a website, Superfish communicated with both the browser and the website. Because it was running on the same computer as your browser and your browser was set up to use it, Superfish was able to negotiate one key to talk to your browser and a second key to talk to the website you were viewing without you or the website noticing anything untoward. Even when users were viewing encrypted websites and would have presumed their communications were protected from eavesdroppers, Superfish was actually decrypting what they sent and reading it before re-encrypting it and sending it on its way. And to add insult to injury, the software was poorly engineered just like XCP. It left the computers that ran it vulnerable to further attacks.[74]

Prosumware

Superfish was software that was distributed in a standard way but that went on to perform questionable activities. The diametric opposite is prosumware: software that is spread using traditional malware techniques but whose payload is designed to help users rather than to harm them. As early as 1993, a virus called Cruncher was released that compressed files on the computers it infected with the aim of saving disk space.[75] More recently, 2014 saw the discovery of prosumware called Linux.Wifatch.[76]

Wifatch mostly infects network routers and CCTV cameras. There is a server that scours the internet attempting to log into machines by trying out commonly occurring insecure passwords. We shall see in the next chapter that a surprising number of machines on the internet have either empty passwords or simple passwords like *123456*.

Wherever it gets in successfully, the scanner program transfers Wifatch to its victim machine and installs it there. The infected machine is then part of a botnet that its masters could easily use for villainous purposes. However, the anomalous nature of Wifatch does not stop with the fact that it infects Linux rather than Windows. Its authors' aim is actually to improve the security of the machines it targets.

Wifatch starts by closing off the attack path to other people by disabling the program it has just used to infiltrate its target. It then scans the router for pre-existing malware using an up-to-date virus signature database. Any infections found are promptly removed. And the router's owner receives a friendly message advising him to change his password to something sensible. In 2015, the authors of Wifatch anonymously published the program code of this helpful payload on the internet in case anybody wanted to learn from it.[77]

Despite the good intentions of the people who write prosumware, the prevailing view is that the world would still be better off without it, both on ethical and on technical grounds. Computers belong to their owners and it should remain their decision whether they want to perform virus scans or create more space on their hard drives. And even if Wifatch does look considerably more expertly written not only than most malware but also than a lot of commercially available software, there have been several instances in the past of tame strains of malware doing inadvertent damage because their authors' assumptions about how infected machines would work were not quite right. If the same thing happened with prosumware, its creators would want to solve the problem. However, they would not be able to distribute a simple update as the authors of a misbehaving legitimate program would, because fixing a bug would require a second attack that could quite conceivably be blocked by antivirus software even if the first attack had got through.

Zero-days and other vulnerabilities

We have already mentioned that some drive-by downloads have been facilitated by browser design faults that attackers managed to exploit to get software installed secretly. More generally, vulnerabilities—construction errors in programs that can be used to trick them into behaving differently from how their authors intended—play a crucial role in software-related hacking and cyberattacks.

Many viruses, worms and trojans abuse vulnerabilities in order to get around the safeguards provided by antivirus software and operating systems. But at least as important as the exploitation of vulnerabilities by malware is their direct use by human actors. Backdoors into software can enable hackers to take over somebody else's computer as they communicate with it over the internet, or to get software running on a machine in their physical possession to behave in a way that its creators had not envisaged.

Just as the emergence of a new type of malware leads to a scramble on the part of antivirus software vendors to add its signature to their databases, the discovery of a previously unknown vulnerability in an operating system like Microsoft Windows or in an application like Microsoft Word results in a rush to plug the gap. The offending program code is updated and the new version is distributed to as many computers as possible as quickly as possible.

A vulnerability that has not yet come to the attention of the authors of the software that contains it is known as a zero-day. Because they offer an uncontrolled back route into the innards of computers running the affected software, zero-days command a high price on the black market: commercial malware authors can easily pay hundreds of thousands of dollars for a powerful zero-day. In an attempt to try and persuade people to remain within the bounds of the law and tell them first, software companies will often reward researchers with payments of the same order of magnitude.[78] As we shall see in Chapter V, nation states also hoard zero-days because they can be used to mount cyberwar attacks. What do these highly valued vulnerabilities consist of?

At the most basic physical level, the only thing the processor at the heart of a computer does is to manipulate sequences of bits—the ones and zeroes we introduced in the previous chapter. It is how specific groups of bits are defined and used that allows this purely electronic activity to be translated into actions that affect the outside world. The program instructions that tell the processor what to do are themselves made up of bits. Other sets of bits could be sent to a screen to be displayed as an image, to a hard drive to be saved as a file, or to another computer over the internet. And all the information that is stored electrically in the computer's memory is maintained there in the form of bits.

Everything keeps working as long as the right strings of bits are consistently interpreted in the right ways. Imagine the computer's memory contains a picture of a Picasso painting ready to be shown on a screen. Something goes wrong so that the bits that make up the image are sent to the processor to be run as a program instead. It would be a tremendous coincidence if the Picasso bits turned out to make up a working program.

When the processor tried to do whatever they happened to instruct, it is almost certain that it would run into an error almost immediately. However, the important point is that there would be nothing intrinsic to the bits themselves to mark them out as an image rather than a program. Bits are bits.

To be of any use, most software interacts with the outside world, accepting information from users and other programs and responding with more information. For example, if the software is the Windows calculator, it receives the numbers and arithmetical operations the user types in and replies with the results of its calculations. The information flowing to and from a program is represented as bits, just like the instructions that make up the program itself. When a typical software-based vulnerability is exploited, a program is expecting to receive some sort of information from its user such as a name, but the attacker manages to supply the program with a string of bits that somehow ends up altering its instructions and changing what it does.

A good developer can write his programs so that this is not possible. Securely written software keeps information that it has received from the outside world strictly separate from its original structure. In practice, though, the checks that would ensure this are often forgotten. This means supplying a program with something that looks very different from the information its author had expected it to receive can sometimes make it behave in a way its author had not intended.

Buffer overflows, Code Red
and Homebrew Wii

One of the first instances of malware that worked by exploiting a vulnerability was a worm called Code Red.[79] It spread rapidly around the world in 2001, targeting a certain type of Windows server. During a given period each month, infected machines would try and overwhelm the White House web server by all issuing requests to it at the same time. The Code Red story represents an early example of what is known as a distributed denial-of-service attack, which we shall look at in more detail in Chapter IV. When security researcher Kenneth D. Eichman finally figured out how to curb the malware, the White House thanked him with a lunch invitation.[80] Code Red had been taking advantage of a type of software vulnerability called a buffer overflow.

Another buffer overflow facilitated an attack on the Nintendo Wii games platform in 2008.[81] While the Code Red worm had used the technique to infect computers against their owners' wishes, the Nintendo Wii vulnerability was deliberately exploited by individual video console users. The consoles were designed only to run software that was licensed by Nintendo; it was not intended that other people should be able to develop new games to run on a Wii. Although various people had managed to get around the platform's control mechanisms and play their own games, this had required making physical modifications to the console, and anything that involved a screwdriver remained firmly outside the scope of what most people were willing or able to try. The situation changed when a buffer overflow vulnerability was discovered in one of Nintendo's games that ended up giving console owners a purely software-based way of taking over control of their machines.

To grasp how buffer overflows work, we first need to take a closer look at how computer memory is structured and what computer processors do. Memory is where a computer stores all sorts of information. It is a vast battery of bit values—zeroes and ones—held in place with electric current. It might help to imagine it as being like an unimaginably enormous pad of squared paper.

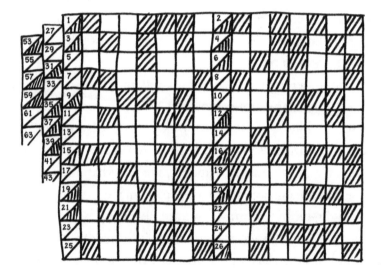

Each square stores a single bit and can either contain black pencil marks (value one) or be empty (value zero). The processor interacts with the squares in groups of eight that are generally referred to as bytes. It refers to each group with an address number that depends on how far the group is from the beginning of the first page. The first group on the first sheet is *1*, the second group is *2*, then *3*, *4* and so on right through to the last group on the last sheet. (Technically speaking, memory actually starts with a *0* address, but it is not normally used.)

Although a computer determines the position of a bit within its memory electronically, you might find the paper-pad analogy easier to follow if you imagine that the top left-hand corner of each group is indelibly printed with its address number. The eight bits held at an address combine to determine its value. There are 256 different permutations of eight digits where each is either a zero or a one. Because human beings find reading and communicating strings of bits difficult, people normally refer to each possible combination using a different number between 0 and 255. *0* denotes *00000000*, *1* denotes *00000001*, *2* denotes *00000011*, and so on.

The number at one memory address might be used to keep track of how many times a button has been pressed in a web browser, while another group of addresses might store somebody's surname, with each letter represented by a specific pair of address values. In Chapter I, we saw that a letter can be represented by a group of sixteen bits, which corresponds to two of the eight-bit byte numbers we are discussing here.

When a program accesses and alters information, the values at the individual memory addresses where that information is stored are transferred on to the processor chip. They are used in calculations whose results are then transferred back in the other direction from the processor chip to memory locations. The processor can change the value of bits in memory just as squares on a pad of paper can be filled in with a pencil or rubbed out with an eraser.

As we mentioned earlier in this chapter, the instructions that make up a program are themselves numeric values. They are stored somewhere within memory and the processor works through them to find out what to do. The processor might read the bit string *00101001*, which corresponds to the number *41*. Each action the processor knows how to perform is associated with its own number, so that the number *41* might mean "increase the value of one number copied on to the chip from memory by the value of a second number copied on to the chip from memory."

If the processor reads the number *41*, it knows that the next two groups of eight bits it will read will specify which values copied on to the chip from memory it is supposed to add together. It will interpret these next two groups of eight bits as identifying two such values, although in a different context they would designate two completely different actions in their own right. Once these two groups of bits have been read, the add action will be complete and the next group of bits the processor reads will once again be construed as an action code.

Memory therefore contains both numbers that make up programs and numbers that represent various types of information that those programs are using and creating. A program will sometimes store its information in the same area of the computer's memory where it is itself located, and sometimes at completely separate memory locations.

The Nintendo Wii vulnerability centred around a game called *The Legend of Zelda: Twilight Princess* that featured a horse that was normally called Epona but whose name could be changed via a little-used option to something else chosen by the player. When a player entered a new name, the game console checked that the name was not longer than a maximum length. However, it was possible to save a game to the hard drive half way through in order to re-load it later and continue playing.

Somebody analysed the program that ran the game. He realised that it failed to check the length of the horse name when a half-played game was reloaded from the hard drive.

Imagine the program is about to command the processor to read a new horse name from the hard drive, where it is stored as a sequence of numbers. It is about to update its own version of the horse name by incorporating these numbers one by one into its own structure within memory, placing the first number from the hard drive into the first address where its own horse name is stored, the second number from the hard drive into the second address, and so on.

A well-written program would not embark upon this action until it had ensured that the new horse name was short enough to fit into the area of memory reserved for it. However, the person who wrote the *Twilight Princess* game forgot this check. Say the intended maximum length was twenty addresses. If the game program now reads in a new horse name that is actually thirty addresses long, it is not only the twenty addresses intended for the horse name that will be changed. The ten addresses immediately following them will be as well. This is the essence of the buffer overflow.

The hacker changed a half-played game directly on the hard drive. He replaced the horse name the program had saved with a fake horse name consisting of a word of exactly the maximum length followed by a program. When the half-played game was re-loaded, the whole overlong horse name was copied to memory. And crucially, because the area of memory immediately following the area designated for the horse name was used by the game to store instructions that were to be sent to the processor, the hacker was then able to make the Wii console do whatever he wanted. The processor understood the numbers that had made up the second part of the fake horse name as part of the program that it was to perform.

A half-played *Twilight Princess* game with an overlong horse name was made generally available to Nintendo Wii users over the internet. The horse name contained a program that instructed the Wii console to load new games not licensed by Nintendo. Suddenly, anyone who owned *Twilight Princess* was in a position to run such games, known collectively as Homebrew Wii, without having to risk breaking his console by physically tampering with it. This was not good news for Nintendo's business. Just like the Code Red attack on the White House, however, its impact on society at large was fairly limited.

Heartbleed

In April 2014, on the other hand, a buffer overflow weakness was discovered with far more profound effects. A significant proportion of all the computers connected to the internet were suddenly put into a situation where what was in their memory was exposed to the world and could be stolen at liberty, secrets and all.

OpenSSL is an open-source library that consists of program instructions for the private/public key encryption mechanism explained in Chapter I.[82] An open-source library is a piece of software available for developers to incorporate into their own programs free of charge and is typically created and maintained by a community of online collaborators who welcome contributions from anyone with the right combination of skills, knowledge and enthusiasm. Because open-source software comes into being outside the bounds of budgetary pressures and gives the top experts in each specialised field an ideal opportunity to put their abilities on show, the quality the most popular projects attain increasingly outstrips anything produced by commercial software companies.

Open-source software is freely accessible. Anyone can examine the programs that make it up. This is a significant advantage from a cybersecurity viewpoint because it means it can be scoured for vulnerabilities just like the open encryption methods discussed in Chapter I. On the other hand, people write it in their spare time, and any legal liability they retain for what they produce is so limited as to remain largely theoretical. This means that when open-source software is produced, the focus can often be even more on developing new features and even less on doing so securely than when software is written by businesses. And because an open-source library is designed to be copied all over the place, the ramifications can be frighteningly wide-ranging when it transpires that a library contains a vulnerability that nobody noticed when it was written.

In March 2012, a new version of OpenSSL had been released. It included an option that allowed a program or person on one machine to check that OpenSSL was still working properly on a second machine by sending it a so-called heartbeat request. To show that everything was still up and running while doing as little as possible, the second machine was simply to send back unchanged whatever string of information it had received from the first machine. It achieved this by copying the information from the request into an area of memory and then copying the same information back out of that area of memory into the response.

The vulnerability was found just over two years later by two researchers working independently from each other, one at

Google[83], the other at a Finnish company called Codenomicon.[84] The problem was that the amount of information OpenSSL copied back out of memory to form the response did not depend on how long the request had been. Rather, it depended on how long the request had claimed to be. Each heartbeat request contained information about its own length, and the OpenSSL library failed to check whether the stated value corresponded to the number of bits that the request actually contained. The software took the asserted length of each request at face value and used it to determine how many bits to copy back out of memory to generate the response.

An attacker could use a heartbeat request that was much shorter than it professed to be to trigger a buffer overflow. A request that really only contained enough bits to occupy one thousand addresses could claim to be fifty thousand addresses long. When the request was copied into memory on the victim computer, it would overwrite the pre-existing contents of the thousand addresses it occupied. However, the pre-existing contents of the forty-nine thousand addresses that directly followed those thousand addresses would remain untouched but would nonetheless be copied back out and returned to the sender as part of the reply.

Heartbleed thus enabled an attacker to steal a copy of whatever happened to be in the portion of the recipient machine's memory that directly followed the addresses where the request information was temporarily stored. Although there was an element of chance in what was returned, he could send as many heartbeat requests as he wanted until the copied information contained something interesting. Depending on what the machine was doing at the moment it processed the heartbeat request, this could mean passwords, bank details, or anything else a computer might happen to be processing.

It was bad enough when this happened to somebody's laptop, but even worse when the target was the server a company was using to run its website. We shall see in the following chapter that when a server wants to prove its identity over the internet, it generates a secret private key that it keeps hidden within its memory and uses to sign messages destined for other computers. The whole system is based on the premise that any message that was signed using your private key must have originated from you because you will never have told anybody else what it is. However, a significant proportion of overlong heartbeat responses now included private keys that computers were just in the process of using to sign messages, and an attacker who had gained access to your private key could use it to impersonate you. The vulnerability had gouged a gaping hole in the very encryption mechanism that OpenSSL had been designed to facilitate.

Codenomicon christened the vulnerability Heartbleed. It has been characterised as the most catastrophic bug in the history of the internet in terms of its potential impact. Some 17% of the world's web servers were open to attack at the time it became common knowledge, as were many standard desktops and laptops running widely used software that incorporated OpenSSL.[85] This included the word processing package LibreOffice.[86]

The absence of the instructions that should have checked the length of the heartbeat request has been estimated to have cost businesses worldwide at least $500m.[87] We can presume that many companies were hacked using Heartbleed without ever finding out. Among the more high-profile victims who realised was the U.S. hospital chain Community Health Systems.[88] Attackers used the bug to obtain a user name and password that got them into the company's network. Once inside, the hackers managed to gain access to a database containing the records of some 4,500,000 patients. The details included names, addresses, birth dates, phone numbers and social security numbers.

Sneaking commands into input data

Programming a computer using only numbers would be both tedious and very hard. Developers write almost all software using computer languages that consist of words and symbols that are translated into the numeric code understood by the processor. Such high-level computer languages have several similarities to human language. They are made up of commands that can be seen as equivalent to sentences. A sentence like *Peter gave Mary a ball* contains a verb—*gave*—that specifies an action in which the nouns *Peter*, *Mary*, and *ball* participate. In the same way, a computer command consists of at least one word or symbol specifying an action to be performed and usually further words denoting the things that the action is to involve. A command might tell the computer to add two numbers together or to send a picture to your monitor.

The length of each word within a high-level computer language is not normally important. This means a hacker cannot take over control of a program in its human-readable form by supplying an overlong piece of information; the buffer overflow technique only has a chance of working once the program has been changed into numeric processor code.

However, high-level computer languages can be vulnerable to a different sort of problem. Sometimes a program in its high-level form includes incomplete commands that are only finalised just before they are translated into processor code and executed: they can contain empty placeholders that have to be filled in with information supplied from outside the program. A command might tell the processor to "send an E-mail to ?". The program then has to replace the question-mark with whatever addressee the user has specified before the command can be converted into numeric code and sent to the processor.

If the program fails to check that the text it is incorporating into its command really consists of a single noun and nothing more, it may be presenting an inadvertent blank check to the outside world. A user may be able to change what the command does by supplying more words that have a meaning in whatever computer language it is written in. This technique is called injection.

Injection vulnerabilities are not restricted to the realm of computers. They can potentially occur wherever incomplete orders are imbued with premature authority. Imagine an ailing monarch in the days before telecommunications who knows that he will have to leave his realm for several weeks, but fears unrest if his subjects get wind of his absence.

Normally he issues a decree from his sick bed every Sunday that is read out on his behalf. He cannot allow a Sunday to pass without a proclamation, because that would lead to suspicions about whether he was still in town. However, he cannot put out the decrees in advance either, because each one includes a list of guests who are to be welcomed over the course of the week to come. His solution to the problem is to write a batch of decrees before he leaves that bear his seal but that each have a large gap where the guests would normally be listed. Each week, his secretary is to enter the names of the expected individuals into one of the ready-made decrees.

If his secretary is inclined to abuse the situation, he is not restricted to entering lists of names into the gap on each decree. He can add anything he likes and it will be accepted on the basis that it clearly bears regal authority. If he is clever in his use of language, he can even complete the sentence into which the king intended him to insert the names and start a new one, perhaps granting himself all sorts of special powers. The only restriction is that whatever he writes has to make sense when followed by the predetermined text that follows the gap. Despite the fact that no technology is involved, this story depicts a classic injection weakness.

Cross-site scripting and Lionaneesh

Returning to the modern day and the internet, when you use your browser to interact with a website, the browser sends the web server responsible for the website a request specifying whatever you want to see, and the web server replies with the content for the browser to display. As we shall see in Chapter IV, the scheme describing the structure of the messages that go backwards and forwards is called Hypertext Transfer Protocol (HTTP), which is why the Universal Resource Locator (URL)—the address that appears at the top of the browser window and that specifies to the browser which page to retrieve from which website—starts with http.

Among other things, the HTTP reply that comes back from the server contains a structured document that tells the browser how to display the web page in question. Such documents are arranged in a format called Hypertext Markup Language (HTML). HTML is not a programming language in that an HTML document is not a list of commands that are carried out one after the other. Instead, an HTML markup document consists of the text that the browser is to display interspersed with elements called tags that have special meanings. Some tags specify that objects like images and buttons should be included on the web page, while others denote the style of stretches of text. Tags are enclosed by the angle brackets ‹ and ›, also known as the lesser-than and greater-than symbols. For example, the ‹i› tag causes whatever text follows it to be shown in italics, while the ‹/i› tag switches italics off again, so that the HTML

```
a book called <i>Cybertwists</i> about hacking
```

would be shown in the browser as follows:

```
a book called Cybertwists about hacking
```

A web server that is cobbling together an HTML document to send to your browser might incorporate some text that you have entered into a previous page. The first page might have asked the question `What is your name?` and the answer might be included within a subsequent greetings page, as in `Hello, Peter`. If the server fails to check that the name that was entered is free of HTML tags, the website will be vulnerable to an injection attack. A user could specify his name as `<i>Peter</i>` to get the website to display it in italics. He could also add a button or image to the greetings page. Because there is a tag that tells the browser to stop processing the document, he would even be able to prevent everything on the page after his name from being shown.

Although it is hardly good news for the website that the user can make it do things that were not intended, the alterations that this technique allows are limited by what can be done with HTML tags inserted at the relevant point within the document. However, one can make much more wide-ranging changes to the whole HTML document using a language called Javascript.

Unlike HTML, Javascript is a genuine programming language with commands that are carried out one after another. A Javascript program is added to a HTML page using a tag that tells the browser to stop understanding HTML and start understanding Javascript until it encounters a second tag that tells it to switch back to HTML. If it is possible to get a web server to add new HTML tags to a page, it is usually also possible to persuade it to incorporate a Javascript program.

It is Javascript that enables programmers to create websites that are a pleasure to use. Without it, a web page would remain completely unchanged once your browser had first shown it. The intended purpose of Javascript is to tell your browser to modify content it has already displayed in response to something you have done. For example, when you make a selection from a list of types of hotel on a travel website, a Javascript program might specify that additional option lists specific to the type of hotel you chose should appear elsewhere on the page.

However, it is also possible to write Javascript commands that tell the browser to change a page immediately after it has first displayed it and before the user has had a chance to do anything. The original content will then be shown for a fraction of a second before it is removed and replaced by the altered version. In an extreme case, a hacker could use this technique to strip everything from the normal page and display something completely different.

The type of attack where Javascript is injected into a web page is known as cross-site scripting (XSS). You might ask at this point whether being able to make your browser display a website that looks different from how its author intended is really serious enough to count as hacking. After all, is not the hacker the only person who gets to see what he has done? **Whatever your personal view on this point, please bear in mind the warning in the preface. Many countries' laws regard cross-site scripting as illegal!**

In fact, however, there are some slightly more complicated sorts of cross-site scripting that do indeed affect other people. For most websites, information that has been entered on one page and is to be displayed on the next page is stored and managed on the central web server; the browser never gets to see what is going on. However, a minority of websites use the browser to feed through user-specific information from one page to the next. This works by the browser taking something the user typed into one page and incorporating it into the URL it sends to the server to request the next page. For example, a server could be instructed to display a greetings page for the customer *Jane* using the URL http://www.mywebsite.com?name=Jane.

If the server program fails to check that the URL it receives does not contain any HTML tags, it will probably be vulnerable to cross-site scripting, because a hacker will then be able to inject a Javascript tag into the URL as part of the specified customer name. The weakness this represents is more serious than cross-site scripting that relies on information being entered into a form as a website is being used, because an attacker can use it to direct other people to an affected version of the web page by placing a link to such a poisoned URL on to another website or by sending it around in an E-mail.

This version of cross-site scripting was used in 2011 by an Indian hacker with the pseudonym Lionaneesh. He adulterated the World Factbook website maintained by the US Central Intelligence Agency (CIA) using a link that contained a Javascript program.[89] When you clicked on the link, you were directed to a version of the site that sported a prominent banner inviting the reader to follow Lionaneesh on Twitter. The aim of the hack was to embarrass the CIA and show off Lionaneesh's skills. This is one step up from self-hacking, but still some way off from doing any concrete harm to anything other than the reputation of the victim organisation.

However, URL-based cross-site scripting also has the potential to facilitate fraud. When a website or E-mail shows a link to a second website, the link's text is often identical to the URL that your browser loads when you click on it. However, it need not be. A perfectly legitimate link might sport the text *BBC News* and lead to the BBC News site http://news.bbc.co.uk. A devious cross-site scripting attacker could create a link that shows a normal URL, e.g. https://cybertwists.com, but that actually points to a second URL that still specifies the same website but that also includes injected Javascript. When a victim clicks on the link, the beginning of the URL that appears in his browser will still look correct. This means he will probably have no reason to suspect that he is retrieving anything other than the genuine website. In reality, though, the content of the page that he will see will be controlled by the hacker.

Cross-site scripting vulnerabilities can be exploited to do still more serious damage when a web server stores content supplied by one user and displays it to subsequent users. If a website has a guestbook facility allowing people to leave comments and fails to check that the comments do not contain HTML tags, a comment could be injected containing a Javascript program that alters not just the guestbook but also the rest of the page that contains it. If you are an innocent bystander trying to use the site, you will then always see the attacker's version of the page as opposed to the original version, regardless of the fact that you have entered the correct URL.

Viral tweets

A Javascript program can also be written to enter silently a new comment into a text box and then press the button that submits that comment. If somebody leaves a guestbook comment that contains a Javascript program that itself leaves a new comment, the first person to view the page will find he has unwittingly left an additional comment, giving two in total. The second person to view the page will then leave two additional comments—one for each existing comment. The third person will leave four comments, the fourth eight and so on. The number of infected comments will increase exponentially, eventually bringing the website to its knees because of the size of the page its server is having to transmit.

Snippets of Javascript that repost themselves when they are viewed present a particular problem for an online-E-mail or social media website where each user maintains his own page. They self-replicate much like traditional strains of malware. A user inadvertently viewing a script posted on somebody else's personal page will suddenly find that it has been posted on his own personal page without his knowledge and is now visible to all his followers. Twitter fell victim to exactly such a script in 2014. The main Twitter website was immune to the problem, because if somebody tweeted something that contained angle brackets, the Twitter server made sure it sent them to your browser in such a way that they were not interpreted as HTML tags. However, the same was not true of the Tweetdeck website designed to help more advanced users manage their Twitter accounts.

An Austrian teenager using the pseudonym Firo stumbled upon the Tweetdeck cross-site scripting vulnerability by accident when he discovered that it was possible to use code to tweet a red heart.[90] Realising that the same mechanism could be abused by hackers, he notified Twitter, who took Tweetdeck temporarily offline so they could fix the problem.

However, another user had beaten them to it. He extended Firo's tweet so that it now not only featured a red heart, but also retweeted itself whenever it was viewed on Tweetdeck. Because the main Twitter website displayed tags as normal text rather than getting browsers to do whatever they directed, anyone viewing the tweet on it would see the Javascript tag and the program it contained. A Tweetdeck user who viewed the tweet, on the other hand, would only see the red heart, but his browser would run the program, which would make it forward the tweet on to all his followers.[91]

Although anyone is free to choose between using Tweetdeck or the main Twitter website, the additional features Tweetdeck offers mean it is more likely to appeal to the professional or semi-professional author with a large number of readers. Within a short space of time, the script had been retweeted by over 83,000 Tweetdeck users including such heavyweights as *@NYTimes* and *@BBCBreaking*. This last user alone had more than 10 million followers at the time, most of whom must have been somewhat puzzled by the cryptic-looking Javascript code and red heart![92]

Cookies and tokens

Still more worrying than viral tweets is the fact that an attacker can sometimes use cross-site scripting to make your browser send him pieces of information about you and what you are doing as you access a website. Cookies are snippets of text that a web server uses to park information on a browser in between different occasions when it is accessed from that browser. Whenever somebody using a browser is viewing a website and the server responsible for the website sends a new page for the browser to display, the server is allowed to ask the browser to store cookies on its behalf at the same time. The browser will return these cookies in subsequent communication with the website: whenever a browser requests a page from any server, it automatically transmits with its request any cookies it has previously received from that server.

A web server might employ a cookie to store an option that the user chose on one of its pages so that it can refer to the user's decision several clicks later when some other page is generated. Alternatively, it might use cookies to allow it to remember what a user did on one day for reference the next time he re-accesses it from the same computer. It is general good practice for websites to store cookies in such a way that they cannot be accessed by Javascript code.[93] However, if a website fails to take this precaution and also happens to be vulnerable to cross-site scripting, an attacker will be able to use injected Javascript commands to make a browser send all the cookies it has stored for that website to some other, completely unrelated website without the user noticing anything untoward.

As we shall see in the following chapter, when a user has successfully logged into a website with a user name and password, the website typically creates a random string of letters and numbers called a token. The web server remembers the token and also sends it to the user's browser to be stored in a cookie. Because this cookie is automatically transmitted back each time the user requests more website content from the server, the server can compare the token in the cookie to the list of tokens it has remembered to find out who the user is and to verify that that user logged in with the right password.

If a hacker has been able to use cross-site scripting to make your browser run some Javascript that sends him the token cookie for some insecure website you are logged into, he can go on to write a program to send a request to the website pretending to be your browser returning that token cookie. The website will then treat him as you and he can continue using the site as you—quite possibly with access to all sorts of personal information—without needing any prior knowledge about your password, who you are or where you are.

SQL injection

Cross-site scripting makes individual browsers carry out extra programming instructions as they display web content. Although we have seen that it can be employed to cause significant damage, it can only ever affect one user at a time. An attack tends to have a somewhat greater impact when it causes extra instructions to be run on the central web servers on which website content is created and managed and from which that content is supplied to all the browsers that request it: such an attack puts a hacker in a position to access and possibly to alter information that pertains to a large number of people.

Most websites that have users maintain information about them in a database, a collection of tables that you can imagine as equivalent to Excel spreadsheets. When you shop online, the website you use might store details of the products you have browsed so it knows which advertisements to display to you in the future. On the other hand, a social media site might record the names of contacts whose pages you have viewed so it can build up a picture of your relationships. Although a website database is occasionally located on the same server that generates and supplies the web content, it is normally based on a separate one within the same company network as that server.

Imagine somebody is searching a social media platform for people registered under a certain name. He types the name into a search field on his browser, which requests a list of people with that name from the server on which the social media website is hosted. The server then works out which data it needs to answer the question and sends a request for that information to its database. The list of matching people is returned from the database to the web server, which then uses it to produce the page content that is finally sent back to the browser and displayed to the person who initiated the search.

The language the web server uses to communicate with the database is called Structured Query Language (SQL). If the web server fails to check that what the browser has requested it to look for is a genuine name, it might be possible for a hacker to enter additional SQL code into the search field. The web server might then unwittingly inject this extra code into the SQL command it sends to the database, changing what it asks it to do. This type of attack is called SQL injection.

Say you are using an online banking website to search for past transactions where you have transferred money to a company called *Tommy Tilers*. You would have already logged into the website and it would have established that your account number was *13579*. You would then have entered the name *Tommy Tilers* into a search page. The web server might retrieve the relevant information by sending the database an SQL command that means "Give me all rows you have where money was transferred from account 13579 and the recipient was called Tommy Tilers".

Because the structure of SQL is closely modelled on the English language, SQL injection feels even more like the trick in the above story about the king and his secretary than cross-site scripting does. A hacker might enter into the search field SQL corresponding to the English phrase *Tommy Tilers or where the payer name was at least one letter long*. This would lead to the web server sending the database an SQL command that means "Give me all rows you have where money was transferred from account 13579 and the recipient was called Tommy Tilers or where the payer name was at least one letter long." Because it is not possible for a payer name to be empty, the database will now return its complete store of past transaction records, regardless of whether the account number was *13579* or the recipient name *Tommy Tilers*, and the web server will forward all this information back to the hacker's browser.

When it is being used legitimately, the online banking website will often only be expecting to retrieve and show a small amount of information at once. An attacker may therefore have difficulty making it display its entire store of transaction records in one go even if he has managed to use injection to produce an SQL command that returns such a huge volume of data. Rather, he may have to inject a large number of different SQL snippets to retrieve the information systematically row by row.

Just as a written sentence ends with what is called a full stop in the UK and a period in the USA, SQL has a punctuation mark that signifies the end of one command and the beginning of the next. An attacker performing SQL injection can sometimes use this punctuation mark to make the server send the database a second command that is completely independent of the original command the programmer intended. By entering into the password field SQL that corresponds to the English *Tommy Tilers. Then delete the database*, the hacker can make the server send the database an SQL command that means "Give me all rows you have where money was transferred from account 13579 and the recipient was called Tommy Tilers. Then delete the database."

Destroying a website's database may sound like a worst-case scenario, but there will usually be a backup copy available that can be used to recover it. In today's knowledge economy, the damage caused is typically greater when SQL injection is used to steal a database's contents. Remembering that a database is a collection of tables that are similar to Excel spreadsheets, someone who has gained access to the database behind a website will use various techniques to find out the names of the various tables and the column headings within each one. His aim is gradually to build up his own copy of as much of the database as he can. The information is then either sold to criminals or merely posted online to show off the supposed prowess of the attacker.

LinkedIn and TalkTalk

SQL injection may make its perpetrators feel clever, but the reality is that it is very simple to carry out and certainly not a hallmark of any great technical ability. Nonetheless, it is usually the technique behind headlines where big-name companies have had all their data stolen. In June 2012, Russian hackers captured and posted online nearly 6.5 million user names and passwords from LinkedIn, and there is strong evidence that they used SQL injection.[94] (As we shall see in the following chapter, the fact that their booty could subsequently be used to access people's accounts stemmed from the fact that the passwords had been stored in an insecure format.)

Just investigating what had happened cost LinkedIn between $500,000 and $1m.[95] One of the biggest problems for organisations in the wake of an SQL injection attack is working out exactly what information has been stolen. Even if the database machine has kept a log of what was accessed when, the SQL injection technique may have been used to build up a copy of the organisation's data over an extended period of time. Evidence of the illicit activity will then be mixed up with records of normal day-to-day business.

A company buckling under media pressure to issue comprehensive details of a breach is unlikely to have the time to wait for its staff to dig out all the historical details. The British internet service provider TalkTalk experienced this problem when it fell victim to SQL injection in 2015. Initially, the company could only declare that it had been attacked and that credit card and bank account information belonging to any of its customers could potentially have been stolen.[96]

It eventually transpired that the bank account numbers of only a small fraction of TalkTalk customers had been purloined.[97] This was hardly good news, but the original fear that the attack would enable credit-card fraud on a massive scale turned out to have been unfounded: in fact, no directly usable card numbers had been accessed. By the time this had been clarified, however, TalkTalk's reputation had already suffered immeasurable damage.

The company later estimated the total cost of the data breach to have reached up to £60m, which corresponded to over $90m at the time.[98] And a year later in October 2016, the British Information Commissioner's Office fined the company an additional £400,000—some $500,000—for failing to protect its customers' personal data.[99]

Why so many companies fall victim

NASA[100], the World Trade Organisation[101], the Wall Street Journal.[102] There is a long list of organisations that have fallen victim to SQL injection, and a still longer list of organisations that have suffered unspecified attacks that sound as though SQL injection was probably to blame. This does not even begin to address data theft that remains under the radar. SQL injection is without doubt the hacking technique that is most costly to companies, individuals and society in general. It also generates the most media attention.

And yet it is actually something that could be simply prevented if whoever wrote the server program followed a couple of straightforward rules. SQL code contains symbols that would most definitely never form part of anybody's name, address or credit card number. Checking that these symbols do not occur in whatever text a user has entered before incorporating it into an SQL command is an easy way of avoiding the problem. There are also simple ways of building SQL that explicitly distinguish between the original command and the information being included in it. Given how easy it is to banish SQL injection completely and definitively from a website, it seems almost unbelievable that large institutions and corporations are still falling prey to it left, right and centre.[103]

When developers write software, their focus is generally on what they are trying to get it to do rather than on security issues. Just as the draft version of a book contains various types of errors, most programs are born insecure. The most effective way of toughening up software before it is released to the general public is a so-called penetration test in which somebody tries to hack it in a legal and controlled fashion and sees how far he can get. As long as the person carrying out the test has the appropriate skills, he has a very good chance of finding any places where the program is vulnerable to classic attacks like cross-site scripting and SQL injection, because he will try out precisely the same tricks as a real hacker would.

The sheer scope of large software products like Microsoft Windows make it unrealistic that a new version will ever be released completely free of vulnerabilities. In practice, a few complex attack scenarios will probably always slip through the net of even the most tenacious penetration tester and surface at a later date as zero-days. However, if LinkedIn or TalkTalk had performed adequate security testing on their much less extensive systems, it is most unlikely that they would have fallen victim to such a basic problem as SQL injection. Why have companies so often failed to take steps to eliminate low-hanging fruit that attackers can take advantage of with the minimum of effort and knowledge?

The essential problem is that executives have tended to underestimate the likelihood of their companies being hacked as well as the probable scope and ramifications of any attack that might occur. Slowly but surely, though, this finally seems to be beginning to change. More and more firms are accepting the additional costs of making sure that newly created software fulfils basic security requirements, even if they still tend to shy away from the more substantial investment of checking older systems retrospectively.

This mind shift has not only come about because instances of data theft are getting more and more media attention and the penny has begun to drop with board members that it might not be such a good idea for the popular consciousness to associate their brands with vulnerable software. Regulatory frameworks, too, are becoming stricter. From May 2018, organisations operating within the European Union that fail to protect their customers' data adequately are liable for fines of up to €10m (around $12m) or 2% of their global annual turnover, whichever is greater.[104] Alongside such figures, the £400,000 TalkTalk fine pales into insignificance. For financial reasons if nothing else, information security is set to play a much more important role in software development and operations over the years to come. If whatever software is created is to be created secure, it will have to become either more expensive or less extensive in the functionality it offers.

III. IDENTITIES

Most computer systems involve identities of one sort or another. You access websites using personal accounts, send E-mails from and to specific addresses and rely on the fact that your internet banking website is really being run by your bank. In all these cases, usurping the relevant identity often sets the scene for further crimes. In this chapter, we examine the various methods used to determine identity and the cyberattacks that target them. We start with knowledge-based means of authentication like PINs and passwords and then go on to look at biometrics and bank cards. The chapter concludes by describing the certificate system that is used to manage and prove identities within the internet.

Brute force and UK phone mailboxes

In 2011, the then UK Prime Minister David Cameron ordered a public inquiry into phone hacking.[105] For many journalists, stealing private information from the people they were reporting on had become a regular way of working. The central technique they used to achieve this was eavesdropping on mailboxes.

The intrusion of privacy the mailbox hacking entailed was bad enough. Worse still, reporters covering their tracks often meant that a message never got to be heard by its intended recipient. Journalists would often delete new messages once they had listened to them, because allowing messages they had accessed to remain in a mailbox risked arousing the suspicions of its owner: mailbox systems distinguish between new and old messages when they play them, and if you were played an old message that you had not heard before, you would conclude that someone else must have already listened to it.

A reporter could carry out an attack from the privacy of his own office. He needed no more than his target's telephone number to work out the number to dial at her phone provider company in order to access her mailbox. The mailbox would be protected by a PIN, but some people had chosen easily guessable values like *1234* or their dates of birth, while others had failed to change their PIN from defaults such as *0000*.[106]

Not all victims had been so imprudent. Many had in fact taken the precaution of changing their PIN to a sensible value. However, some providers' systems were set up in such a way that each and every customer was completely at the mercy of journalists nosing around regardless of the PIN he had used. These phone companies had failed to put a limit on how many times a caller was allowed to try and guess the correct value.[107] At the same time, they had restricted the range of permissible PINs to the numbers between 0000 and 9999. The two decisions would turn out to be a fatal combination that basically opened up messages to anybody who wanted to listen to them. You just had to invest a few hours in a brute-force attack where you looped through up to ten thousand possible numbers until you hit on the one that worked.

An internet-based system normally locks an account for a certain period of time if too many unsuccessful attempts have been made to log into it. This prevents brute-force attacks where a hacker who is allowed to keep guessing indefinitely loops through a long list of possible passwords until he hits on the correct value. The unwanted side effect—that the genuine user is temporarily shut out as well—is felt to be a price worth paying for keeping her information safe.

The same consideration should have been all the more valid for mailboxes. Phone companies that failed to use a comparable protection mechanism left their customers totally defenceless. While an internet user can reduce his risk of falling prey to a brute-force attack by using a password that is long, complex and unique, a mailbox user selecting a PIN has no such option. He is restricted to numbers rather than combinations of letters, numbers and special characters, and things get really bad when the PIN has to be composed of exactly four numbers.

Sony Pictures

Brute-force password hacking hit the headlines in November 2014 when a vast quantity of data was stolen from the Sony Pictures film studio.[108] Shortly after the breach, the United States Computer Emergency Readiness Team (US-CERT) published details of an attack "targeting a major entertainment company".[109] They described a sophisticated worm that proliferated between Microsoft Windows servers via a facility called Server Message Block that allows files stored on a server to be accessed from remote computers. Server Message Block access is password-protected, but, whenever the malware jumped from server to server, it was able to try out a vast number of possible passwords until it found the one that happened to be protecting its next target. Here too, then, it was the lack of a limit on the number of incorrect password attempts that had left systems open to attack.

Responsibility for the hack was claimed by an anonymous group who called themselves the Guardians of Peace.[110] They disclosed various titbits of gossip that seemed to be calculated to discredit film stars, Sony executives and the movie industry in general. They also leaked the full-length versions of several films that had not yet been released.

Then in December, almost a month after details of the attack had originally entered the public domain, the group issued a threat regarding an upcoming comedy blockbuster called *The Interview*.[111] The film mocked the North Korean leader Kim Jong Un and included a scene in which the helicopter in which he was travelling was obliterated when it was shelled by a tank. The group's warning marked out any cinemas that screened the movie as possible targets of terrorist attacks, which led to it being pulled by major cinema chains throughout the United States.

The FBI later claimed to have linked the Guardians of Peace to the North Korean state.[112] Although the technical evidence the Americans published to support this was somewhat patchy, the fact that the principal aim of the attack seems to have been to interfere with the release of *The Interview* makes it likely that the perpetrators were genuine sympathisers of the Kim regime. Even if, technically speaking, it remains within the bounds of possibility that the attack was actually carried out by a disgruntled Sony employee or some other person who was just pretending to be a North Korean, it is hard to see why someone with a general grudge would have had such a specific motive.

Predictably, the DPRK authorities vehemently denied the allegation on an official level.[113] However, in a pattern we shall see repeated several times in this book, it looks as though in reality one of their goals may well have been to show the world what they could do. The Guardians of Peace name was used to issue both the original news of the attack and the later threat that attempted to suppress the film. If the perpetrators genuinely wished to remain undercover, why did they choose to speak with the same voice on both occasions? Had the North Korean government simply claimed that independent hackers had sent them a copy of *The Interview* to which they were now reacting, they would not have been so clearly linkable to the original data theft.

Password hashes

Rather than trying to work out passwords by repeatedly attempting to log into a system in the intended way with different possible values, it is more efficient for a hacker to use techniques like those described in the previous chapter to breach that system and to go on to steal the passwords from the database where they are stored. This gets around any safeguards against brute-force attacks and potentially gives him access to the passwords of all the users of the system in one go rather than merely to passwords of individual users. However, software authors are mindful of this danger as well. A system designer will almost always take steps to ensure that the passwords for a system are stored in such a way that they cannot be used directly to log into it. As we will see in the following discussion, though, these steps are tricky and often implemented in a way that is far from watertight.

In the previous chapter, we saw how, in June 2012, Russian hackers used SQL injection to access the login details of millions of accounts belonging to the LinkedIn social network. They went on to publish around 6.5 million passwords together with the associated user names. That the SQL injection attack had worked in the first place was bad enough. What commentators found even more shocking at the time, and what formed the basis of a hefty lawsuit that was eventually settled in early 2015, was that it had been so easy for the hackers to transform the information they had found in the database into a list of usable passwords.[114]

This was possible even though LinkedIn had not kept the passwords in their simple, unencoded form. They had rather used a standard mechanism to protect them whereby when a new user registers with a website, the password he specifies is converted into a hash value by putting it through a hash function. The U.S. agency NIST discussed in Chapter I maintains and publishes descriptions of standard hash functions just as it does for standard encryption functions.[115] The hash values these functions create are sequences of bits that are often expressed as strings of digits where each digit is either a number or one of the letters between A and F. For example, one popular hash function would convert the password *cybertwists* into the following hash value:

```
e5e10c33f4e8e4a5f7f746af398622c80eb178f9b3721e68d
cbeb13f414811ec
```

Rather than storing the password itself, the system stores the password's hash value. When the user enters his password at some later time to log into the system, the password he types in is put through the same hash function that was used when he enrolled. If the resulting hash value matches the stored hash value, the system knows that the user must have entered the same password on both occasions and can let him into his account.

When you are logging into a system that requires a password, you cannot use its hash value instead. The hash value would then itself be put through the hash function, producing a new value that would not match the stored one. Storing hash values rather than raw passwords thus prevents anyone who manages to hack into a system and steal the user names and passwords from using that information directly to log in as other users.

Like other sorts of texts we have discussed in the previous chapters, a password is represented within a computer as a sequence of bits, or ones and zeroes, divided into groups that are perhaps 16 bits long depending on the standard being used. Each group represents the character at a different position within the password—a letter, number, or symbol—and each of the various characters the computer can display is signified by a different 16-bit combination. The sequence of bits that denote the characters that make up a password is what is put into the hash function.

A hash function works in a similar way to the block-based encryption described in Chapter I: values of the bits in the sequence are switched (ones become zeroes and zeroes become ones); sub-sequences within the sequence are replaced with new sub-sequences; and parts of the sequence are swapped around according to a predetermined pattern. The impenetrable string of ones and zeroes that results is the hash value. And another similarity to encryption is that a hash function is designed so that the outputs it produces reveal nothing about the texts from which they were generated. If two long strings of bits that are identical except for one single digit are put through a well-designed hash function, the hash values that emerge from it should display no detectable similarity.

How are hashing and encryption different? The crucial distinction is that a hash function only lets you travel in one direction. Information encrypted using the methods described in Chapter I can be decrypted again: someone in possession of the right key can use it to retrieve the original text. On the other hand, once a hash value has been generated from a piece of information, the aim is that there should be no possible way for anyone to recover the original piece of information from the hash value. This aim is achieved by using bit-mangling techniques that result in this one-way quality.

There is another important way in which hash functions differ from encryption functions. Whether what you put through a hash function is just a couple of letters or an entire book, the hash value that is generated is always the same length, which typically ranges from 128 to 512 bits depending on which technique is being used. This makes hashing more secure because it means that a hash value does not betray the length of the text that was used to generate it.

When a hash function receives a very short word, it pads it out with extra zeroes and ones before it operates on it to ensure that the resulting hash value will be exactly long enough. In the contrary case where the original text is much longer than the target hash value, the constant length is achieved as follows. Recall how, in block-based encryption, the text to be encoded is split up into blocks containing perhaps eight letters each. A list of bit-mangling steps is carried out on the bits within the first block of the original text to obtain the first block of the encrypted text. The bits in the second block of the original text are subjected to a change step whose details are based on the encrypted version of its predecessor, the first block, and it is the bits that result from this change step that are put through the list of bit-mangling steps to obtain the second block of the encrypted text. The same technique is then applied to the third, fourth and subsequent blocks, so that encrypted information percolates through from each block to its successor.

A hash function processes information block for block in a similar fashion.[116] However, when a hash function operates on a long original text and generates a correspondingly long sequence of encoded bits, they do not all need to be retained in the hash value. Because there is no requirement to be able to get back to the original text, it is sufficient to use one or more transformed blocks from the end of the sequence. Although these do not directly encode the whole original text, they will still reflect it in its entirety because the processing of each block took the preceding block's results into account. The hash value of a long text is like a fingerprint formed by whatever emerges when the hash function reaches the last few letters.

From an unlimited number of texts of different lengths emerge hash values of a single fixed length. Whatever the exact details of how a hash function works, this means there is no way it can possibly rule out converting two completely different original texts into the same hash value. Known as a collision, this is a theoretical eventuality that some people worry about when they work with hash functions. Personally, I try not to lose too much sleep over it. Modern hash functions are designed to avoid collisions, and they generate hash values that are long enough to mean it is just not going to happen. Even with a relatively short hash length of 128 bits, there are two to the power of 128 different possible values. It puts things into perspective when you consider that this is trillions of times more than the estimated number of atoms in the observable universe—around two to the power of 83.[117]

LinkedIn had put its users' passwords through a hash function before storing them, but this alone was insufficient to keep the original password values safe. Hashing is different from encryption in that there is normally no key involved. Because the key with which an encryption technique is configured determines the details of some of the change steps that are applied to each block when a text is encrypted, different encoded versions of the text will result if the same encryption method is used on two occasions but with different keys. The same does not apply to keyless hash functions. If you know the hash function somebody is employing, you can predict the hash value that will be generated from a given password. And there are only a small number of standardised hash functions in common use.

Rainbow tables

If you had access to the LinkedIn database and you knew the hash function LinkedIn had used, you could have searched the database for the hash value that resulted when a specific password like *123456* was put through the function. Wherever you had a hit, you would have known that the account in question must be using the password *123456* and would then have had all you needed to log into it. The same technique would have enabled you to gain access to a large number of accounts. You might have begun by finding out the hash values of the ten passwords people most commonly use and searching for them in the database.

In the event, the hackers will quite possibly not have needed to calculate the hash values of any passwords themselves. They are more likely to have consulted an electronic translation dictionary pre-generated for the hash function LinkedIn was using. Such dictionaries list words and character combinations together with the hash value derived from each one. They take the sting out of the mathematical impossibility of discovering the text that was used to generate a given hash value. With the right dictionary, you can simply look the hash value up.

A relatively short dictionary might contain the hash values for standard words in a certain language or languages. To make sure your password did not feature in such a list, you could use an acronym based on the first letters of each word in a phrase. *NIarabacah*, which is derived from the phrase *Now I am reading a book about cyberattacks and hacking*, would not feature in a simple, word-based hash list.

Neither would a subtly changed everyday word: the hash value generated from a password like *ElEffAnt* bears no resemblance to the hash value the underlying noun *elephant* would have been transformed into. If you mutate a word in a way nobody else has ever thought of, you will call into being a hash value that nobody else has ever used. In practice, though, this is easier said than done. Human beings tend to think alike, and many hash dictionaries contain entries for altered versions of common words.

In any case, avoiding bona fide words offers no protection when a more comprehensive list has been generated to cover random permutations of letters, numbers and special characters. A rainbow table is a type of structured dictionary that aims to offer translations for most hash values generated from character combinations up to a typical password size.[118] Only unusually long passwords remain out of reach, and while an acronym produced from a twenty-word sentence may not be retrievable via a rainbow table, it is hardly easy to remember or quick to type in either.

Salts

How could LinkedIn have made the hash values of its users' passwords less vulnerable to being looked up in rainbow tables? At the very least, they should have added some other text, called a salt, to each password before hashing it. They could have used *linkedin* as a salt. Say a user specifies the password *password123*. The system would add *linkedin* to the end and submit the resulting text *password123linkedin* to the hash function. The hash value that would emerge from it would not only be totally different from the well-known one generated from *password123*; it would also be based on a longer character combination. Both factors would make it considerably less likely to be found in a publicly available dictionary.

Better still would have been to use a different salt for each account. Say I register with a system as user *rphudson* with the password *security*. The system chooses a random salt for me, for example *gofU5efV*. It adds the random salt to my password and puts the resulting text, which in this case is *securitygofU5efV*, through the hash function. The hash value that results and the random salt are both stored in the database alongside my user name. When I next try and log in, the system can add the stored random salt to whatever password I type in, put the compound text through the hash function and check that it obtains the expected result.

The advantage of this procedure over using the same salt every time is that if a second user has also chosen *security* as his password, it will not be apparent to a hacker who has gained access to the user database that we are using the same password. Different salts will have been used in the two cases, and this will have led to different hash values being generated.

The time required to attack a single password within a database that uses individual salts is comparable to the time required to attack all the passwords stored in a database that does not; individual salts would have prevented the LinkedIn hackers from gaining access to such a huge number of passwords. However, if they had wanted to target a single, specific user, perhaps a celebrity or business leader, they would probably still have been able to recover even a well-chosen, acronym-based password from the hash value stored for his account. There is modern hardware that is capable of generating enormous numbers of hash values in a relatively short space of time.

The attackers could have looped through all possible combinations of letters, numbers and special characters up to a certain length. They would have added the random salt stored for the account to each combination, put the resulting sequence of characters through the hash function, and checked to see whether the resulting hash value matched the one in the database. Again, the only thing that would have saved our celebrity's skin would be if he had happened to have come up with an unusually long password: an unlikely scenario because of the practical difficulty of using one.

Work factors

To protect hash values against this type of brute-force attack, some systems do not immediately store the hash value that is generated from each password. Instead, they hash the hash value again to generate a second hash value, and then again to generate a third hash value, and repeat the process perhaps hundreds of thousands of times. The number of repetitions is known as the work factor.

The idea is that because a possible password has to be put through so many hashing steps to find out whether it matches the value in the database, looping through the whole process for large numbers of letter combinations ends up taking too long to be practicable. Imagine a machine that previously needed a week to calculate the hash values for all combinations under ten characters in length. Once a large work factor has entered the equation, the computer will no longer be able to complete the process during its owner's lifetime, because it will now need to put each permutation through the hash function 100,000 times.

Even then, however, the time required to work through a large number of letter combinations could theoretically be reduced back down to a few days or weeks by getting thousands of computers to tackle the problem at once, each one covering a different group of permutations. To make setting up the hardware necessary to achieve this too costly to be worthwhile, one work-factor based hashing method, *scrypt*, requires the use of large amounts of memory for its calculations: compared with processors, memory is relatively expensive to buy.[119]

The drawback is that all this extra work does not only serve to slow down hackers. The genuine system also has to carry it out every time it checks a password that somebody has entered.

This increases the time it takes to reply to a user who is trying to log in. In a world where websites aim for speed, this is hardly an effect somebody designing one is likely to welcome. As a compromise between security and usability, people responsible for password systems normally try and set a work factor that makes hashing a password slow enough to thwart an attacker, but fast enough that users do not notice a big difference. They typically end up settling on a delay of between a quarter and half of a second.

Timing attacks

Introducing a work factor solves one problem, but without great care it can inadvertently lead to another one. For many systems, it is not just users' passwords that are confidential, but also the identities of the users themselves. For example, there are multiple reasons why a company does not normally publish a list of its employees' names, including the risk that such information could be abused by scammers.

A system with a confidential user base has to avoid revealing whether the reason why an attempt to log into it failed was that the user name did not exist or that the password was wrong. Otherwise, an attacker could loop through all letter combinations that might form user names. He would enter each permutation in conjunction with a dummy password. By recording the reason why each login attempt failed, he could derive a list of the users on the system.

A website that has been designed naturally without regard for the issue we are about to describe will probably start by establishing whether the user name that was typed into its login page has an account on the system. If it does not, the user can be immediately notified that the login attempt was unsuccessful. If it does, on the other hand, the next task will be to generate the hash value for the password and to compare it to the one stored in the database for the user in question.

Using a work factor means the hashing step takes a measurable amount of time like half a second. This will lead to the system being noticeably slower to respond in the scenario where it has checked both the user name and the password than in the scenario where it has only checked the user name. A hacker can use the time it takes to receive an answer from a failed login attempt to distinguish between the two situations. If the answer comes back quickly, he can conclude that no hashing work was carried out and that the problem lay with the user name. If it takes longer, on the other hand, he knows that the user name must have existed and that it was the incorrect password that led to the access request being rejected. Performing this test for a large number of potential user names will enable him to build up a list of accounts on the system.

This is an example of a timing attack. All that a program has to do to prevent it is always to calculate the hash value for whatever password was typed in, even when it has already been established that the user name that was entered at the same time does not exist. This is a simple enough step, but one that whoever is designing a system is unlikely to think of without the benefit of bitter experience, whether his own or somebody else's.

Cross-site request forgery
and Facebook profiles

A website does not require its users to enter their login details every time they navigate to a new page. Once a web-based application has successfully authenticated you, you will expect it to remember who you are until you log out again. As described in the previous chapter, this is commonly achieved using tokens and cookies.

Recall that a web server transmitting a new page to be displayed on a user's browser is allowed to store a cookie on the browser at the same time, and that when a typical web server ascertains that somebody has entered a correct user name and password, it will generate a random token. It will remember the token locally, but it will also add it to a cookie when it transmits the next page back to the browser. All subsequent requests the web server receives from the same browser will contain this cookie. Comparing the token in the cookie to the list of stored tokens enables the web server to work out who the user is and to confirm that he must have logged in successfully. In most cases, the technical meaning of you being "logged into" a website is that your browser has received from that website a cookie that identifies you.

Websites vary in how long they go on accepting cookies after they have issued them. Some websites only regard a cookie as valid for as long as there is regular communication from the browser that has received it. If a browser remains silent for a defined interval of time, perhaps twenty minutes, and then sends a request, the request will still contain the cookie, but the web server will ignore the token it contains. This has the effect of automatically logging out inactive users. Other websites give their users a "remember me" option where the cookie remains valid indefinitely.

There is nothing to stop a website you are using from silently sending a request to a second website in the background from within your browser, but if the two websites have unrelated addresses, your browser will prevent the first website from reading the response, a feature known as the same-origin policy. However, the request to the second website will still automatically incorporate any cookies the second website had previously sent to the browser.

This is a problem for very popular websites like Facebook. Take anybody who is now viewing any website anywhere in the world. There is a good chance that he accessed Facebook from the same browser a few minutes ago and that his browser is currently in possession of a valid Facebook cookie. A malicious website might try and take advantage of this. It could send Facebook a request for a certain message to be posted on to the wall of whatever user is currently logged in. For every user who happens to be logged into Facebook when he views the malicious website, the request Facebook receives will contain a cookie identifying the user despite the fact the user is unaware the request was ever sent. And because the request is designed to write information, the fact the malicious website cannot read whatever Facebook sends back is irrelevant.

This is known as cross-site request forgery. Websites such as Facebook use additional techniques that we will not go into here to prevent it from really enabling attackers to write to victims' accounts. These techniques verify automatically that any request attempting to perform an action that would change information, as opposed to merely retrieving it, originated from a genuine user and not from a rogue website abusing cookies within a genuine user's browser.

However, in 2015, it was discovered that it was nonetheless possible for a rogue website to use cross-site request forgery in conjunction with a timing attack to gather information about a Facebook user logged into the same browser.[120] Facebook posts can be targeted so they are only displayed to users who fulfil specific demographic criteria. The author can stipulate the age range, gender and/or geographical location of his target audience. As you use Facebook, your browser requests a number of posts of which some are relevant to you and some are not. The Facebook server determines whether each requested post is appropriate to what it knows about you. If it is, the targeted post is sent back to your browser. If it is not, an almost empty answer is returned instead.

The vulnerability lay in the fact that replies from Facebook took measurably longer to arrive when they carried targeted posts than when they contained almost empty answers. A second website running in the same browser could take advantage of this to build up a profile of whoever was logged into Facebook. It simply had to send Facebook a succession of requests for posts with known target demographics. It could never read what came back, but it could still determine whether or not a response had contained a post by measuring how long Facebook had taken to answer.

For example, if the present author had logged into Facebook, a second website carrying out the attack might have observed that full answers were being returned whenever it requested posts that were intended for men between 40 and 50 living in Germany. This is hardly a major issue for most people, but nevertheless demonstrates the convoluted routes via which information that is only destined for specific, authenticated users can leak out to the world beyond.

Security questions

Although passwords are the authentication option that are used on most websites on a day-to-day basis, they are often not the only one. During the 2008 U.S. presidential election campaign, University of Tennessee student David Kernell managed to gain access to the private Yahoo! E-mail account of vice-presidential candidate Sarah Palin.[121]

The technique he had used was strikingly simple. Kernell posed as the legitimate account owner—in this case Sarah Palin—and pretended she had forgotten her password. To confirm Palin's identity, Yahoo! demanded the answer to two security questions Palin had set up for this eventuality. She was asked to confirm her date of birth and name the place where she had met her spouse. Because Palin was a public figure, a simple Wikipedia search and a bit of guesswork sufficed to provide Kernell with the information he needed. The one-year prison sentence Kernell received will have given him ample time to reflect on the fact that the simplicity of a cyberattack has no bearing on its illegality or on the severity with which it is punished.[122]

Such security questions can form a very weak link in an otherwise robust login system. A user has to recall his password every time he logs into an application, which is generally fairly often. The answer to a security question, on the other hand, is stored when a user registers with the system and is only needed if and when he forgets his password. This may be several years later. If a security question is to be of any use, then, it has to be considerably easier to recall than a normal password, which is typically only possible if the answer is some piece of information that the user does not need to make an effort to remember because he knows it anyway. You are often required to select a security question from one of several options in a dropdown menu. Quintessential candidates are your mother's maiden name or the name of your first teacher.

It is notoriously difficult to find information that somebody can reasonably be expected still to know in ten years' time but that nobody else has access to. If someone is trying to hack an account belonging to a member of his own family, he will have intimate knowledge of her life history. And if he wishes to gain access to the account of a former classmate and lifelong neighbour, a security question that demands the name of her first school or the town in which she was born is unlikely to pose much of a challenge.

At the same time, genuine users find it difficult to reply to a security question with an answer that exactly matches the version they stored several years previously. The challenge is especially acute for answers that consist of several words and contain punctuation: a comma that was present when an answer was originally specified might be absent from the version that has now been entered by somebody trying to regain access to his account. There are ways to reduce this problem. For example, answers can be converted to capital letters and have all their spaces and punctuation marks stripped out before they are put through a hash function. Provided that the underlying answer is correct, the generated hash values will then match regardless of any stray commas or capitals.

This is still of no help if the two responses being compared diverge in spelling or grammar. To cover this scenario, some early security-question implementations allowed users to communicate with a helpdesk employee who would use his judgement to determine whether a submitted answer corresponded to the stored information. No new system would be designed like this. A security answer that is to be displayed on a helpdesk screen has to be available in the database in its immediately readable plaintext form; it cannot be put through a hash function before it is saved.

Even in recent years, however, it has transpired that some long-standing systems were still storing security answers in their unencoded form. In September 2016, it was revealed that Yahoo! had been the victim of a cyberattack two years previously.[123] It eventually transpired that the criminal activity dated back to an earlier breach in August 2013 and that details had been stolen relating to all of the company's approximately three billion user accounts.[124] All the passwords had been put through a hash function, in some cases using a work factor. However, it is striking that some of the security answers were in plaintext.[125] We can surmise that this was probably due to a desire to allow human intervention when checking them.

Because of the many problems around security questions, more and more websites including Google have moved away from them altogether.[126] When you register a new account, you are asked to specify a phone number or second E-mail address instead of the answer to a security question. In the event you should ever forget your password, the website sends the phone or second E-mail address a code that you are asked to read and type back into the website. The fact you are able to reproduce the code demonstrates that you still have access to the phone or second E-mail address, which is an indication of who you are that is not quite so simple for others to hijack.

Initial passwords

Some large companies and institutions offer their employees automatic mechanisms to regain access to their accounts when they have forgotten their passwords similar to those used by online mail services like Google and Yahoo!. Especially in smaller organizations, however, it is more common for there to be an administrator who can set and reset passwords on behalf of users. Such setups are often prone to exhibit a second type of chink in the armour of password authentication.

When a system's administrator creates an account for a new user, it would be bad practice if he were to ask her what password she intended to use for the account and then to set it for her. He would then know her password and could exploit it at some future date to masquerade as her. Instead, the administrator generally specifies an initial password to the new user with the expectation that she will change it the first time she logs in. Because of the difficulty of imparting a complex string of letters to the new user, the administrator will often select a value that is at once simple and predictable.

A similar situation occurs when a physical machine like a server first comes into operation. Because its new master has never logged into it before, it cannot possibly know the password he will wish to use. His initial access must be possible either without a password at all or via a default one that has somehow been specified externally to the system, perhaps in an instruction manual.

In both cases, the infant account only becomes secure when its new owner changes the password to a value he has chosen himself. A system should force its users to take this step. If it does not, a significant proportion of people will typically carry on using the initial password, giving hackers a simple route into their accounts. This was the case for many victims of the phone mailbox hacking discussed earlier in this chapter. They made it easy for journalists to access their information by continuing to use default PINs like *0000*.

In 2002, an attack using default initial passwords triggered a political scandal of a magnitude that seemed ridiculous in comparison to the unsophisticated techniques employed by the perpetrator. Scottish hacker Gary McKinnon shut down an entire network consisting of some 2,000 computers belonging to the U.S. military[127], causing some $800,000 of damage in the process.[128] His actions gave rise to a decade of legal wrangling that culminated in 2012 in Theresa May, who was the British Home Secretary at the time, refusing a U.S. request to extradite him. He had mental health issues and she was of the opinion that subjecting him to the stress of a trial and sentence in a foreign country posed too great a risk of him committing suicide.[129]

McKinnon was convinced the U.S. authorities had in-depth knowledge of alien life and technology that they were deliberately concealing from the public. His motive for breaking into their systems was to look for documents that would prove his theory right. In glaring contrast to his mission, the steps he had to take to gain access were almost unbelievably down-to-earth. He started by obtaining a list of U.S. government computers. He knew which operating system they were running and tried to log into each one in turn using its default initial administration password. This happened to be a blank string and, amazingly, it was still valid for some of the computers on McKinnon's list.[130]

That this situation was possible was a clear fault in the design of the operating system. Administrators should have been forced to change the blank initial passwords to some other value the first time they logged in. As it was, they were not, and the fact that some people continued to use blank passwords may have been the result of laziness or indifference. It is, however, just conceivable that it was at least partially a conscious choice. An administrator might have judged the possibility of an intruder being allowed into the system to be a risk worth taking in return for the near certitude that a genuine user would never find himself inadvertently locked out of it. Things are so much easier if everyone knows that the required response to a password prompt is the enter key. With blank administration passwords, there is nothing to remember; it is easy to explain to new staff how to access the system.

Permissive Action Links

It might seem naïve to speculate that armed forces could have made a deliberate decision to use blank passwords. However, it has been claimed that precisely such an attitude was demonstrated by the U.S. Air Force managing access to the most critical system imaginable. In Chapter V, we shall look at the wider security issues around nuclear weapons; here we are concerned specifically with their launch codes.

In June 1962, the then President John F. Kennedy ordered the military to begin securing the country's nuclear missiles to make it more difficult for a rogue group of soldiers or technicians to carry out an unsanctioned attack. The new safety mechanism was an eight-number combination lock called a Permissive Action Link.[131] The idea was that the code required to prime a weapon would only be revealed to staff on the ground when they were actually being ordered to do so. Because the danger of weapons being used without authorisation was felt to be most pressing on foreign soil, American missiles deployed in Western Europe were the first to be upgraded.

When the system was rolled out at home, however, a section of the military was evidently more worried about ensuring their ability to follow through on a genuine nuclear strike order than about reducing the risk of an accidental Armageddon. The codes on all Permissive Action Links on the Minuteman intercontinental ballistic missiles were secretly set to *00000000* to ensure that nothing would need to be communicated in the heat of a nuclear exchange.[132]

As the years passed, people's understanding of the codes and what they had originally been intended to achieve seems to have faded. A note was even added to the standard pre-launch instructions requiring operators to check that none of the digits had been inadvertently set to some number other than zero. It was not until 1977 that Bruce Blair, a former launch officer turned whistleblower, brought the situation to the attention of the politicians in charge. The system was finally put to its intended use shortly afterwards. In 2014, it was reported that the U.S. Air Force had denied that any of this had ever happened.[133] We will probably never know for sure, but Bruce Blair, who was actually there at the time, does seem a more reliable source than the military officials who issued the rebuttal some forty years later.

Replacing the real codes with dummies did not only serve to keep in existence the risk the Permissive Action Links had been designed to reduce. It actually created a more dangerous situation than would have resulted if there had been no codes at all. Whoever designed the missile launch procedures will probably have relied on the assurance the Permissive Action Links provided. Without them, other security mechanisms might well have been set up in their place.

British nuclear weapons are still not protected by any secret codes.[134] The missiles are thought to form a more effective deterrent when enemies know that they cannot be put beyond use by destroying the command structures of the nation that owns them. The UK's conscious decision to rely on discipline rather than technology to reduce the risk of an illicit launch is clearly preferable to the way American military officials hoodwinked their political masters, but it remains controversial. In the 1960s at least, the social class of the naval officers involved appears to have made a significant contribution to the perception that they were trustworthy. The Royal Navy's curt response to a suggestion to install Permissive Action Links on its weapons was that "[it] would be invidious to suggest... that senior Service officers may, in difficult circumstances, act in defiance of their clear orders."[135]

Home router default passwords

In the previous examples, default initial codes have consisted of zeroes or empty strings. Their weak nature would at least have been obvious to anyone wishing to toughen up the systems that used them. Worse still are situations where an initial password looks like a random, unique value but is really anything but: a long, complex-looking password is liable to arouse misplaced trust.

A British Telecom customer in early 2008 examining the wireless network name (SSID) and password with which his

Home Hub router came preconfigured could have been forgiven for thinking that both were complex, arbitrary values that he was safe to go on using. In fact, it was soon to transpire that the two values were actually related to each other. Both were derived from different parts of a code generated by putting the router's serial number through a standard hash function. A router normally broadcasts openly the SSID it is using. By looping through the relatively small range of possible serial numbers and observing which serial numbers yielded hash values that matched the transmitted SSID, an attacker was able to build up a shortlist of possible passwords that he could then try out one by one until he hit lucky.[136]

A similar blunder was made preconfiguring EasyBox wireless routers for telecommunications provider Vodafone in Germany. In 2012, security researcher Sebastian Petters discovered that the MAC address of each router could be used to work out its preconfigured network password.[137] As we shall see in the final chapter of the book, a MAC address is a unique combination of numbers and letters that identifies a piece of computer hardware. Anybody can find out a router's MAC address: a router broadcasts its MAC address together with its SSID when it replies to probing requests from computers trying to find out what wireless networks are available in their vicinity. Germans found the revelation that it was so easy for attackers to gain access to other people's wireless networks particularly disturbing. At the time, the owner of a German network was automatically held legally responsible for any crime carried out over it.

Petters had found a description of the mathematical operations that led from the MAC address to the password in a patent application filed by Arcadyan, the Taiwanese manufacturers of the routers.[138] The procedure had originally been designed to enable two new pieces of hardware to identify themselves to each other when they are first used within the same network. The authors seem strangely oblivious to the fact that applying for the patent entailed publishing the details of the very mathematical operations whose secrecy formed the basis of what little security the method had.

In the patent, typing in passwords is regarded as somewhat passé: it "[makes] the user feel complicated, especially when an input error occurs". Now, when a Vodafone customer set up a new router, the supposed advantage that passwords did not need to be typed in did not even apply. He still had to enter the password into his laptop in order to use the wireless network. This makes it something of a mystery why the procedure had been chosen to generate EasyBox initial passwords in the first place. Perhaps it had just seemed like a readily available method of producing a complicated-looking code.

Biometric identification

As an alternative to passwords and passcodes with all their inherent difficulties, some systems root their identification mechanisms in the physical world and instead rely on recognising individuals' anatomical features, or biometrics. This is only an option when the person who carries out an action within a system is the same person who authorises that action, which is normally the case, although there are situations where it does not hold. For example, biometrics would be of no use at all as a replacement for Permissive Action Links. The whole idea is that the missile codes are carefully guarded by high-ranking officials and revealed to operators shortly before a weapon is to be launched. If the system depended on what the boss looked like, he would need to be physically present to prime a missile. Biometrics cannot be passed around.

Perhaps the best known biometric is the fingerprint, which has played a pivotal role in criminal investigations for well over a century. Even if it has yet to be conclusively proven that all fingerprints are unique, there is no documented case of two individuals having prints that are indistinguishable from each other.[139] Because fingerprints are not only determined by genes, but also by random events in the womb, they are not even shared by identical twins. And even if there is sometimes an element of doubt around smudged or partial impressions recovered from a crime scene, high quality, clear images in the hands of skilled forensic investigators provide a highly effective means of identifying people.[140]

Unfortunately, fingerprint comparison is one area where computers still have a long way to catch up with the human brain. A fingerprint scanner confirms your identity by comparing a current image of your finger to a second image that was recorded at some point in the past. A trained human being could use the data to determine with a high degree of accuracy whether you were really who you claimed to be. An automatic fingerprint matching system, on the other hand, gets it wrong relatively often. Although things are improving all the time, the performance of older systems for which figures are readily available was not particularly convincing.[141]

A scanner might mistakenly analyse somebody else's fingerprint as matching yours. Or, conversely, it might fail to perceive the similarity between an image taken from me today and one taken from me last month. This makes a fingerprint-based system unsuitable as the sole means of authenticating people. Even if you can live with the risk of the wrong people being allowed in, you still need a fallback procedure for when the right people have been locked out.

There are other reasons why fingerprint-based identification has not always had a particularly good press. In 2005, Malaysian car thieves cut off the end of an accountant's index finger in order to operate the fingerprint recognition system that started his top-end Mercedes.[142] And two years later, and somewhat less dramatically, the German Chaos Computer Club demonstrated that you could deceive a fingerprint-based supermarket payment system by printing out another customer's fingerprint on to a piece of plastic using a standard laser printer and sticking the plastic on to your own finger with wood glue.[143]

It is important to bear in mind that such problems relate to specific scanner models rather than to finger-based biometrics in general. They are gradually being solved as the technology progresses. In 2015, the company Qualcomm presented a new type of scanner that uses ultrasound to build up a three-dimensional model of the finger[144], and when the UK supermarket Costcutter introduced finger scanning as a means of payment in late 2017, the system was based on the pattern of veins within the finger rather than on traditional prints.[145] Such newer systems cannot be deceived by simple pictures; they are able to confirm that they are dealing with a real finger that is still attached to a living human being.

There are other systems that use different biometrics to give more accurate results than can be achieved with even with the more modern types of finger scanning. This is not because the features they compare are any more unique, but rather because computers do a better job of capturing and analysing them. Automatic iris scans can identify people much more reliably than automatic finger scans.[146] Contrary to the frankly ridiculous claims of some alternative medical practitioners who believe that the iris offers them a window into all sorts of details about a patient's current state of health, its structures are actually fixed in the womb just like fingerprints. In the absence of eye diseases, they stay the same throughout your life.

Automatic retinal scanners examine the pattern of veins at the back of the eye and are more accurate still, making an error only about 0.00001% of the time.[147] Unfortunately, however, using them on a large scale would pose significant practical problems. A retinal scan takes several seconds and you have to get very close to the scanner. The procedure is actually harmless, but many people are understandably averse to subjecting their eye to the whims of an unknown machine. Confronted with a retinal scanner at a strange airport in a foreign country where they do not speak the language, most passengers would probably try and do everything possible to avoid having to use it. And although it is not necessary to make physical contact between your eye and the scanner, it is also difficult to prevent people from doing so. A retinal scanner as a standard means of identifying passengers at an airport would probably turn out to be a horribly effective way of spreading conjunctivitis.

E-passports

Biometric passports, also known as e-passports, are being issued by an increasing number of nations. The relevant international standard allows a variety of features to be stored, including fingerprints and iris information.[148] However, the biometric technology that is most widely used to authenticate passengers at airports is the recognition of facial features like the distance between your eyes and the size of your nose. This may seem surprising given that such measurements do not identify people uniquely. However, the theoretical distinctiveness of the biometric under examination is irrelevant. It is the capabilities of the scanning procedure that matter. Even if fingerprints are unique and facial features are not, a facial-feature scanner that makes mistakes ten percent of the time is just as acceptable as a fingerprint scanner that makes mistakes ten percent of the time.

For passport authorities, facial features have two considerable advantages over other biometrics. Firstly, while registering for a system that relies on fingerprints or iris patterns entails going to a scanner to have the initial images taken, facial feature information can be obtained from a photograph. This is a decisive argument in countries like the UK where there is no requirement to turn up anywhere in person to apply for a passport: unlike in the U.S. or Germany, you can obtain one by post. Secondly, the political discussion around using facial features tends to be somewhat less heated than for other biometrics because no new information is being gathered from passport applicants.

Just like many systems analysing fingerprints or irises, current facial-feature scanners find it difficult to tell a real person apart from a model. At an airport, they are supervised by staff, so the fact that today's technology is worse than human beings at detecting fakes is not a genuine practical problem. At the same time, human officials are far from infallible and it would be useful if tomorrow's automatic authentication mechanisms could learn to outperform them. In 2010, a young man succeeded in hoodwinking airport staff and boarding a flight from Hong

Kong to Canada, where he later claimed asylum. He had used a silicone mask to disguise himself as an elderly white American.[149]

Storing biometrics safely

Any biometric technology that is to enter general use in a wide range of situations will need to be at least as good if not better than human beings at distinguishing fakes from real people; it will have to be able to ensure that an attacker who has gained access to your biometric details cannot use them to usurp your identity. Keeping the information safe in the first place is a non-starter, because you cannot keep your biometrics secret. Every time you touch a door handle, open your eyes or speak, you risk giving away details of your fingerprint, iris or voice to anyone who has the right technology to capture them. In 2014, the German Chaos Computer Club demonstrated that they could recover both the fingerprints and the iris details of politicians from photographs.[150] And purloined biometrics are compromised until the day their owner dies. While you can simply discard a stolen password and replace it with a new one, you are stuck with your fingers, eyes and larynx for life.

It is also challenging to store information about physical features in a form that is resistant to theft. Biometrics cannot simply be put through a hash function like a password can, because two images captured from the same individual on separate occasions will never look exactly the same. One picture of my index finger will produce a totally different hash value from an almost identical second picture of the same index finger. There is then no way of determining that the hash values were generated from matching prints.

One approach to this problem is to generate a collection of facts about an image and then to apply a hash function to the collection of facts rather than to the image. Research is also underway into methods to warp a biometric image in a controlled fashion before the facts are generated about it. Provided the same distortions are carried out before each time a person's features are analysed, the information that ensues will match on repeated occasions, but the resulting cancellable biometrics will also share some of the transitory nature of passwords: if the data about my warped features is stolen, I can render it useless by starting again with a new set of distortions.[151]

Such security features may or may not eventually prove to be an effective way of keeping biometrics safe from being stolen from the server where they are stored. Either way, though, the knowledge that information is protected from falling into the wrong hands does nothing to reassure those who are just as worried about placing it into the "right" hands in the first place. As the accuracy, usability and security of the various biometric procedures improves, the concerns shift more and more to issues of privacy. The strong historical association of fingerprints with law enforcement hardly helps. In the last analysis, biometrics are unlikely ever to replace other forms of identification on a large scale simply because so many people are reluctant to lay themselves open to being tracked by their employers, by their governments or by companies providing them services.

Something you have and banking scams

Passwords ("something you know") and biometrics ("something you are") are two of the three main methods a system can use to establish identity. The third relies on objects people possess like keys and swipe cards ("something you have"). The received wisdom in security circles is that controlling access to anything critical should involve checking at least two out of these three: a system is then protected from attackers by dual fortifications. We have seen that the range of situations in which biometrics are appropriate is rather limited. The combination most often used in practice is therefore "something you know" in conjunction with "something you have".

These are the two methods of identification that are typically required when you identify yourself to your bank. When you access an ATM (cashpoint), you have your bank card and know your PIN; and when you use internet banking, you know the password or passcode you use to log in and have the transaction authentication number (TAN)—the confirmation code you are required to enter when you transfer some money. Depending on which country you are in and who your bank is, a list of TANs may have been sent to you in advance in the post. Alternatively and particularly in European countries, your TANs may be sent by text message to your phone as and when they are needed. You will have given the bank your phone number when you set up your account.

Despite the use of "something you have", however, scammers have mounted successful attacks on both these authentication methods. Large amounts of money have been stolen in a variety of countries by adding illegal skimmers to vulnerable ATM models. A camera concealed somewhere where it can record what is entered into the keypad allows a criminal to obtain her victim's PIN. At the same time, a magnetic card reader mounted on to the front of the card slot enables her to steal the magnetic strip information required to manufacture a duplicate of his bank card.[152] She then has all she needs to plunder his account at some other ATM.

And in 2015 in Germany, the bank accounts of a number of customers of telecommunications provider Deutsche Telekom were ransacked over the internet.[153] For the scam to work, the attacker had to have already gained access to a victim's internet banking account by some means or other, perhaps using the key loggers described in Chapter II. Having gleaned the victim's phone number from his online profile, the attacker would call Deutsche Telekom. She would pretend to be a shop owner ringing on behalf of the victim. The story was that he had lost his phone and wished to reassign his number to a new SIM card. In reality, though, the new SIM card was in her phone. The redirection of the text messages then allowed her to carry out transactions in his name.

That both these tricks worked demonstrates that the distinction between "something you know", "something you are" and "something you have" is much more blurred than it seems on first analysis. In the world of computers, everything ends up as a string as ones and zeroes. Biometric scanners can be fooled using models because it is not actually physical features that are being compared at all; it is information about physical features. In the same way, when TANs are sent to a phone, the crucial factor in authenticating its owner is less the phone itself than its owner's entitlement to have text messages that have been sent to a certain number directed to that phone. The difference between an object and a piece of information is even less meaningful where the object is no more than a means of holding the information, which is the case for a bank card that stores its details on a magnetic strip.

Secure tokens

One solution to this problem is to get "something you have" to create a new piece of information each time it is used to authenticate its owner. It is still the ones and zeroes supplied by an object that are used to prove who has it. However, the code that is generated and transmitted on any given occasion is useless to a bystander who manages to observe it. It will never be valid again.

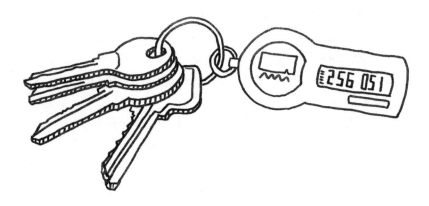

Many companies use SecurID Tokens to authenticate employees who are working remotely.[154] These are pocket-sized gadgets sold by the company RSA that are designed to fit neatly on to a keyring. A token has a small screen that displays a six-digit number that changes every 60 seconds. An employee uses the token to log into his company's systems over the internet. He reads the number off his token's screen and types it into his company's website. Within the company network, the number is forwarded to a machine that generates the same numbers within the same timeframes and can check that the number the employee entered was valid.

Stored within each token is a secret number called a seed. Each minute, a complex mathematical function is used to combine the seed with the current time in order to generate the six-digit number the token displays. The token is designed to be tamperproof: if it detects that somebody is trying to access its internal circuitry, it deletes the seed from its memory. This makes it very difficult to obtain the seed from the token. In the top-end version of the system, the company-located machine that checks the six-digit number is also a specially built server that is designed to respond to tampering in a similar way.

Despite all these precautions, the SecurID system of U.S. aerospace giant Lockheed Martin was successfully hacked in 2011. Although exemplary action on the part of the Lockheed Martin security department prevented any data from being stolen as a result, the attackers had managed to create duplicate SecurID tokens. They did this by hacking neither the server at Lockheed Martin nor the tokens belonging to individual employees, but rather the systems at RSA itself.[155]

The internal workings of the RSA system are not in the public domain, and RSA never fully revealed the details of the data that was stolen, nor of how the information had enabled the hackers to attack Lockheed Martin. However, when a company that is using the RSA SecurID system issues an employee a new token, somebody has to register the token by supplying the relevant seed information to the company machine that is used to check the six-digit numbers. Perhaps the hackers had found a database of token serial numbers and the matching seeds; another possibility is that there is some way of deriving a token's seed from its serial number, and that it was details of this mapping that the hackers had stolen.[156] Either way, a photograph of the back of a token showing its serial number would then have sufficed to allow them to duplicate the numbers it generated.

Whatever exactly the SecurID attackers did, their ability to recreate tokens using knowledge stolen from RSA resulted from the fact that the same information a token used to generate its six-digit numbers had to be available on the machine where they were to be verified. This is like an everyday lock. The information represented by a physical key has to be represented by the corresponding keyhole as well, and it is conceivable that someone could develop an imaging technology to scan a keyhole and work out what shape to make a key to fit it.

Something only you have, EMV and chipTAN

An ideal sort of "something you have" would contain a piece of information that only it possesses and that is stored nowhere else on the planet. Only when this is the case can keeping guard of an object completely guarantee the safety of the data it contains. This holy grail of objects used for identification—"something *only* you have"—is made possible by the asymmetric encryption based on private and public keys that was described in Chapter I.

There, we pictured a physically impossible lock with a pair of keys where the strong key—which corresponded to a private key in the world of encryption—had to be involved at least once in any cycle of locking and unlocking the door. Now we can extend the analogy and imagine that the internal structure of the lock itself, as if by magic, corresponds to the weak key and reveals nothing about what the strong key looks like. If there were only a single copy of the strong key for such a door, the information it represented would be unique in the universe.

A private key stands alone as something that somebody can check I have without needing to know it himself. I can use my private key to encrypt a piece of information that I then send him. My possession of my private key is proven to him by his ability to decrypt the information using the corresponding public key. This means my private key can be generated and stored exclusively on an object I retain and does not need to be duplicated anywhere else.

Europay, MasterCard and Visa (EMV) is used to secure all bank cards in the European Union as well as an increasing number of bank cards in the United States and other countries.[157] EMV cards have the status of "something only you have". Rather than relying on the magnetic strips that criminals used to copy, the cards contain tamperproof microchips that use encryption to identify themselves to ATMs. The microchip uses a private key deep within it to encrypt some information that it supplies to the ATM. The ATM then obtains from the bank the corresponding public key for the bank card in question, uses the public key to decode the encrypted information and checks that it ends up with the expected format and content.[158]

And some banks in Germany and Austria offer a similar method for creating transaction authentication numbers (TANs) called chipTAN.[159] When a customer is using an internet banking website and requires a TAN, he slots his bank card into a handheld machine. The website encodes information including details of the transaction which the customer somehow communicates to the handheld machine, most typically by the handheld machine taking a photograph of his screen. The handheld machine displays details of the payee and the transaction amount for the customer to verify. It then communicates with the microchip on the customer's bank card, whose private key is used to generate a TAN from information about the transaction. The TAN is displayed on the handheld machine, the customer types the TAN into the website, and the website verifies the TAN using the public key stored for the bank card.

The chipTAN method has important features above and beyond the simple use of asymmetric encryption: the handheld device displays transaction details supplied by the bank for the customer to compare to what he entered on the website; and it is these details that the private key is used to encrypt as opposed to a random code generated within the handheld device. Unfortunately, the procedures used by other banks do not always incorporate the same safeguards. It has been shown that a number of ostensibly similar card reader systems are vulnerable to various types of crime because their designers have relied too much on the security inherent in the EMV chips and paid too little attention to the communication that accompanies their use.[160]

EMV also enables secure payment with contactless cards. If you own such a card, it is true that anybody with the right hardware can steal small amounts of money from your account simply by getting close enough to your wallet. However, the scope for fraud this offers is severely limited by the fact that the funds have to be transferred to a trackable bank account. The more decisive security feature should be the impossibility of cloning the card because of there being no way of accessing its private key. In 2013, however, it was shown that it was possible to skim other information from a chip-based card and use it to build a non–chip-based replica that the contactless terminals in use at the time were quite happy to accept instead: they supported both systems and had no way of checking which one was in use for a given bank account.[161]

Certificates

Pairs of private and public keys are the normal way in which computers identify themselves to one other over the internet. Before a server starts communicating with other machines, a private key is generated and stored on it or, alternatively, on a tamperproof module connected to it. The private key remains a secret known only to the server and never leaves home. Whenever the server sends out messages, it uses the private key to generate digital signatures for them, appending a signature to the end of each message. This enables messages from the server to be confirmed as authentic elsewhere in the internet by checking that the signatures can be decrypted using the corresponding public key. What exactly do these signatures consist of?

Encrypting complete messages with a private key would demonstrate conclusively which machine sent them. However, recall from Chapter 1 that, because asymmetric encryption is slow, it is not normally used to encrypt entire messages. In order to prove where the content of a message came from without having to encode all of it using costly asymmetric encryption, the sending machine puts the message through a hash function. It then uses its private key to encrypt the resulting hash value. The result is the signature that is added to the end of the message. The recipient can verify that a message, a signature and a public key belong together as a triplet by recalculating the hash value for the message content, decrypting the signature using the public key, and checking that the same sequence of bits results both times.

If the computer you are communicating with today can use a signature to demonstrate it knows the same private key as the one you were in contact with yesterday, you can be sure you are talking to the same machine, unless the private key happens to have been stolen, perhaps using a loophole like the Heartbleed vulnerability described in Chapter II. However, in the anonymous world that is the internet, you are still left with the problem of not knowing whether that machine's owner is really who he says he is.

Imagine a new bank opens and decides to offer its customers internet banking. It generates a pair of keys—private and public— with which to run its website. A customer communicating with the bank using its public key can rely on the fact that a third party will not be able to read his messages while they are in transit. However, uncertainty remains around whether the public key really originated from the bank: whether it is really the bank that is receiving and reading the messages. Using techniques described in the next chapter, an imposter could be redirecting internet requests destined for the bank to his own server. He could be supplying bank customers with his own public key in lieu of the genuine one generated by the bank.

This danger is forestalled using certificates. These work as follows. The bank specifies to a certificate authority its public key and the web domain it is using, which might be https://www.betterwisemans.com. The certificate authority checks that the domain really belongs to the bank and then issues the bank with a certificate, which is an official confirmation that the bank's public key and web domain belong together. The certificate authority signs the bank's certificate with its own private key, enabling customers' browsers to check that the certificate is valid using the corresponding certificate authority public key.

A standard browser like Firefox, Internet Explorer or Chrome comes with a pre-installed list of certificate authority root certificates, which are based on their public keys. A certificate for a website like the one belonging to the bank may be signed directly by one of these root authorities. Alternatively, a root certificate authority may have issued a certificate for an intermediate certificate authority that then goes on to issue the certificate for the bank. There may even be multiple intermediate layers involved. The system enables a browser to verify that a certificate is genuine by following the signatures up the chain of trust until it reaches one of its pre-defined root authorities.

The special status of a certificate authority stems solely from the fact that it has persuaded the major operating-system and browser manufacturers that it can be trusted with the task of validating third parties.[162] It is important to appreciate that, from a mathematical point of view, there is nothing to differentiate the private and public keys associated with a certificate authority from those used by a normal web server or individual.

Phishing, spear phishing and whaling

Websites are divided into those that encrypt the information they supply and those that do not. Unencrypted website addresses start with http://, while encrypted website addresses start with https://. The extra letter stems from the fact that the version of the Hypertext Transfer Protocol (HTTP) that transmits information in an encrypted form is called Hypertext Transfer

Protocol Secure (HTTPS).[163] Browsers expect an encrypted website to prove its identity using a certificate. A browser typically displays a padlock next to the address whenever it is showing a page sent from an encrypted website that supplied a genuine certificate. It will also display a security warning if it encounters an encrypted website that fails to do so.

The fact that somebody has been issued a certificate for `https://www.better-wisemans.com` demonstrates that he controls that web domain. However, this does not show that he is really the webmaster of Better Wisemans bank. We saw in the example above that the bank's address was actually `https://www.betterwisemans.com`. It could be that `https://www.better-wisemans.com` was set up by an imposter with the specific aim of masquerading as the bank. This practice is known as phishing. A few victims might have the misfortune to fall into the trap by chance by mistyping the address; the hoaxer is also likely to try and direct his victims to the fake site by sending them an E-mail that contains a link to it.

You are viewing `https://www.better-wisemans.com`, having followed a rogue link from an E-mail or another website. Not only does the address look right. The page contents look just like your bank's website as well. You have no reason to doubt that you are communicating with your bank. In reality, however, you are interacting with a criminal who is doing his best to imitate its website. He may be hoping you will reveal confidential information that he can then forward on to the real bank website to gain access to your account. Alternatively, he may aim to use the fake site to infect your computer with malware via a drive-by download as described in Chapter II.

Phishing tends to be especially successful when the message sent as bait does not resemble indiscriminate junk mail, but has rather been carefully tailored to a specific victim's interests, hang-ups or proclivities, a technique that has been somewhat amusingly christened spear phishing. Even if you generally avoid following links within mails from unknown senders, there will almost certainly be some particular message content that will catch your attention to an extent where you will find it very hard to resist.

In 2008, thousands of U.S. executives were sent mails claiming that their companies had been issued a subpoena from the United States District Court in San Diego and containing a link where the full-text version could be downloaded. The fake legal document that then appeared came complete with a key logger that infected their machines and went on to transmit information about their subsequent dealings to the scammers.[164] When spear phishing has high-profile individuals as its target, it is sometimes known by a third term that continues the angling theme: whaling.

Extended validation and free certificate services

To try and combat such practices, some certificate authorities offer extended validation services. These involve the certificate authority checking not only that the organisations for which it issues certificates control their web domains, but also that those organisations really correspond to the legal entities that the web domains appear to name. This is a process that takes place outside the world of computers and the internet. Once an organisation has been successfully vetted, it can incorporate the extended validation results into its certificate, where they are viewable by people accessing its web pages.

Browsers will typically try and show when a certificate demonstrates legal identity as opposed to just domain ownership, perhaps by displaying the company's name as well as the padlock next to the address or by displaying the address itself against a green background. However, the distinction will probably not be clear to many internet-based customers. People are often prone to trust any site for which the browser does not actively generate a security warning. Even if the genuine Better Wisemans Bank site does use an extended-validation certificate to identify itself, most victims of a phishing attack are unlikely to notice that the counterfeit site does not.

Additionally, the whole certification system suffers from a lack of consistency between the stringency of the checks performed by different certificate authorities. Browsers trust all certificate authorities to the same degree and are incapable of taking advantage of the value added by a more robust certification procedure. Because stricter verification will generally be more expensive to carry out, this has tended to lead to the checks performed by certificate authorities becoming less and less rigorous over the years.

For the first two decades of the internet's history, verifying the ownership of a domain in order to grant a certificate was a bureaucratic and partially manual process that cost money and acted as a barrier that prevented many smaller websites from using encryption. In late 2015, however, a new certificate authority called letsencrypt began offering free certificates that were based on a completely automatic verification process.[165]

The owner of a web domain sends the letsencrypt certificate authority a request to issue a certificate testifying to the link between his web domain and a public key. The certificate authority starts by sending a random string to the web server in charge of the domain. The web server encrypts the random string using its corresponding private key and makes the resulting encrypted string available on a page within the domain. The certificate authority then downloads this page and checks that it can decrypt the string again using the public key it is being asked to stamp as valid. If it can, this proves the claimed link between the domain and the public key, and the certificate can be granted.

While this is a positive step in that it makes certificates available for free, the certification process is itself now vulnerable to the very uncertainty it was designed to combat in the first place: whether the communication partner is the genuine owner of the domain in question. It could be argued that letsencrypt is much less likely than a typical user to fall victim to its traffic being redirected to the wrong server, and that the automatic procedure offered by letsencrypt is no less rigorous than the often perfunctory checks other certificate authorities carry out manually or semi-automatically.

However, things got a lot worse in June 2016 when a serious security hole was discovered in the procedure on offer from a copycat free certificate service, StartEncrypt.[166] While letsencrypt specified the location of the page within your web domain where it required you to serve the results of the private-key encryption, StartEncrypt let you choose any page you liked. This was a fatal error. There are websites like Dropbox that serve millions of pages and hand over control of each one to a different user. Now any one of these customers could use StartEncrypt to obtain a valid certificate for the whole website. He could then masquerade as the entire Dropbox service.

The advent of free certificate services has brought into focus the inflation to which the whole setup has fallen victim. Issues like the StartEncrypt bug devalue the great majority of genuine certificates used on the internet. Perhaps a partial solution would be to educate ordinary web users about the limited gradation the system does offer: it would help if a typical customer knew not to accept a bank website as genuine unless his browser shows that its certificate attests to extended validation.

Certificate revocation

If the private key that corresponds to the public key endorsed by a certificate is stolen, or if an organisation that has been issued an extended validation certificate turns out to be bogus, there is a mechanism whereby certificate authorities can revoke certificates. A revocation is a declaration that a cryptographically valid certificate should no longer be accepted. Until quite recently, browsers would maintain lists of revoked certificates and add to them with periodic updates that they fetched from certificate authorities.[167] Nowadays, however, as the speed and capacity of the internet grows, a gradual shift is underway to a real-time system whereby every time a browser receives a certificate, it checks the certificate is still valid by sending a query to the certificate authority that issued it.[168]

On discovering that a certificate has been revoked, a browser will display a warning message to its user asking him whether he wishes to go on using the website and advising him not to. This sounds good in theory. The difficulty is that certificate warning messages do not always indicate a real issue with the authenticity of a website. They can also result when the way the website is being run does not quite correspond to specifications. For example, a genuine company might be using a valid certificate for the wrong set of web pages. A user who does not understand the technical details of a warning message about a certificate ends up having to make a subjective judgement about what he trusts more: the website and its certificate, or the warning message.

In 2001, an imposter claiming to work for Microsoft persuaded the VeriSign certificate authority to issue two certificates for the company.[169] Although the certificates were revoked shortly afterwards, a concern was that, if one of them were to have subsequently been used, many people would have been likely to ignore the resulting warning messages. The Microsoft domain was too well-known for there to be any doubt about its identity, and the certificates clearly identified Microsoft as their owner. In the interests of making users more cautious, the messages browsers show when they identify a problem with a certificate have tended to become more and more dramatic over the past years, with some browsers no longer giving users the option of proceeding at all in the face of serious issues.

The worst-case scenario is when hackers take over an entire certificate authority and issue fraudulent certificates in its name. This happened to the Dutch certificate authority DigiNotar in September 2011.[170] It was clear that criminals had issued a large number of fake certificates on DigiNotar's behalf and that some of them were for major companies like Mozilla. However, DigiNotar was unable to compile a reliable list of them or of the affected web domains. This meant that revoking individual certificates was not a solution. The only way to protect users from unknown illicit certificates was to expunge DigiNotar's own public key from their browsers. The removal of the entire certificate authority then inevitably led to unnecessary warning messages being generated for a large number of actually valid websites.

We have seen that asymmetric encryption is an unparalleled means of authentication in that it enables proving an identity without having to surrender the proof in the process, and that the certification paradigm provides a way of linking private-key-based identities with the concrete world. However, the DigiNotar story highlights the problem that every chain of trust has to end somewhere: in practice, there will never be any means of guaranteeing that whoever is at the root of the chain is both perfectly trustworthy and perfectly immune to being hacked himself.

IV. MESSAGES

This chapter starts by focussing on various types of cyberattack that target the mechanics of how information is fetched and transmitted over the internet. It then goes on to explore ways of using the internet without betraying where you are. This is challenging because internet communication normally relies on the location of the participants in each conversation being openly indicated at the top of each message: even if the contents of a letter are secret, the envelope has to remain readable so that the postman knows where to deliver it. Techniques to get around this are complex and themselves open to intriguing modalities of hacking, and we will take a closer look at the cat-and-mouse game between internet criminals endeavouring to conceal their whereabouts and the law enforcement agencies and secret services trying to unmask them. We will also describe the Bitcoin system and how it extends anonymity to financial transactions.

Smurf, Fraggle and the Ping of Death

Whenever a message is sent over the internet, the bits (ones and zeroes) that make it up have to be arranged in such a way that it can be understood when it is received. The forms different types of messages take are called protocols. The protocols in use across the internet are standardised by the Internet Engineering Task Force (IETF) under the auspices of the international and non-profit Internet Society (ISOC).[171] They fulfil a variety of roles, such as conveying requests and responses between browsers and web servers (Hypertext Transfer Protocol, or HTTP, which we discussed in previous chapters); allowing your phone or laptop to talk to wireless routers (IEEE 802.11)[172]; and enabling different routers to collaborate in working out the best path for a message to take as it traverses the wider internet (Border Gateway Protocol, or BGP).[173]

Perhaps the most fundamental protocol is simply called Internet Protocol, or IP.[174] IP messages identify their source and destination computers using IP addresses that you can think of as being much like postal addresses. The most commonly used type of IP address, an IP version 4 address, is composed of four numbers between 0 and 255. For example, at the time this book was written, the IP address of the web server that supplied information about it was 217.160.57.21.

Communication reaching a computer has to be taken care of by a program that can understand the right protocol, and an internet message is labelled with a port number that tells the computer that receives it what sort of message it is so that the computer knows which program to channel it to. When you write a new program that communicates over the network, you can get it to listen on any port number you like, but software designed to process the standard internet protocols normally sticks to generally agreed port numbers. This means that although you may not know exactly which program is answering the messages you are sending to a certain machine, you can still presume that you can direct HTTP messages to port 80 and BGP messages to port 179.

In the very early days of the internet, there was little to stop anybody contacting any machine he wanted and sending it a message destined for a standard port and structured according to the corresponding standard protocol; any checks on a message's provenance and content were performed as it was being processed rather than beforehand. However, this approach soon changed when people realised that there were manifold ways of stopping a remote computer from functioning properly by feeding it a malicious message crafted using one of the standard protocols.

The 1990s saw a spate of denial-of-service or DoS attacks. (The abbreviation DOS is also used to denote disk operating systems like Microsoft's MS-DOS, but the two things are in no way connected.) Names like "Fraggle"[175] and "ping of death"[176] denoted various types of nasty communication that were designed to bring the target computer to its knees, typically by sending it an excess amount of information or by giving it an excess amount of work to do. Perhaps the most celebrated case was the Smurf attack.[177] This involved contacting a large number of computers with messages that claimed to be from the machine that was under attack and then watching as it creaked and snapped under the cumulative weight of the replies.

Denial-of-service attacks do not involve reading or changing any information: the hacker neither requires nor obtains access to the machine he is targeting. Stopping a system from working normally for a while is perhaps less spectacular than the SQL injection data thefts described in Chapter II, but it is nonetheless a frequent goal of disgruntled employees and political activists. The denial-of-service attack is also sometimes used in conjunction with more effectual crime to draw attention away from the main theatre of operations, or to overwhelm a monitoring system to prevent it from observing what is going on.

Firewalls, DDoS attacks and Anonymous

Nowadays, most types of denial-of-service attacks are prevented using firewalls. A firewall is either a program running on a computer or a dedicated machine within a network. In both cases, it observes the messages going to and fro and stops anything in its tracks that does not appear to be legitimate. One of several reasons why Smurf attacks are usually no longer possible today is that a well-configured firewall will only allow a reply message through if it can match it up to a request message that was previously sent in the opposite direction.

A firewall protecting a server can conclude that an IP address from which a huge number of requests are originating probably belongs to a machine from which somebody is trying to mount a denial-of-service attack. Blocking all traffic from that IP address for a certain period of time thwarts the attack while keeping the server available for everybody else. However, if the requests that make up an attack all come from different IP addresses, there is nothing a firewall can do to stop them, because it cannot distinguish a request that forms part of the attack from a message from a legitimate user. It has no way of knowing which traffic to let through and which traffic to block.

Such an assault in which a large number of separate machines overwhelm a web server with requests is called a distributed denial-of-service or DDoS attack. It is typically carried out using a botnet that has been appropriated using malware as described in Chapter II, where we looked at a specific example of a DDoS attack where the target was the White House.

Just as any river or lake will flood eventually if it rains hard enough and for long enough, no website is completely immune to such raw aggression, however well its software has been programmed and however powerful the hardware it is running on. You can carry out a successful DDoS attack against any target you like if you have a big enough botnet. This is why DDoS is the favourite tool of hacktivist groups like Anonymous. In 2010, Anonymous conducted a campaign called Operation Payback in which it used the technique to attack a number of websites belonging to organisations that were trying to enforce music copyrights.[178]

Protocols and covert channels

A firewall is generally set up with complex rules that allow messages through depending on the IP addresses from which they were sent, the ports for which they are destined and the protocols according to which they are structured. For example, a web server will need to accept HTTP requests on port 80 from anywhere on the internet to do its job, but it will almost certainly reject unexpected messages from elsewhere in the world that are designed to make changes to its operating system. However, this job of distinguishing good traffic from bad is greatly complicated by the fact that practically all messages that make up internet traffic actually contain structures from several protocols at once.

Imagine a stream of bits that leaves your computer as your browser communicates with a web server. The message is initially destined for your local router. The protocol according to which it is arranged depends on whether you are using a cable network or a wireless network, but in both cases the message will contain initial bit sequences called headers that are used to manage communication between your computer and your router, followed by the bits that make up the actual contents or payload. In this case, the payload is itself a complete message in the IP protocol that is what will traverse the wider internet. This IP message has its own headers specifying the IP address from which it is coming and the IP address to which it is going. It also has its own payload.

This inner payload is once again a message in its own right with yet more headers, this time following a protocol called Transmission Control Protocol, or TCP, that is used to set up and maintain two-way communications between a pair of machines in a way that proves that neither party is faking its IP address and that ensures a message cannot get lost unnoticed.[179] And the TCP payload is in turn a complete HTTP protocol message that contains the actual information your browser wants to send to the web server. Believe it or not, this is still a relatively simple example!

It is a bit like a system of communication within a large corporation where letters are placed in open envelopes of one colour that can themselves be placed in envelopes of a second colour. These envelopes can then be placed in envelopes of a third colour and of a fourth colour and so on. A red envelope might be used for sending things from one building to another. If the person who takes out its contents finds a blue envelope, he knows it has to go to a secretary. If he finds a green envelope, on the other hand, he knows it is destined for the chairman of the board.

Because most letters for senior management go via the secretaries, a green envelope would normally be placed into a blue envelope before being enclosed by a red envelope. In a really urgent case, though, somebody might take the liberty of putting a green envelope directly into a red envelope to propel its contents straight to the boss. The important point is that any combination of envelopes is possible and will work as long as whoever examines each one is able and willing to do whatever its colour bids.

It is difficult for a firewall to strike the right balance between enforcing stringent controls and allowing adequate leeway for exceptions. In our non-technological thought experiment, an inspector might be tasked with checking that the contents of the envelopes travelling from building to building conform to a certain set of rules. If a yellow envelope is used for communication between trainees, for example, one of these rules might be that a yellow envelope may never contain a green envelope because trainees have no business making direct contact with the chairman.

Our inspector can examine the inner envelopes as much as he likes. The greater the depth to which he goes, however, the more complex the rules will become and the more likely he is to end up blocking a genuine, important letter whose set of envelopes just happen to be arranged slightly differently from what he expects. And as we discussed in previous chapters, it has increasingly become the norm for the payload of many internet protocols to be encrypted, which is like replacing an open envelope with a locked box. Unless a firewall is itself one of the parties performing the encryption, there is then no way for it to examine a message's contents, which may well consist of further inner protocols that will remain invisible to it.

A state-of-the-art firewall controlling the messages between two computers is usually fairly effective at protecting the machine at one end from an attacker working at the other end. If somebody controls both ends of the connection, on the other hand, it will be clear in the light of the discussion about steganography in Chapter I that he will be able to set up some sort of covert channel: a means of communicating whatever information he wants between the two machines while escaping detection by a firewall monitoring the messages as they travel to and fro.

As early as 1997, a program called Loki2 was developed to demonstrate communication via covert channels.[180] Commands used to set up and configure computers were concealed within the payload of a protocol called Internet Control Message Protocol, or ICMP, whose original purpose was just to find out whether other computers were up and running.[181] Most firewalls would block configuration messages, but back then they would normally let ICMP traffic through. An attacker who had managed to gain access to a machine could install Loki2 on it and then continue to control it even after his original entry path had been blocked off.

DNS and the Banamex attack

Attackers have been known to employ a similar technique to access the internet for free over a network that they were supposed to be paying to use.[182] When you access a website, you do not normally type its server's IP address (217.160.57.21) into your browser, although this would work for some websites. Instead, the URL you enter typically contains a domain name that is designed to be memorable for human beings. For example, the domain name of the website that supplies information about this book is cybertwists.com.

The internet contains a network of Domain Name System (DNS) servers whose job is to tell other computers which domain names translate to which IP addresses.[183] Whenever you enter a URL that contains a domain name, your browser has to contact a DNS server to find out the matching IP address. Only then can it send the web server located at that IP address the request for the content you are trying to access.

If you try and browse an external website from your hotel room, you will often find you are redirected to a hotel website that requires you to enter your credit card details before you can go any further. The system that does this is typically triggered by you sending a message structured according to the HTTP protocol that your browser uses to communicate with web servers.

However, before you get to this point, your computer has already contacted some DNS server with a request containing the domain name of the website and obtained a reply specifying its IP address. All this takes place over a separate DNS protocol. The trick hackers have used to get around the paywall involves sending DNS messages that encapsulate disguised HTTP traffic to a machine somewhere in the internet that has been set up to extract HTTP messages from DNS messages, forward them on to their final targets and then conceal whatever is returned within DNS replies.

And criminals have also used DNS to attack businesses and other internet users. In 2008 in Mexico, false DNS information was used to commit fraud against the Banamex internet banking website.[184] The attack was fairly typical in that it was based on the phishing technique described in the previous chapter. On this occasion, however, the phishing did not rely on the user typing in or being redirected to a domain name subtly different from the genuine one; you were vulnerable even if you had entered the correct URL letter by letter. How did the scam work?

A home router that connects your local network to your telecommunications provider is typically configured via a local website that the router itself generates and serves to your browser. The hack was possible whenever somebody was using one of the main brands of Mexican home router with its default password. When you used your browser to access the router's local website, it would specify your password by incorporating it into the URL. If the local IP address of the router was 192.168.1.254, the URL would have looked something like this, where ... denotes whatever configuration page on the router your browser was accessing:

```
http://192.168.1.254/...?password=admin
```

In the previous chapter, we introduced the idea of cross-site request forgery based on cookies. Here, the fact that the password was tacked on the end of each URL left this brand of home router susceptible to a strain of cross-site request forgery that took advantage of default passwords instead. Another website controlled by the hackers took advantage of the weakness: unbeknown to you as you browsed it, it surreptitiously communicated with your home router configuration website.

The attack would have no effect unless you happened to be using the type of router in question and to have failed to change the default password to something more sensible. However, for the significant proportion of people for whom both these conditions were met, a silent request would reconfigure the router to point to a counterfeit DNS server that was controlled by the hackers. Whenever a browser subsequently tried to resolve the domain name of the Banamex website, the fake DNS server would return an IP address that led the browser to an equally fake website where users were tricked into delivering their financial information directly into the hands of the hackers.

Several years later, the attack was duplicated almost to the letter in Brazil with a different combination of criminals, home routers and target websites.[185] The fact that this sort of thing is possible demonstrates very clearly why the encryption-based signatures that we discussed in the previous chapter offer the only means of knowing with any useful level of confidence whom you are talking to over the internet.

Cache poisoning

A genuine DNS server run by an organisation like your internet service provider needs a source for the information it provides to its customers. For any given web address, there exists a DNS server somewhere on the internet that is responsible for providing a definitive answer to the question of what the corresponding IP address is. The so-called authoritative name servers that map the internet are arranged like a tree. Imagine an internet service provider's DNS server has just found out the IP address for cybertwists.com from the relevant authoritative DNS server. Beforehand, it had to ascertain the IP address of that authoritative DNS server by asking the DNS server that was authoritative for the top-level com domain, and it had previously found out where that was via a request to one of over a dozen root servers. Much like the public keys of the certificate authorities we looked at in the previous chapter, the IP addresses of these root servers have to be made known to a DNS server before it can start work.

If your internet service provider had to do go down the chain of authoritative name servers every time anyone accessed a website, the internet would rapidly grind to a halt because of all the DNS traffic clogging it up. Instead, DNS information can be stored for future reference by any machine that uses it or that gets to see it when it is transmitted. Remembering information locally in this way is called caching.

When you enter the domain name of a new website that has just gone online, your browser will try to find out the matching IP address by sending a DNS query to the pertinent authoritative name servers via your computer's operating system, your home router, your internet service provider and possibly further machines. The directory entries will be routed back to your browser along the same path and are likely to be cached by every computer they pass through. Any of these machines that receives a subsequent query for the same domain name within a certain period of time will then reply with the answer from the first query without checking with anybody else further down the chain that the information is still correct. The reply to a DNS query specifies the validity period of the assertions it makes, which tells its recipients how long they may cache it for.

This makes everything run nice and quickly, but there is a catch. If a hacker knows by some means or other that a computer has just sent out a DNS query, he can supply it with a fake answer by sending it a reply that reaches it more quickly than the genuine one returned by whomever it asked, a technique known as a man-on-the-side attack. And if the machine that takes delivery of the false response maintains a cache of DNS answers, its cache will have been poisoned and it may well end up forwarding the incorrect information it has received on to other people for some time afterwards.

The Kaminsky vulnerability

This type of attack has been known about since the dawn of the internet, but for a long time it was not seen as particularly serious because it was only thought to work for domain names that a DNS server did not already know about. If a server received a DNS request for google.com, it would almost certainly already have the relevant entry in its cache. Because it would respond from the information it already possessed rather than passing the query on to a second server, it would not send out a request that an attacker would be able to try and fake a response for.

On the other hand, a server that received a DNS request for some obscure domain would be unlikely already to hold a relevant entry in its cache and could be relied upon to issue a request that a hacker could respond to with false information, but even if the attack succeeded the fake information would probably never be returned to anybody else for the whole time it was remembered, because nobody else would ask for it.

In late 2008, however, Seattle-based researcher Dan Kaminsky stunned the security community by pointing out that the technique could not only be used to supply the wrong IP address for an individual DNS name. It was also possible to send a fake response that claimed that a whole parent domain that contained the name in question was now being serviced by a new authoritative DNS server.[186]

If a hacker wanted to poison a DNS server's cache entry for cybertwists.com, he could make up a non-existent domain dummy.cybertwists.com and send his target server a query for it. Because the target server could not possibly have any information in its cache about the fake domain, he could be sure that it would forward his query on to a second server. He could then try and reply to this query more quickly than the second server and send an assertion that the whole domain cybertwists.com now had a new authoritative name server.

The authoritative name server he specified would be another machine that he controlled, so that all subsequent queries about that domain would then be fielded to him. Theoretically, the technique could even have been used to poison the entry for the whole top-level com domain as well. Kaminsky's discovery raised the spectre of attackers forging DNS information about whole swathes of the internet.

Why was the DNS protocol susceptible to this trick? In most cases when two machines communicate over the internet, they start by exchanging a sequence of messages backwards and forwards that each party uses to demonstrate to the other that his IP address is really what he says it is. As we mentioned earlier in the chapter, the protocol that achieves this is called TCP and an example of when it is used is when your browser contacts a server to download a web page. TCP is a bit like me calling you on the phone, giving you my details and hanging up, and you calling me back to reassure yourself I have not given you a fake number.

DNS requests, on the other hand, do not normally use TCP because it would make a process that can already be somewhat long-winded even slower. Instead, the contents of DNS messages are themselves supposed to demonstrate that an answer has come from the same server that was asked the question. When a machine sends out a DNS request, it generates a number that forms part of the query, and it will only recognise as valid a response that cites the right query number. One might imagine that this would prevent the sort of attacks we have just been discussing: because a hacker is normally unable to view the requests his victim machine is sending out, he should have no way of knowing which query number to specify in his fake responses.

At the time when the Kaminsky revelations broke, however, many computers assigned DNS query numbers sequentially. If the last number used was *464*, the next one would be *465*, then *466* and so on. A hacker could make use of this knowledge as follows. He would have already registered his own DNS server as authoritative for some domain that he himself owned, say hackerownedsite.com. He would send a request to the DNS server he was attacking and ask it for the IP address for his own domain. Shortly afterwards, the victim DNS server would forward his request on to his own DNS server and he would be able to observe the query number it used.

He would then immediately go on to try and employ the Kaminsky attack to poison the victim DNS server's cache entry for some other domain, say sitetobepoisoned.com. He would send the victim server a request to retrieve the IP address for dummy.sitetobepoisoned.com. Because the victim DNS server would then forward the request to the DNS server responsible for the sitetobepoisoned.com domain, the hacker would not get to see it. However, he would know that the victim DNS server was likely to have specified a query number one, two or three numbers higher than the one it had just used for his own domain. He could then send several responses in rapid succession with these query numbers and would have a good chance of getting in with the right one in front of the real answer.

Even servers that used randomly selected query numbers were not totally immune to the problem. The range of possible values that DNS allowed was small enough that flooding the network with fake answers sporting query numbers chosen at whim still gave an attacker a fighting chance of hitting the jackpot. Unfortunately, permitting a larger range of query numbers was not a realistic option, because the vast number of people using DNS throughout the world precluded a sudden change to the way it worked. Instead, the problem ended up being solved with a somewhat inelegant form of jiggery-pokery. As well as avoiding sequential query numbers, whenever a computer issued a DNS request, it was to choose at random a port number where it specified that it was expecting the reply.[187] The combination of random port number and random query number decreased to an acceptable level the likelihood that a fake answer would happen to match the corresponding question. Early 2009 saw a mad rush to update DNS software and hardware to conform to this new procedure.

DNSSEC

Using random ports and query numbers is only a temporary workaround. The long-term solution is called Domain Name System Security Extensions (DNSSEC) and it is based on private and public key pairs: the asymmetric encryption described in Chapter I.[188] DNSSEC builds chains of trust for DNS itself that are similar to those that the certificates described in Chapter III create for the websites that DNS is used to locate. A server that has received a DNS record for a domain that is using DNSSEC can verify the record's signature using the public key of the responsible authoritative name server. That public key will itself have been signed by the authoritative name server for the top-level com domain, whose own public key is verifiable using a root public key. There is a list of root public keys that have to be known to a DNSSEC server before it is first used, just as the IP addresses of the DNS root servers are used to set up DNS servers in general and just as a browser has to be preconfigured with details of root certificate authorities.

Introducing DNSSEC in a big-bang style has never been on the cards. It would have brought the internet to a grinding halt. The old DNS system has to keep working as well, and all DNS servers continue to accept unsigned records. However, the idea is that if a DNS server knows that DNSSEC is being used for a domain, it will not accept any new unsigned information concerning that domain. If you are a website operator, you have an interest in your DNS records being signed using DNSSEC because it makes it much more difficult for traffic destined for you to be misdirected.

The adoption of DNSSEC is gradually gathering pace, but has not occurred as quickly as many would have hoped when the standard was first introduced. More and more authoritative name servers are signing their records, but this is only any help if the DNS servers that retrieve and store the information they provide go on to take the trouble to validate the signatures. The practicalities of this step have proven a stumbling block for many server operators, who seem to have tended to give up when initial tests did not go quite as smoothly as they had hoped. People generally prefer an insecure system to one that runs erratically. The percentage of DNS queries worldwide that are validated using DNSSEC signatures has lumbered up from circa 9% in early 2014 to still no more than around 12% in early 2018.[189]

And until unsigned DNS has been completely abandoned and no pockets of the internet remain where it is still regarded as valid, the assurance DNSSEC offers will only ever be of any use if you are sure you can trust the frontline DNS server from which you get your information. DNSSEC would have offered little protection against the Banamex hack described above. Once the attackers had cleared out the cached DNS entries from your home router, it would have forgotten which domains it had previously known to be issuing signed records; and Windows versions in use at the time would only cache DNS information on local computers for up to a day even if it specified longer validity periods.[190] As soon as this day had passed, the fake DNS server that the criminals used to feed you false IP addresses could have pretended that none of the domains you were viewing was yet DNSSEC-compliant; the hackers would have had carte blanche to return you whatever IP addresses they wanted.

Fast flux and the Storm Worm

The idea behind DNS is that information about domains can be distributed and cached because it does not change very often. The system is designed to publish and disseminate relatively static entries that state which domain name is being serviced by which IP address. However, some botnets use DNS to achieve the exact opposite of its intended use: to conceal the whereabouts of the servers that control them.

In 2007, thousands of computers in the United States and Europe fell victim to a piece of malware called the Storm Worm that spread via E-mail attachments in a similar fashion to the Love Letter and CryptoLocker trojans described in Chapter II.[191] The infected computers that made up the resulting botnet received their orders from a domain name that they queried on a regular basis. Under normal circumstances, the DNS entry linking this domain name to its associated IP address would have led investigators straight to the commanding server, because an IP address falls under the responsibility of a service provider who can locate the computer that is using it.

In this case, however, the botnet owners were using a technique called fast flux. This involved changing the DNS entry for their domain on a very frequent basis and each time declaring it to be valid for a very brief period of time to prevent it from being cached. At any given moment, the DNS entry would specify the IP address of an infected machine somewhere within the botnet that was being used to issue commands to the rest of the botnet. However, anybody trying to take down the whole Storm Worm system by locating and disinfecting that victim machine would have had too little time to act, because the control function would have been transferred to some other computer moments afterwards.

Georestrictions

When you browse the internet, the requests you generate have to specify your own IP address so the server with which you are communicating knows where to send its replies. Because most service providers operate within individual countries, this normally means that whoever you are talking to can work out where you are in the world.

Some countries have public television services that offer online programmes but that refuse to transmit them to IP addresses located outside their borders in an attempt to prevent foreigners from watching.[192] Circumventing such georestrictions is technically simple even if the legal situation in many jurisdictions remains somewhat murky. Rather than travelling to wherever you want to watch television, you can stay put and connect to a virtual private network (VPN) service located in the target country. This is a server that pretends to be a normal home computer, accesses the television content on your behalf and relays it back to you.

There is a whole industry facilitating clandestine television viewing across international borders. In 2015, researcher Jason Mander of the company GlobalWebIndex claimed that British Broadcasting Corporation (BBC) programmes intended for domestic UK audiences were being consumed online by some 65 million people in other countries who were not supposed to be watching them.[193] Given that the entire population of the UK at the time was also 65 million, this would be a sensationally high figure.[194] There is no way of validating it, but even a number two orders of magnitudes lower would demonstrate the existence of a multi-million-dollar business sector constructed solely around people watching UK television abroad: a typical annual subscription to a VPN service costs about $100.

The BBC's response on learning about the hordes of foreigners who were daring to access their programmes was to announce a crackdown.[195] The organisation regularly attempts to block VPN services, presumably by rejecting requests from IP addresses that guilty relay servers have been observed to use in the past. However, it does not normally take long before the servers are moved to new IP addresses and *Doctor Who* is once again being enjoyed across the globe.[196] One might imagine that there are a handful of network technicians at the BBC who are tasked with suppressing foreign viewing. They are probably never in with much of a chance against the much better-resourced VPN service companies, who seem to be consistently successful in outflanking them.

It remains one of life's greatest mysteries why the BBC makes no effort to monetize the tremendous interest in its content that exists throughout the world. There can be little doubt that most customers of VPN services would far rather pay an annual subscription to the BBC itself, which could then use their cash to make new programmes. The BBC's argument is that the rights it purchases on films only apply to the domestic UK market. However, a cursory examination of the figures involved makes it hard to believe that the extra revenue from viewers abroad would not dwarf any additional fees that media companies might demand on learning that it was now legal to consume UK television from countries where everybody knew people had long been doing so anyway.

Traffic analysis

People watching *Top Gear* in Asia is of no relevance to UK national security. However, if it were and if the police were to obtain a warrant to wiretap VPN services, they could find out viewers' locations by observing the traffic going to and from the relay servers. Even if the content you send and receive over the internet is encrypted, any message you transmit to your VPN service still has to bear your IP address in unencrypted form. Otherwise, the VPN service would have no way of knowing where to stream your television programme in reply. The envelope may be sealed, but anyone can read what is on the outside to find out who the sender and addressee are.

Whether or not you are party to what is being said, just knowing who is talking has a very significant surveillance value that is commonly underestimated. So-called traffic analysis played an often understated role in the Allied effort to glean useful information from the Enigma messages described in Chapter I.[197] The best-case scenario was obviously being able to listen in on and understand detailed plans of an upcoming military operation. However, even when the Bletchley Park teams could not decode the contents of a broadcast they had eavesdropped on, they could usually still work out who was transmitting to whom, and the simple observation that a group of army units had suddenly started to communicate more intensively than over the preceding days was frequently sufficient to permit an educated guess that there was something major in the offing.

The preamble to each Enigma message was transmitted in unencrypted form just as an IP message header is today. It included a three-letter code called a discriminant that would be specified in the codebook together with the rotor, wiring and plugboard configurations with which the sender and recipient set up their machines. While the discriminant confirmed to the recipient that he was using the same codebook as the sender, it was useful to enemy analysts because messages that shared a discriminant normally originated from the same section of the German military. And there were other ways of working out which messages belonged together. As we saw in Chapter I, preambles also included non-encrypted callsigns that identified the sending and receiving stations, and some radio operators transmitted their Morse code with distinctive rhythms.

Even today, how the Bletchley Park teams collated, managed and employed the information the preambles provided is much more patchily documented than the well-known tale of rotors, wirings and plugboards. To some extent, this may be simply because gathering and analysing the data effectively was mostly a feat of pure organisation about which there is little to say that is technically surprising. However, there remains the tantalising possibility that details of the Bletchley Park traffic analysis could, even today, remain concealed as classified information with a relevance to modern intelligence work.[198]

Gordon Welchman, the architect of the Bletchley Park traffic analysis programme, published his memoirs in 1982. They focussed chiefly on the main message decoding techniques. Interestingly, though, although these had already been public knowledge for several years, the British intelligence agency Government Communications Headquarters (GCHQ) branded him "a disastrous example", and the American NSA—his employer at the time—permanently revoked his security clearance. Was their real objection to his book not that it explained how Bletchley Park had cracked Enigma, but that it simultaneously drew attention to the still all-too-relevant issue of traffic analysis?[199]

Onion routing and Tor

In 2001, the U.S. Navy published a patent for a technique called onion routing that is designed to allow people to communicate over the internet in a way that protects them from traffic analysis.[200] Within a few years, the idea had been opened up for general use and the concept had been embodied in a software platform called Tor, which stands for "The Onion Router" but also happens to be the word for *gate* in several European languages including German.[201]

You can connect to and make use of the Tor infrastructure from any normal computer. It is made up of Tor servers, or onion routers, that are distributed around the world; anyone can volunteer to contribute a server he owns to be used as an onion router. Tor takes the limited privacy offered by communicating over a VPN service to its logical conclusion: a message between two points within the internet is sent on a complex detour via several onion routers to throw observers off the trail; and the details of the path it takes are themselves protected using encryption.

Tor's maintenance and funding was a collaborative effort between the U.S. Navy and such unlikely bedfellows as human rights organisations and press freedom groups who saw the software as a vital tool to keep journalists and activists working under repressive regimes safe from exposure.[202] The popular impression of Tor came to be dominated by this anti-establishment tinge, with many people unaware that the platform was actually the brainchild of the American military.

As Michael G. Reed, one of Tor's inventors, hinted in 2011, the intelligence community was more than happy to allow the system to be used by the general public, because that way the chatter of spies could blend in inconspicuously against the background noise generated by the left-wing activists and teenage geeks with whom they then shared the infrastructure.[203] It seems quite plausible that the military establishment then went one step further and actively engineered the journalistic spin that made it look as though such alternative types who were using Tor to communicate were also its original designers and creators.

The term "onion routing" stems from the fact that what the servers at each point in the Tor network do is akin to peeling off the outer layers of an onion. Imagine you want to send somebody a parcel. Because you want a reply when it has been delivered, you have no option but to identify yourself as the sender on the back. The parcel is already locked with a key that you share with the addressee, so there is no danger of anyone taking a peek into its contents, but you are also anxious that the post office should not be able to observe the communication between you and the recipient.

To resolve this conundrum, you make use of a network of volunteers dotted around the world who are willing to go to the trouble of forwarding parcels around so that other postal service users can enjoy anonymity. You address the parcel to its eventual destination, specify one of the volunteers, whom we shall call Peter, as its sender, and lock it in a second box, using a different key. You then address this second box to Peter, naming Sue, a second volunteer, as the second box's sender. Using a third key, you then lock the second box in a third box which you address to Sue; this time the sender is Adrian. The fourth box, which—you will not be surprised to learn—is locked with a fourth key and addressed to Adrian, identifies you as the sender and is what you actually take to the post office.

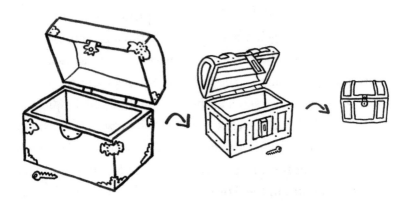

Each volunteer unlocks his or her box with his or her key and sends it on to the next addressee. Adrian, the volunteer closest in the chain to you, the original sender, knows who you are but not who the final addressee is, while Peter, the volunteer closest to the final addressee, knows who she is but not that you were the original sender. And Sue, the volunteer in the middle, knows nothing at all apart from the details of the two volunteers on either side of her, neither of whom have anything whatsoever to do with the actual parcel.

If the chain is lengthened to involve four, five or more participants, any volunteer who is not at one of the two ends will not even have any way of knowing where in the chain he is. He will simply be forwarding a parcel from one volunteer on to some other volunteer. The box he receives might have originally been enclosed by one, two or more larger boxes, and the box he sends on could be harbouring one, two or more smaller boxes.

Each time a volunteer opens a box and forwards on its contents, he keeps the box in reserve in case he is asked to use it to help the final addressee send a second parcel back along the same route to the original sender. Sue previously received her box from Adrian and sent its contents on to Peter. Now she receives a parcel from Peter that is travelling back in the opposite direction. She takes her original box off its shelf and puts Peter's parcel into it. She locks her box, swaps over its sender and receiver labels, and sends it on to Adrian. When you, the original sender, receive the outer box, you can use your bunch of keys to open the boxes one after the other until you finally get through to the parcel at the centre.

The clever bit is that all the keys fit. This would be essentially impossible to achieve in the non-digital analogy we have just used to explain the concept, because you would have to have exchanged keys with Sue and Adrian, the volunteers further down the chain, in advance. This would not only be very inconvenient but also hard to do without risking revealing your identity to them. The virtual world, on the other hand, has a ready-made solution in the form of the encryption techniques that were explained in the first chapter.

In Tor parlance, a chain of onion routers along which two computers communicate is known as a circuit. The public key of each onion router is published along with its IP address. A sender building up a circuit starts by contacting the first router and using a version of the Diffie-Hellman exchange that incorporates the router's public key to agree on a symmetric key. This symmetric key will be used for all further communication between the sender and the router.

The sender then asks the first router to broker messages between it and a second router in order to extend the circuit. These messages are used to negotiate a second symmetric key that the sender shares with the second router but that remains unknown to the first router.

When the sender goes on to transmit a message to the second router requesting it to extend the circuit once again by brokering contact with a third router, the message will be encrypted twice: once using the second router's symmetric key, and once using the first router's symmetric key. This ensures that, although the message will be transmitted via the first router, the first router will not be party to what the sender is asking the second router to do: the first router will have no way of eavesdropping on the identity of the third router.

Traffic analysis is possible with everyday internet communication because the headers that specify who is talking cannot be encrypted even if the message payload is. Tor solves this problem by incorporating the headers of one message into the encrypted payload of a second message, whose own headers are incorporated into the encrypted payload of a third message, and so on.

Sybil attacks, jurisdictional arbitrage and leaky pipes

The anonymity Tor offers is based on the fact that any single onion router observing messages as it sends and receives them will be unable to glean from them any information about who is talking to whom. Nonetheless, with enough resources, a secret service could theoretically compromise the system by running a large enough proportion of the world's onion routers and collating the information passing through them to trace out the communication paths.

The integrity of the Tor network relies on the individual onion routers being operated independently from one another. However, although it can be verified that they are all located at different IP addresses, there is no way of checking that the computers using those IP addresses are not all owned by the same person or organisation: remember that anybody can anonymously offer his server to be used as an onion router. An attack that involves a single individual claiming a large number of distinct identities is known as a Sybil attack after a 1973 book about a woman with multiple personalities.[204]

Even when the onion routers that make up a circuit are being run by several distinct people, if they are all located in the same country, a judge could still conceivably force them to submit to monitoring by national authorities who could then use the collected information to link original senders to final receivers. This danger can be avoided by making sure that the routers that make up each circuit are distributed around the globe, a technique referred to in Tor circles as jurisdictional arbitrage.[205]

With or without Tor, whenever any sort of longer message is sent over the internet, it is split up into a number of physical messages that are reassembled at the other end. While an ordinary network card creates physical messages of various sizes, though, Tor software takes care to send ones that are all the same length. This feature is necessary because without it somebody would be in a strong position to work out which messages belonged together as steps within circuits by observing the traffic throughout the Tor network and matching up the sizes of individual messages sent from onion router to onion router.

However, the fact that Tor messages have a constant size also has the unwanted side effect of giving them a characteristic fingerprint that makes it fairly simple for your internet service provider to identify you as a Tor user, and in many countries, even if there is no way of finding out what you are saying or to whom you are talking, the mere fact that you are using Tor is enough to put you under surveillance.

Despite the fact that all messages are the same length, somebody in a position to monitor the network traffic at various points along a Tor circuit would still have a reasonable chance of working out who was talking to whom by noting the precise times at which each router sent and received messages. This sort of observation falls into the class of timing attacks that we covered in the previous chapter. To make it more difficult, Tor provides a little-used feature called the leaky-pipe topology. I create a Tor circuit that consists of four onion routers and then send the traffic so that half of it is forwarded to its target by the fourth and final router in the chain, while the other half is delivered directly by the third, penultimate, "leaking" one. That way, it will be more challenging for anybody trying to match up what I send with what emerges from either the third or the fourth router.

When you are using Tor to send messages to a target machine, a new circuit with a new chain of onion routers is built up every ten minutes. Most routers are selected at random from a large worldwide pool. However, because the router at your end of each circuit you create can see your IP address, it would be a bad idea if you kept connecting to different ones. If an intelligence service running a small number of onion routers decided to start keeping track of the traffic passing through them, the laws of statistics would then mean that at some point in time you would be bound to construct a circuit with a dodgy router at your end and get your identity logged. This would expose you as a Tor user. To avoid this, a computer connecting to the Tor infrastructure selects a much smaller group of initial onion routers, which are known as entry guards, to use consistently over a period of several months.[206] Although you personally might still have the misfortune to chance upon a rotten entry guard, this ensures that, overall, most people will stay anonymous most of the time.

Tracking down Tor users

Although Tor has a sound theoretical basis, staying hidden when using it requires a lot of discipline and is actually quite tricky in practice. One version of how the FBI finally tracked down the infamous New-York-based hacker Hector Xavier Monsegur, alias Sabu, is that he forgot to use Tor a single time when he logged into a chatroom.[207] And even if your traffic is being successfully anonymised as you use your browser to access a website, you are still liable to blow your cover if you click on a link on that website that downloads and opens a Word or Excel file. Unless you are very careful, you might find that the Office application that is now running alongside your browser has made direct contact with the server using an everyday internet connection that betrays all the information you have been going to such lengths to hide.[208]

Perhaps the biggest weakness of the Tor system is that there is essentially only one piece of software with which most people's skills allow them to use it. Although it is possible to configure a variety of programs to access the Tor infrastructure, the scope for getting things disastrously wrong has led the Tor project to urge people who wish to access websites over Tor to stick to the official Tor browser, which is a modified version of Mozilla Firefox.[209]

Together, Firefox and the Tor extension form a complex mass of code that offers considerable scope for malware infections and vulnerability exploits. If you have read Chapter II, it is not hard to imagine how a security service could take advantage of the fact that practically everybody using Tor relies on the same browser model. You just have to entice your target group to a website that is likely to interest them. You can then make use of a drive-by download or some other vulnerability to reprogram their browsers or computers to bypass the Tor safeguards and to send you precise information about their activities and whereabouts.

In 2013, the FBI exploited a complex and elegant zero-day vulnerability that sneaked additional executable numeric code instructions into Firefox from within the Javascript tag on an HTML page.[210] They used the resulting control over each infected browser to make it send them the IP address of the machine where it was running. This allowed them to unmask a host of people who were using Tor to access child pornography. And in November 2016, it emerged that very similar code was being used to take advantage of a related but subtly different vulnerability: this time, Tor browser users' IP addresses were being sent to a server located in France.[211]

Despite such attacks, we know that, as of 2012 at least, the NSA and the British intelligence service GCHQ had not yet come up with a general means of conquering Tor. The information leaked by Edward Snowden confirmed that the American security apparatus seemed to have set free a beast that it had subsequently found itself unable to tame. The relevant presentation is entitled "Tor Stinks" and the olfactory references continue with the description of a piece of analysis software called ONIONBREATH.[212] What the document shows is that while there are a number of ways of demasking individual Tor users—we will return to these in a moment—the basic Tor concept is sound. Peter Steiner's famous cartoon proclaimed in 1993 that "on the internet, nobody knows you're a dog".[213] It is worth remembering that, with Tor, locating the barking is generally pretty hard too.

U.S. election hacking allegations

Hillary Clinton's 2016 presidential election campaign was marred with E-mail leaks that were made possible because the Democratic Party servers had been hacked, and a document released jointly by the Department of Homeland Security (DHS) and the FBI in December of that year claimed that they had traced the attack to the Russian national security apparatus, codenaming it GRIZZLY STEPPE.[214] In fact, none of the concrete evidence for this that is in the public domain stands up to critical scrutiny.

At first glance, the paper looks substantial, but most of it is actually a list of largely irrelevant general tips explaining how computer administrators can protect themselves against some of the vulnerabilities we discussed in Chapter II. The arguments put forward for ascribing the hacking activity to the Russian government turn out to be few and far between. They are also shaky at best.

Most strikingly, the document is accompanied by a list of IP addresses from which the activity is said to have been carried out. Does this mean that we are really to believe that the Russian Federal Security Service (FSB) would not have the skills to use the internet anonymously?[215] Surely if anybody could be expected to know how to use Tor effectively to cover their tracks, it would be the FSB! Many of the implicated IP addresses were in fact later attributed to Tor routers, which demonstrates that whoever was behind the attacks knew what they were doing, but hardly proves that it was the Russians.[216]

A second press release in January 2017 from the U.S. Office of the Council of National Intelligence focussed on the political evidence that the Russian government had wanted to affect the course of the election.[217] This time no technical details were given on the basis that "the release of such information would reveal sensitive sources or methods and imperil the ability to collect critical foreign intelligence in the future." There is obviously no way of knowing whether or not the U.S. authorities had in fact exposed the culprit definitively via some secret means. It could even be that they had compromised the entire Tor system during the years since the Snowden leak. However, if they really had strong technical evidence that had to be kept secret, it is difficult to explain why they would have resorted to publishing embarrassingly weak technical evidence just a few weeks beforehand.

On the other hand, the security company CrowdStrike had already presented a rather more cogent analysis of the hacks in June 2016.[218] Like the report from the DHS and the FBI, their document had mentioned APT28, alias Fancy Bear, and APT29, alias Cozy Bear, hacker groups commonly associated with the Russian state. But CrowdStrike had presented somewhat better evidence, listing a dozen pieces of malware that had previously been used by the two groups and had now been involved in the attack. The DHS went on to publish comparable information in February 2017.[219]

Although this certainly constituted a stronger case than IP addresses, however, it would still not stand up in a court of law. Nothing comes even close to having been proven beyond reasonable doubt, because somebody else in the know could easily have reused the right software to make it look as though the Russians were responsible. However, the balance of probabilities is still that Russia was really behind the leaks. The most likely explanation is that, as with the North Koreans as mentioned in the previous chapter, the Russians are actually quite happy for people to suspect strongly that they were to blame because of the power this allegation reflects.

Hidden services, introductions and rendezvous points

Tor enables you to run a hidden service: a website that users and customers can only connect to over Tor, normally with the Tor browser, and whose own IP address remains secret as well as theirs. As a hidden service owner, you choose a chain of onion routers and use them to create a circuit just as you would in the normal Tor case where you want a message anonymously forwarded on to somebody somewhere on the internet. However, a hidden service's circuit ends with an onion router rather than with a target computer: this router then acts as an introduction point for clients.

A customer connects to your introduction point router using his own Tor circuit that he has built up to it. He sends a message destined for you up his circuit to the introduction point router, and the introduction point router forwards the message back down your circuit to your hidden service. Your introduction point router does not know where your hidden service is located. And because there is nothing to distinguish a hidden-service circuit from any other Tor circuit, the other onion routers that make it up have no way of knowing that they are involved with a hidden service at all.

This setup would have been sufficient to allow hidden services to be provided and used anonymously. However, the designers of the Tor system were concerned that responsibility for whatever a hidden service was doing could have ended up being attributed to the person running its introduction-point onion router. He would have had no way of proving that all he was doing was passing messages to an unknown machine down a chain of servers; theoretically, he could have just been pretending to be communicating with the hidden service over a Tor circuit while actually running it himself.

Tor prevents such allegations by using a more complex architecture that makes them impossible. Instead of communicating solely via the introduction point, you connect to a hidden service by first setting up a circuit with an onion router you yourself have chosen, which is known as a rendezvous point. You then let the hidden service know where your rendezvous point is by sending it a single message via its introduction point.

Remember that the Diffie–Hellman technique allows two people to agree on a secret key by each sending the other a number. In this case, the customer sends the hidden service his number via the introduction point, and the hidden service replies with its number via a circuit it builds up to the rendezvous point. A common key results and encrypted communication can begin via the two circuits linked by the rendezvous point despite the fact that the two numbers used to generate the key were sent over different paths.

The Tor system maintains a directory of hidden services that fulfils a similar function to DNS but that works quite differently from it. The DNS system is designed to spread around information about domain names as widely as possible; the information about any one Tor hidden service, on the other hand, is only kept on a handful of directory servers that are changed daily and that are themselves hidden behind Tor circuits. A directory entry tells a customer which onion router or routers are acting as introduction points for a hidden service. It also specifies the hidden service's public key. A customer uses this key to encrypt the message that it sends the hidden service via the two circuits linked by the introduction point. Because only the hidden service should have the corresponding private key that enables it to decrypt the customer's message, he can then be confident that the reply he receives via his rendezvous point really originates from the hidden service and not from some other server somewhere within the Tor system.

You access a hidden service by entering its name into the Tor browser just as you would enter a normal website's DNS name into it, or indeed into any other browser. However, hidden service names have to conform to a much stricter pattern than standard DNS names. They begin with a sixteen-character identifier derived from the service's public key and end with the appendage .onion, which was chosen to look like a DNS top-level domain.

Tying an onion name directly to its public key means that Tor hidden services are immune to the sort of phishing attacks described earlier in this chapter for DNS: it is impossible to persuade directory servers to publish a false public key and introduction point for another hidden service and get messages destined for that hidden service diverted to your own server, because doing so would necessarily entail changing the hidden service's name at the same time. However, this stringent standard has disadvantages as well. It is difficult to get an onion name right when you type it in, and almost impossible to remember it. For example, search engine DuckDuckGo uses the onion name http://3g2upl4pq6kufc4m.onion.[220]

Some sites partially get around this problem by generating large numbers of private keys until they hit on one whose corresponding public key translates to an onion name that relates to the service they are offering. Because doing this for an onion name spanning all sixteen characters would take impractically long, the names people use typically begin with a meaningful word before degenerating into gobbledegook. For example, a hidden service for financial trading might use the onion name http://torbroker8g3xziu.onion.

Tor hidden services are probably the most extreme example of what the popular press means by the term "dark web". However, the term is not technically specific, but can rather refer to any internet services that are somehow hidden from general view. A typical website aims to be easy for visitors to find. It is likely to have a meaningful domain name, it will probably answer to requests on one of the standard ports for web traffic, and even if you try and access it in a different way from what it expects or fail to provide a required password, it is likely to tell you what you are doing wrong so that you can try again.

If, on the other hand, I run a website that has no domain name and can only be accessed via its IP address, that runs on an unexpected port, and that replies if you include a certain password in your request but pretends not to exist otherwise, I have already created a service that is highly concealed. If I then switch to running it as a Tor hidden service, an additional shroud of darkness descends on the scene in as much as I do not know where my customers are located, my customers do not know where I am located, and a third party observing the traffic is unable to work out that we are having a conversation.

Demasking hidden services

Once any onion router has been running smoothly for a reasonable period of time, its owner can volunteer it to be used as a hidden-service directory server. In 2014, the Tor project revealed that somebody had been taking advantage of this opportunity to find out the locations of hidden-service customers.[221] The culprits had been performing a Sybil attack in as much as they have been shown to have been controlling a significant proportion of the world's onion routers, and a user was exposed whenever, by chance, the attackers had in their throes both the directory server he was accessing and the entry guard: the onion router closest to him within the circuit he built up to that directory server. As with any other Tor circuit, the two machines were linked by intermediaries and had no way of communicating directly, but what the rogue onion routers did was to use Tor's own messages to create a particularly crafty type of covert channel.

When a Tor user wishing to find out the introduction point for a hidden service contacted a directory server that happened to be carrying out the attack, the directory server would encode the name of the hidden service the user was trying to access as a string of bits that it then communicated back down the chain to the entry guard. For each zero bit, it sent it one type of administrative Tor message, and for each one bit, it sent it a second type of administrative Tor message. Although these messages were encrypted and a subversive entry guard could not read their contents, it only had to be able to distinguish one type of message from the other to be able to recover the name of the hidden service from the sequence. Because the entry guard already knew the IP address of whoever was trying to browse that service, it could then work out who was doing what.

And in 2016, it was demonstrated that some organisation seemed to be running directory services in order to use the facts they managed to its own ends.[222] Researchers provided the Tor directory system with details of hidden services that did not really do anything and that were not advertised anywhere outside Tor. They christened these services *honions*, a portmanteau of *honeypot* and *onion*. There should have been no way of anybody ever finding them, because there are too many sixteen-letter names to try them all out one by one. That many honion services were in fact accessed led to the conclusion that information about their whereabouts were being leaked by directory servers. One possibility is that the aim was to attack the servers where hidden services ran, perhaps using malware or vulnerabilities to get them to reveal their IP addresses in the same way that Tor browsers have sometimes been persuaded to divulge their whereabouts to law enforcement authorities.

Blockchain, Bitcoin and Ethereum

For the first few years that Tor existed, you could only use it to hide online as long as you did not wish to purchase any goods or services. Spending money involved your bank account and meant revealing where and who you were. This situation was overturned in early 2009 with the creation of the Bitcoin system, which extended online anonymity to financial transfers. Designed by an unknown individual or group using the pseudonym Satoshi Nakamoto, bitcoin is a virtual cryptocurrency that is different from traditional forms of payment in that there is no central bank that issues it.[223] (Convention has it that the capitalised *Bitcoin* is used to refer to the system, while the lowercase *bitcoin* is preferred when discussing the currency.)

Bitcoins have a purely virtual existence. A consignment of bitcoins is a history of transactions that record when it was transferred from one person to another. This history begins with the event that brought the coins into existence and assigned them to their initial owner: as we shall see, bitcoins come into being as a result of the deliberately costly operation of the system that is used to deal in them.

The Bitcoin network makes use of the blockchain pattern, which in its most basic form is no more than a cheap and simple way of storing a large stream of information as it is generated and of ensuring that the information is accurately recorded for posterity. A blockchain is based on the hashing technique that was described in the previous chapter. Each time a certain amount of new material has been amassed, it is lumped together to form a new block. The new block is signed off with the hash value of all its contents concatenated together. This hash value is then used as the first piece of information in the subsequent block, whose own hash value will later be used as the first piece of information in the block after that, and so on.

The integrity of a blockchain relies on lots of people having copies of it and being able to recalculate all the hash values. As long as everybody knows what the hash value of the latest block should be, it is impossible for any surreptitious alterations to be made to information stored further back in the chain. They would set off a cascade of changes to the hash values of all the blocks from that point onwards that would percolate through to the end and alter the generally known final value, making it immediately apparent that something was amiss.

The Estonian state stores many of the details of its ongoing national life on a blockchain.[224] Officially, the aim is to increase transparency and efficiency, but the system also makes sure that information like land ownership would survive in virtual form should the tiny country ever be invaded. The blockchain idea is also poised to revolutionise the world of commerce. It provides a means for business partners who may not trust each other to work with a common store of information: it makes it impossible for one party to change anything without giving the other party proof of what happened.

Returning to Bitcoin, its blockchain stores information about who has paid which coin amounts to whom and when. Thousands of computers share information about current transactions, disseminating them through an enormous improvised network. Each of these machines has a copy of the blockchain up to that point, and any one of them can extend the chain by conflating the transactions that have not yet been set in stone into a new block, signing off that block with a hash value and distributing the block through the rest of the network.

Crucially, though, signing off a block is not just a case of calculating the hash value of that block's contents as they stand. A valid hash value has to begin with a certain number of zero bits. The final item in each block is a meaningless string of bits chosen by the person who is signing it off, and a huge number of possible final items normally have to be tried out until somebody happens to hit on one that sets the hash value of the whole block to something that fulfils this requirement.

This brute-force process takes time and, unfortunately for the environment, energy. One researcher estimated that the electricity used worldwide searching for Bitcoin hashes in 2014 was equivalent to the entire consumption of Ireland.[225] The resources required to take part in the Bitcoin system make it much more expensive to carry off a Sybil attack on Bitcoin than on Tor. Controlling more than half of the Bitcoin network is not simply a case of posing as a large number of distinct participants. It rather entails paying for more power than everybody else put together.

Finding valid hash values for new blocks is getting harder all the time. Every 2016 blocks, the number of zero bits that will be required at the beginning of each hash value within the next 2016 blocks is calibrated based on how long it has taken to find the previous 2016 blocks. The value is set so that, however many people are using the system and whatever the power of currently available hardware, the average time between consecutive blocks being mined remains consistent at around ten minutes. (The number 2016 has nothing to do with the year 2016; it happens to be the number of blocks that come into being over a two-week period.)

The energy used to generate Bitcoin blocks gives them an intrinsic value that forms the basis for the Bitcoin financial system. The process of wasting electricity to sign off a block is known as mining, and if you mine a block that ends up being immortalised in the Bitcoin blockchain, you automatically become the proud initial owner of a certain number of new bitcoins that are regarded as having been minted with that block.

The transaction information stored within the blocks relies on the asymmetric encryption described in Chapter I. Each time you trade in bitcoin, you use a new private key you have generated, a corresponding public key and an address derived from that public key. You incorporate an address you control into a block you are mining so that—should you be lucky enough to stumble upon a valid hash value—the address will attest to your ownership of the newly minted bitcoins.

At some later date, you spend these bitcoins by transferring them to somebody else. Firstly, you create a transaction in which you add to the existing information about the coins an address supplied by the recipient. Secondly, you sign the transaction using the private key from which you created your own address when you were mining. Thirdly, you disseminate the transaction. Everybody else will regard your signature as valid because it will correspond to the address in the existing coin information. When the recipient wants to transfer the coins to a third person, he adds an address belonging to that third person to the coin information that emerged from your transaction and signs the coin information with his own private key, and so on.

Unlike with web domain certificates and DNSSEC information, there is no higher authority that signs your public key or address to confirm that you are who you claim to be, because the whole idea is that you remain untraceable. In the Bitcoin world, a private key is not just used to prove your identity; it is your identity. In fact, because the Bitcoin system is designed to make use of a different key-based identity for each new transaction, it is not even possible for somebody to work out what Bitcoin users are doing by collating the records of their various activities within the blockchain. The flipside of this privacy is that, should you ever mislay a private key, you will have lost the bitcoins it protected and will have absolutely no way of ever getting them back. They will remain in limbo until the end of time. Equally, if somebody manages to steal the private key for your bitcoins, there is nothing to mark you out as the rightful owner over the thief. Either of you can then go on to spend the funds.

Bitcoins can be swapped for dollars, pounds or euros just like any other currency. You can buy bitcoins using a traditional payment method such as a bank transfer, but there are also bitcoin ATMs where you can obtain them in exchange for cash.[226] This facility is important because it gives ordinary users who do not mine coins or operate hidden services an easy way of taking part in the bitcoin system without revealing their identities.

It may seem counterintuitive that the side products of electronic calculations should have a market value, until you consider that the materials that make up banknotes are not worth much in their own right either. However it has come into being, any means of payment is ultimately worth no more or no less than what people think they will be able to buy with it in the future, and bitcoin is convincing enough to endow it with a durable worth. That said, bitcoin exchange rates have a volatility unmatched by even the most unstable of national currencies. Bitcoin's dollar value soared almost fourteenfold over the course of 2017, but its upwards trajectory was strikingly erratic.[227] And in 2013, the bitcoin exchange rate had plummeted by nearly 40 percent over the space of just a few hours when the Chinese government forbade its banks from dealing in bitcoins.[228].

As a built-in inflation safeguard, the number of bitcoins that are brought into existence with each block is halved every 210,000 blocks, which corresponds to a period of approximately four years. For example, at the time of writing in 2018, the mining block reward was 12.5 bitcoins; this was scheduled to be reduced to 6.25 bitcoins in June 2020. And coin creation will cease to accompany block creation completely once 21 million bitcoins have been generated, which should occur in 2140. When this date finally comes around, there will be no escape from what will by then be an ancient stipulation: everybody knows about it and there is no central bank that can reverse it.

Although the Bitcoin system allows information to be incorporated into a block for free and this was the norm in the earliest days of its operation, competition for blockchain space means that nowadays miners will only accept transactions in return for payment. Strictly speaking, a miner does not have to wait for a block to fill up before he can sign it off, but transaction fees provide him with a strong incentive to include in it as much information as he can up to a maximum size. Fees will have to suffice as the sole motivation for operating the system when coin creation stops in 2140.

Whenever bitcoins change hands, the transaction will be distributed through the network and the recipient will hope that it will be included in the next block that is signed off and disseminated. If you do fail to make it into one block, though, you can just wait for the next and subsequent blocks. When you distribute a new transaction, you declare how much bitcoin you are willing to pay to have it processed: as long as you have not been too stingy, somebody is bound to accept it eventually, unless whoever is trying to transfer the coins has already spent them in an earlier block, in which case miners will refuse to admit the transaction.

If two or more Bitcoin miners manage to sign off a block more or less simultaneously, each will try and propagate his new block to as many other computers as he can in the hope that it will become part of the canon. The important point is that everyone else taking part in the system then has a strong incentive to reach and stick to an agreement about which of the candidate blocks to accept and which to reject: if you bet on the wrong horse and start mining a block that is based on another block that does not end up forming part of the permanent chain, you will go empty-handed even if you manage to produce a winning hash value.

Theoretically, a small group of Bitcoin miners could get cut off from the rest of the network because of technical problems with the underlying internet infrastructure. They would then unwittingly start to produce an alternative continuation of the blockchain that would not match the main one. However, the system is designed to ensure that such a situation will be immediately resolved once the two groups are able to talk to each other again. A version of the chain that took more energy to create is always recognised as taking precedence over one that took less energy to create. This means the main branch will always win over a temporary local branch because many more people will have been mining on it during the separation period.

If somebody is assigning bitcoins to you and you have just observed the transaction being incorporated into a new block, you cannot be completely sure that you are not just participating in a temporary local chain that will later be rejected by the rest of the system. If you were really unlucky, you might then discover that the bitcoins you thought were yours had also been transferred to somebody else in a parallel spend that was already set in stone on the main chain. This would render your own transaction invalid and you would go empty-handed.

It has been shown that internet infrastructure routing issues that prevent Bitcoin traffic from reaching its intended destinations can be observed on a regular basis, although they are never normally wide-ranging enough to cut off completely a section of the internet from the rest of the network.[229] Even if network problems did occur to a sufficient extent to have a practical impact, however, the crucial point is that the architecture of the internet is designed to restore connectivity as quickly as possible: an extended lack of communication is even less likely than a momentary one. Your status as the undisputed owner of bitcoins that you have accepted as payment, then, solidifies as the length of the chain increases following the block where the transfer was captured.

The small risk that your transaction has been recorded on a temporary local chain is unlikely to lose you any sleep if you are only trading small items like cups of coffee. On the other hand, if you have just accepted bitcoin as payment for a property sale, you are well advised to wait for a while before handing over the keys. Standard Bitcoin software regards a transaction that was captured at least six blocks ago—around an hour ago—as confirmed, while new bitcoins are not available for spending until the block where they were minted has had at least a hundred additional blocks appended to it in the chain.

A whole host of alternative cryptocurrencies have sprung up since the invention of Bitcoin. Some of them offer additional features. The Ethereum blockchain allows its coins to be irrevocably linked with computer-program snippets called smart contracts.[230] These specify a sequence of predetermined actions that are to be carried out if and when a certain set of circumstances should come into being, and can be designed to execute of their own accord without any prompting from their original authors. And the Zcash blockchain is designed to hide not only the identities of the participants involved in each coin transfer, but also the amounts spent on each occasion.[231] It aims to rule out the possibility that its users could be unmasked using traffic analysis based on the sizes of the recorded transactions.

Many of the other so-called altcoins—cryptocurrencies other than Bitcoin—offer little in the way of new features and seem to have been started up by hopeful individuals who had realised that the creator of a successful cryptocurrency generally ended up rich because he was able to mine a large number of the initial coins without much competition: of the almost 1,400 cryptocurrencies listed at the beginning of 2018, more than 400 had total market capitalisations of less than $100,000.[232]

AlphaBay, Silk Road and the Dread Pirate Roberts

It did not take long for criminals to realise that the combination of Tor hidden services and cryptocurrencies like bitcoin gave them the opportunity to trade in all kinds of contraband with what they thought was impunity. The challenge of selling illegal items online was reduced to disguising them in the post, which was especially simple for drugs given the relatively small amount of space they took up. The first and most celebrated website for mind-changing substances was called Silk Road. As one 30-year-old disc jockey told the British Daily Mail newspaper in late

2012: "Why would I want to try and score from some dodgy dealer in a nightclub when I can just get it delivered to my doorstep? It's a no-brainer."[233]

Silk Road did not attempt to solve the logistic problems of procuring and delivering drugs. It merely provided a platform to link buyers and sellers, complete with reviews and reliability ratings, and creamed off a portion of the profits from each transaction into the bargain. When the FBI finally took it offline in late 2013, it turned out to have been run by Ross William Ulbricht, alias the Dread Pirate Roberts, a then 29-year-old American whose LinkedIn page was peppered with high-minded ideals like "a world without the systemic use of force" but who later turned out to have twice tried to hire hitmen to settle business scores.[234] Ulbricht was arrested as he administered Silk Road from a California library. During the two-and-a-half years that it was online, it had netted him more than $28m.

The government investigators unmasked Silk Road by looking back through the history of the internet to find the very first recorded mentions of the site. They had correctly postulated that whoever created it was likely to have written something about it to drum up initial business. A hidden service that is known only to the Tor directory servers is no more likely to amass customers (as opposed to authorities trying to attack it) than this book would attract readers if I kept it on my laptop. It has to be advertised in a place where people will find out about it, and advertisement is the antithesis of anonymity.

Two very early posts discussing Silk Road bore the user name *Altoid*, as did a forum post several months later that aimed to recruit Bitcoin experts and invited them to send their CVs to Ross Ulbricht's normal E-mail address.[235] And once law enforcement officials were on the right track, they had little difficulty in finding further pointers to confirm their suspicions. Fired up less by the money than by the intrinsic challenge and excitement of what he was doing, Ulbricht just could not bring himself to keep the enormity of it all under wraps. He had fake ID cards made with his own photograph although anybody's picture would have done, and when Homeland Security questioned him about them, he volunteered the information that he could have been "hypothetically" sent them via a website called Silk Road.[236]

The Dread Pirate Roberts' fatal mistake was to trust too heavily in the theoretical cover provided by the Tor technology. A manhunt was always bound to ensue as soon as his site became popular, and he seems to have failed to realise that his only hope of escaping detection was to lead a double life in which he kept his Silk Road activities scrupulously separate from the rest of his existence.

Silk Road was soon replaced by a Silk Road 2, and, when that was taken down a year later, further drug-dealing sites were hot on its tracks. The business model is probably too lucrative for the demand to remain unfulfilled for long. In July 2017, the AlphaBay drugs platform was servicing a transaction volume an order of magnitude higher than Silk Road ever had when its alleged creator, Canadian Alexandre Cazes, was unmasked by a catalogue of ingenuous errors strikingly similar to those committed by the Dread Pirate Roberts. Far from learning the lessons of the Silk Road story, Cazes had outstripped Ulbricht in his foolhardiness. He had sent customers a welcome E-mail bearing a Hotmail address that he had previously used in conjunction with his full name to post to a technology forum.[237]

The evil side of the dark web

Unfortunately, Silk Road and AlphaBay represent the benign end of the crimes committed over the dark web. The anonymous connectivity that Tor provides seems to engender a particularly raw brand of evil. It has facilitated some of the cruellest abominations imaginable. The paedophilic crimes of which Australian-born businessman Peter Scully was accused in 2015 in the Philippines are so heart-wrenchingly sickening that the country considered re-introducing the death penalty just for him because any other punishment seemed so insufficient.[238] Even words like "depraved" and "murderer" seem to come nowhere near to depicting the tragic horror of what happened.

And yet the Tor project itself offers no assistance whatsoever in tracking down such monsters.[239] This stance is looking increasingly outdated. The internet has taken on such a fundamental role in the world's affairs that, like it or not, those who design, maintain and manage its infrastructure now find themselves burdened with a social responsibility that was unthinkable just a few years ago. Although aiming to enable online anonymity is an ethically valid goal whose importance has greatly increased in the light of the Snowden revelations, it is hardly an absolute ideal that outweighs basic humanity. When you are running a system that is being used to enable people to pay to watch toddlers being tortured to death, it is time to take a step back and reconsider.

The main argument against building some kind of facility into Tor that would allow the worst of its users to be exposed are that it would be impossible to do so without destroying the integrity of the overall system. On the other hand, anyone who has worked in systems design for any length of time has experienced situations where something that was originally billed as technically unworkable goes into successful production a few months later following liberal helpings of money, time and management pressure. Just because there are justified objections to an initial idea does not mean it cannot eventually be realised in some modified form.

The technical infrastructure behind both Tor and Bitcoin relies on consensus between the majority of their participants. It is consensus that allows both systems to tolerate the presence of small numbers of individuals who are not abiding by the rules. The Tor project claims that any move to ban certain types of content would get bogged down in a "quagmire of conflicting personal morals".[240] However, just as a democratic state tries to resolve ethical, legal and moral dilemmas by consensus rather than simply accepting anarchy as the lowest common denominator, there is no reason why the consensus mechanisms already present within the Tor design could not be used to try questionable hidden services by virtual jury: if an overwhelming proportion of randomly chosen people agree that a particular hidden service is so despicable that it should be shut down, there is a strong case for doing so.

I do not claim to have anything approaching a thought-through change proposal, but a request to uncover a hidden site could be handled by somehow polling a large number of people involved with Tor—onion router operators and perhaps browser users and developers as well—and only acceding to the application when a sufficient majority approved. There would need to be a watertight technical guarantee, probably based on encryption, that the information could only possibly be revealed to anybody once all the necessary votes had been cast. Such a system would also require stringent checks and balances to ensure a false indictment could not be used to expose the wrong site.

However, if it worked, paedophiles would be forced off Tor while everybody else could expect to continue to operate with relative impunity. A significant proportion of people believe that drugs should be legalized, so that any attempt to use the facility to find the whereabouts of a Silk Road incarnation would definitely fail to achieve a clear enough result to succeed. And enough onion router owners would value anonymity too highly to agree to surrender the identities of common financial criminals or hackers. But surely almost anyone would agree to almost anything in order to catch a child torturer and murderer.

Another argument Tor cites against an unmasking facility is that the underworld would just find other ways of communicating in secret anyway. This might be true if Tor were to start assisting the police to solve all kinds of crimes committed over it. However, paedophiles would find it very difficult to conceal their activities effectively if they were the only ones to be excluded. A parallel dark web that only they inhabited would be much easier for the authorities to illuminate. After all, the real reason the U.S. military opened Tor up to general use in the first place was to keep their own traffic hidden in among everyone else's chatter.

V. OBJECTS

The cyberattacks we have looked at up to this point have mostly interacted with the internet in its classic manifestation as an intangible cloud; the locations and surroundings of the computers being hacked have not been relevant. In this final chapter, we examine two ways in which the non-virtual and virtual worlds interact to facilitate particular flavours of attack. Firstly, physical methods can be used to hack computers that would remain safe if they were accessible exclusively over the internet. Secondly, computers do not exist in a vacuum: many direct a wide variety of other objects, and a criminal who succeeds in hacking a brain obtains manipulative power over the body it controls as well.

Local networks, Wi-Fi and sniffing

Servers like the one responsible for the website advertising this book have to be directly reachable from the internet. This is not usually the case for normal PCs, laptops and phones that only need to use internet services rather than to provide them. Such machines are more likely to access the internet indirectly. Computers within a home or office are typically grouped together in a cable-based or wireless (Wi-Fi) local network managed by a router that provides the gateway to the rest of the world.

When your computer is connected to a local network, all your communication with the wider internet will be channelled through the router in charge of that local network. In a wireless network, the frequency that links you to the router will carry other computers' conversations as well as yours; the same is true of your cable connection in some older types of wired network. The router labels each message as being intended for a specific machine and presumes everyone else will ignore it. In reality, however, there is nothing to stop anyone from accessing traffic belonging to other people within the same local network, a practice known as sniffing.

This is not that big a problem as long as any confidential information has been encrypted using the techniques described in Chapter I. An eavesdropper can examine all the messages he likes, but, without the right key, he will still not be able to read them. Traffic analysis aside, getting somebody else's post delivered to you is of little use if you have no way of opening it.

In the previous chapter, we described the multiple protocol layers that make up internet communication, and there are various levels at which messages can be encoded. The same VPN technology that can be employed to get around georestrictions is used by many companies to allow employees located remotely to work as if they were on site: because VPN communication involves encrypting network traffic in its entirety without regard for its content, the VPN acts like a wormhole through which messages from the employee are pulled unchanged before being processed within the company network. For everyday internet use, on the other hand, privacy is ensured simply by individual web servers offering content over HTTPS rather than over HTTP so that encryption is used when browsers communicate with them.

As recently as 2012 in North America and 2013 in the rest of the world, however, the Facebook website only employed encryption when users had explicitly switched on the relevant option in their settings.[241] Anyone who had not taken this precaution and who logged into the social network via a public wireless network, perhaps in a coffee shop or hotel, was essentially broadcasting his private business to anybody else in the vicinity who was inclined to tune into it.

Worse still, after a user has logged into Facebook, the site keeps track of him using the method described in Chapter III where a randomly generated token is stored in a cookie. In the days before Facebook messages were encrypted, these random tokens would fill the airwaves of the café as well, and there were tools that allowed people to pick them up and take over the corresponding Facebook sessions. On one particularly memorable demonstration on German television, the presenter wrote on the Facebook wall of each victim inviting all his or her friends to come out for a spontaneous cup of coffee and then watched the chilled-out atmosphere in the café turn to general consternation as the unexpected guests started to show up.[242]

Most wireless networks in homes and offices are not designed for public use and can only be accessed with the right password. However, as we also saw in Chapter III, users frequently continue using the default passwords with which their routers left the factory, and these have often turned out to be predictable.

Another thing that is often overlooked is that a friend or neighbour who knows your home router's network name and wireless password is not only able to connect to it in order to access the internet. He is also in a position to usurp your wireless network by setting up a second router in the vicinity using the same network name and wireless password as you. If he can emit a stronger signal than the genuine router, all the devices in your home are then likely to switch to accessing the internet via his bogus router. In the light of the previous chapter, you will know that he is then in a position to feed you fake DNS information and direct your browser to fake websites.

Large companies typically shield themselves against this type of hacking with a mechanism where wireless routers prove their identity using signatures based on asymmetric encryption as described in Chapter III. In Chapter I, we saw that the standard protocol used by wireless routers is called WPA2, and this additional signature mechanism is called WPA2-Enterprise Edition. Each wireless router signs its messages with its own private key, and the computers that connect to wireless routers employ certificates similar to the ones described in Chapter III to verify the corresponding public keys. However, setting up WPA2-Enterprise Edition is something of a challenge even for professional systems administrators, let alone for somebody managing a simple wireless network at home. At present, the best most home users can realistically do to protect themselves is to be selective when they share their Wi-Fi password with friends and acquaintances.

A cable-based network is intrinsically more secure than a wireless one. It is generally much more difficult to gain illicit access to it without actually breaking and entering. And while we have seen that it is possible to take over the traffic intended for an existing wireless router simply by drowning out its signal, there is no comparable attack on cable circuits. Nonetheless, cable-based networks often represent an attractive target precisely because they are more likely to be used to communicate sensitive data.

I know of one situation where a gardener was working next to the office of a multinational in a European country. Both the company and the country will remain nameless. He was most surprised to come across a plastic cable some centimetres under the ground where he had only expected to find tree roots. The cable, which was terminated with a network plug buried in the soil a few meters from where the gardener had been working, turned out to lead directly into a network that the company was using for developing confidential industrial plans.

Whoever was behind the secret cable had presumably colluded with the builders of the office complex. There was no way of accessing the private network from the internet, but the culprit will have been able to sneak into the grounds in the middle of the night, dig a hole and plug the cable into his laptop. He will have had a good chance of being able to steal a lot of information, because the company employees may well have relied on the fact that the network was safe from prying external eyes and failed to see the need to use additional security measures to protect their files.

TURMOIL, TURBINE and FOXACID

The Edward Snowden revelations in 2013 showed that the NSA and the British intelligence service GCHQ had taken the notion of sniffing and altering electronic messages to a whole new level.

It was no longer merely a local network within a home or office that was under attack; it was the internet itself. The TURMOIL programme consisted of the secret services wiretapping the telecommunication corporations that ran the internet backbone.[243] A leaked presentation states that at least one U.S. communications company, which investigative journalists at ProPublica believe to have identified as AT&T, assisted the NSA in this operation.[244] It remains unclear whether there were also communications companies that were hacked and infiltrated without their consent or knowledge.

The information provided by TURMOIL passive surveillance informed decisions about when to make use of the active TURBINE programme. This included several types of attack whose names began with the word "QUANTUM", although they actually had nothing whatsoever to do either with quantum computing or with the quantum key distribution we will cover later in this chapter.[245]

Observation of the traffic passing through the internet would enable the spies to work out when a target computer was expecting a particular message, and they would then get in first by "shooting" a matching fake message at that computer. For example, the QUANTUMHAND technique involves answering a request to access Facebook with a reply that directs the user to a FOXACID server instead, which then infects his computer with surveillance malware.

On the other hand, a QUANTUMDNS attack supplies users with fake DNS information to direct them to bogus websites in a similar fashion to the attacks discussed in the previous chapter. Presumably, though, the NSA could carry out its attacks without needing to bother with trying to guess DNS query numbers: its operatives could simply read them from the requests they were wiretapping.

MAC addresses, local IP addresses and ARP spoofing

One might have thought that falling victim to government network surveillance would presuppose having used the internet in the first place, but a wireless router can actually gather a surprising amount of information about phones and laptops in its vicinity even if their owners never actively try to connect to it. How does this work?

Before a newly produced laptop or phone is sold, the company that manufactured it assigns it a code called a Media Access Control address or MAC address (the name has nothing to do with Apple hardware) that is then permanently stored on it. A MAC address is composed of twelve digits where each digit is either a number or one of the letters between A and F, for example 00:0a:95:9d:68:16.

A computer uses its MAC address to identify itself whenever it is first connected to a network. Unlike an IP address, which can change as a machine moves around, a MAC address is intended to remain constant. If an IP address is like a postal address, you can imagine a MAC address as being more like a passport number, national ID number or social security number.

Manufacturers are supposed to ensure that every internet-enabled device in the world gets a unique MAC address, and they usually succeed, so that a device's MAC address is like a fingerprint. If your phone is set up to discover wireless hotspots, it will broadcast its MAC address all over the place whenever it is switched on, even when you are not using it. This is because it sends out regular probing requests to find out whether there are any wireless networks available in its vicinity.

In 2014, CBC news claimed that the Canadian intelligence service had been building up profiles of passengers by collecting the MAC addresses of devices like smartphones and laptops passing through a major airport and then comparing them to MAC addresses gathered over the following days by wireless routers at hotels, conference centres and other airports.[246] To protect their users against such tracking, many systems including Windows 10 now offer a feature where the computer sends each new wireless network a temporary random MAC address instead of its real MAC address.[247]

The router in charge of a local network requires an IP address allocated by its internet service provider (ISP) to enable it to communicate with the world beyond. On the other hand, your phone or computer will communicate with the router using a normally temporary local IP address that it is assigned when it first connects to the local network. Local IP addresses belong to specific number ranges that always denote computers hidden behind routers within local networks.[248] For example, any IP address whose first number is 10 is a local address, as in 10.2.2.1. Local IP addresses can only ever be used for local communication; all routers refuse to specify them as the destinations of messages that traverse the wider internet.

Especially within a larger business where a network contains multiple routers and has to be guaranteed to continue to work when individual machines fail, the function of dispensing local IP addresses to new computers when they join a local network is not necessarily performed by routers themselves. The job can also be carried out by a separate machine or machines within the local network. The drawback of this arrangement is that a router will not then know which IP address has been associated with which computer.

When a router receives traffic destined for an IP address that has just been newly allotted or that has not been used for a certain period of time, it will send a query around the network asking for whichever computer has received that IP address to come forward and identify itself with its MAC address. Even in a so-called fully switched network where each machine has a separate cable connection in the direction of the router and cannot normally see other people's traffic, such administrative messages are necessarily broadcast to everybody, and there is nothing to stop a hacker working on some other computer within the local network from replying to a query with false information, a technique called Address Resolution Protocol (ARP) spoofing.

The situation is a bit like an official in a room full of neighbours asking for the person who lives in a certain house to come forward and collect a prize and then giving it to the first applicant without any proof that he really lives there. By claiming a certain IP address, I can go on to receive any messages destined for the computer that had really been assigned it and read them if they are not encrypted. If I also manage to persuade the victim computer that my own machine has taken on the role of the router—that my MAC address is now associated with the router's IP address—the scene is set for a classic man-in-the-middle attack as described in Chapter I: I can change messages before forwarding them on to their genuine target.

IP version 4, IP version 6 and the Carna botnet

The four-number IP version 4 address system permits too few number combinations for today's requirements, because it was conceived when the internet was still a niche communications system dominated by the higher education sector. The first years of the current millennium saw increasingly urgent predictions that IP addresses were shortly to run out, and in February 2011 the last address blocks were finally apportioned.[249]

The mainstream media seemed convinced that the internet was about to stop working, but business actually continued more or less as usual. People often forget that the internet can support many more computers than there are IP addresses, because the same local IP addresses are used over and over again within millions of networks all around the world. And although we shall see later in this chapter that numerous types of gadgets that were previously firmly confined to the offline world are now being designed to connect to the internet, few of these devices will need to access it directly.

Non-local IP addresses, too, have so far been re-allocated by the market efficiently enough to prevent their exhaustion from causing any real pain. For example, Microsoft spent $7,500,000 buying over 500,000 IP addresses from a bankrupt hardware manufacturer around one month after the official supply had run out.[250] Somebody looking to purchase IP addresses will have little difficulty in finding willing vendors: because IP addresses were originally handed out for free, many people have ended up with ranges they do not really need. In 2012, an anonymous hacker created the Carna botnet out of some 420,000 computers that he had been able to access using default or empty passwords.[251] He used the coerced machines to gather statistics about the rest of the internet in a massive unofficial census, and one of the things he found out was that only somewhat over a third of all IP version 4 addresses were in active use.

The IP address crisis may not have materialised quite as quickly as some commentators expected, but it cannot be put off indefinitely. The long-term solution, a standard called IP version 6, has actually been around since the late 1990s, although it has been slow to catch on.[252] The new IP version 6 addresses, which are expressed in a similar fashion to MAC addresses, contain four times more information than the old IP version 4 ones, e.g. 2001:cdba:0000:0000:0000:0000:3257:9652. Just as with the hash values we described in Chapter III, there are many more possible IP version 6 addresses than atoms in the observable universe. They will clearly never run out.

An IP version 6 address is over twice as long as a MAC address, which should itself be globally unique. The original standard for when a new computer or phone joined a network using IP version 6 suggested incorporating the computer or phone's MAC address into the second half of the IP address that was to be assigned to it.[253] This made things very easy for the people writing the network software. It offered a ready-made means of ensuring that two computers would never end up with the same IP address.

However, it was also a gift to intelligence services, social media companies and anyone else trying to profile people's online activities. A machine communicating over the internet using an IP version 6 address that contained its original, unique MAC address would trail a fingerprint just like a phone being carried from one wireless hotspot to the next. This time, though, it would broadcast its identity around the globe rather than just to the nearest coffee shop. It is just as well that IP version 6 did not come into widespread use earlier. It took until 2007 for IPv6 Privacy Extensions, a new technique based on random numbers that keeps MAC addresses and IP addresses separate, to be adopted as a standard.[254] Several more years passed before it was included in the main operating systems.

Quantum key distribution

Physical links between computers cannot only be exploited to breach the security of the messages sent over them. They can also be put to use to guarantee it. Quantum key distribution is a means of two computers agreeing on a symmetric key via an optical fibre cable. The principle behind it will never be broken because it is rooted in the fabric of the universe. It relies on the fact that certain states of a subatomic particle cannot be observed without there being a risk of them being changed as a side effect of the act of observation.

The most tried and tested type of quantum key distribution is called BB84 because it was first proposed by Charles Bennett and Gilles Brassard in 1984.[255] In the procedure, one of the two people who wish to agree on a common key transmits the other person a randomly generated sequence of bit values—zeroes and ones—along an optical fibre in the form of individual photons, or packets of light.

A photon can be transmitted in various physical states. Exactly which particle phenomena are used in BB84 depends on how it is implemented, but it always involves two pairs of states which we shall refer to abstractly as *0a* and *1a* on the one hand and *0b* and *1b* on the other hand. As I send you each photon, I make an arbitrary choice between the *a* state and the *b* state that correspond to whichever of the two numbers I am trying to communicate, so that the bit string *0101* might be rendered as *0b-1a-0a-1b*.

When you examine each photon at the other end, you also make your own random choice between reading its *a* states and reading its *b* states. If you happen to select the same letter as I did, you will observe the photon in whichever of the four states I sent it in, which will allow you to retrieve whichever of the two bit values I was trying to communicate. For example, if I send *0b* and you decide to examine the *b* states, you will observe my *0b* and with it the number *0*.

If, on the other hand, you elect to examine the *a* states, particle physics will arbitrarily determine whether you happen to observe a *0a* or a *1a*. Crucially, the process of you reading the *a* states will also have destroyed the original information I had written using the *b* states: if you then go on to observe the *b* states of the same photon, the result will once again be random.

How can I use this behaviour to send you a symmetric key? After I have sent you a long string of photons in this fashion, we use non-quantum communication to compare notes on which letter each of us used for each photon in the sequence. If we then discard all the photons for which we used different letters, we should end up with a matching sequence of bits formed by the number values of the photons for which we happened to use the same letters.

The crucial point is that an eavesdropper who had managed to tap into the optical fibre would himself have had to make a random choice between the two letters each time he read a photon. He would have been bound to choose the wrong letter, say *a*, on some of the occasions when you chose the right letter, say *b*. Imagine I sent a photon in the *1b* state, the eavesdropper performed an *a* read and then you went on to perform a *b* read. Because the illicit observation would have reset the *b* state of the photon, it would then be fifty-fifty whether you observed a *0b* or a *1b*.

On average, a quarter of the bits in the eavesdropped sequence you and I expected to be identical would in fact be different. The final step in the key distribution procedure is that we demonstrate that no such contamination has occurred. We confirm that our sequences correspond by again using non-quantum communication to compare a certain proportion of the bits they contain, which we also go on to discard. We can then use the bits that remain as our common symmetric key.

What is the point in using quantum key distribution when the Diffie-Hellman exchange already offers a foolproof method for two parties to produce a common symmetric key without using any expensive equipment? Diffie-Hellman is undoubtedly the more elegant way of agreeing on keys that only need to remain secret for a limited period of time. However, as we saw in Chapter I, it is already clear that the Diffie-Hellman procedure will be rendered largely useless by Shor's algorithm once quantum computing becomes available on an industrial scale; Perfect Forward Secrecy is actually far from perfect. This makes Diffie-Hellman an inappropriate way of protecting information that needs to remain concealed for many years into the future. And although new mathematical encryption techniques are now emerging that are quantum-resistant, any mathematics-based encryption standard could potentially be broken at any time. None will ever be able to match the totally future-proof, physics-based assurance of quantum key distribution.

Tricking the quantum sensors

Quantum key distribution is a much more mature technology than the quantum computing we discussed towards the beginning of the book: from 2007 onwards it has been used to transmit a small proportion of election results in Switzerland.[256] Why is it still not in widespread commercial use over ten years later? The main reason is probably cost and effort. Carrying it out requires a dedicated optical fibre link, and setting up a working system meant spending over $100,000 as of 2015.[257]

However, these costs are destined to fall over the coming years, which could make the technique much more generally relevant. It is the nature of the beast that it is difficult to find out exactly which companies and organisations are already relying on the technology, although its current users are presumed to include the U.S. secret services and military. One widely quoted piece of speculation is that a quantum key distribution channel links the White House with the Pentagon, although this notion is just as likely to stem from the fact that these two important institutions are physically close enough for the technique to have worked when it was still in its infancy as from any leaked factual knowledge.

Another reason why quantum key distribution has taken so long to reach industrial fruition is that it has proven challenging to build machines that translate its theoretical unbreakability into practical reliability and security. The very fact that the technique is based on physics rather than mathematics means that the act of carrying it out is liable to generate extrinsic events that can be observed. For example, the practical difficulty of sending and processing individual particles meant that early implementations of the idea sometimes produced superfluous light that eavesdroppers could conceivably have captured and examined without being detected.[258] And in any case, the process of transmitting and reading information at the sub-atomic level never works perfectly. The communicated information will always contain a certain proportion of errors that will need to be identified and corrected using non-quantum messages. The rectification procedure exposes additional weak points that hackers might target.

And in 2010, a group of researchers showed that two of the quantum key distribution systems on the market had been built in a way that left them open to a man-in-the-middle attack.[259] Shining a strong laser beam at the detector that was receiving the sequence of photons could not only be used to send it either a zero or a one; an attacker was also able to use the laser beam to force the detector to make a specific choice between reading the *a* states and reading the *b* states. This would allow him to carry out his own quantum key distribution procedure with the sender while forwarding on to the intended recipient whichever of the four states he had read for each photon. He would end up with a perfect copy of the key shared between the sender and the genuine recipient, which was exactly what quantum key distribution was supposed to be preventing.

This demonstration seemed sensational at the time, and it was indeed an apposite reminder of the danger of simplistically equating theory and practice. However, the threat it presented to real quantum key distribution systems in the field was heavily constrained by the fact that the attacker carrying it out had to have physical access to the detector rather than merely to the optical fibre. In a genuine scenario, a hacker who had managed to break into the building where the photons were being received would have been unlikely to focus his efforts on the quantum key distribution equipment in the first place. He would typically have found the computer next to it a much easier target from which to recover both the generated symmetric key and whatever information that key was being used to communicate.

COTTONMOUTH, TEMPEST and electrosmog

An NSA secret revealed by Edward Snowden that was perhaps more intriguing even than the details of the TURMOIL and TURBINE programmes discussed earlier in this chapter was the existence of a nifty piece of hardware called COTTONMOUTH.[260] Available to American spies from January 2009 for as little as $20 apiece, a COTTONMOUTH connector is designed to be indistinguishable from a normal USB plug with which you would connect your keyboard or mouse up to your PC. However, it contains a hidden wireless transmitter that the internal NSA advertisement describes as providing "air-gap bridging".

A COTTONMOUTH connector gives a spy working in the next building a direct and uncomplicated path on to whatever computer it is being used to attack. It can be used not only to steal data, but also to upload malware. The victim machine might interact with the rest of the world from within a local network. Alternatively, it might not even be connected to the internet at all.

Even now that the existence of COTTONMOUTH is widely known, it is difficult to see what a normal business could realistically do to protect itself from it. In the absence of a specific threat, examining all your USB plugs regularly is unlikely to be economical. And monitoring the airwaves for unexpected wireless communications might work if your business happened to be located in the middle of a field, but, in a typical urban situation where the wavelengths are teeming with electrosmog, there will be little to distinguish COTTONMOUTH traffic from the noise produced by the router two doors down.

As well as deliberately transmitted messages, this electrosmog will contain a large number of legible signals generated as an incidental by-product of the operation of computers, phones and other electronic equipment. In 1987, ex-MI5-spy Peter Wright revealed a number of British state secrets in his book *Spycatcher*, which became a celebrated bestseller after the UK government unsuccessfully tried to ban it. One of Wright's disclosures was that the British had spied on the French government during the UK's application for its ill-fated membership of the European Economic Community (later the European Union). The French were encrypting their traffic, but the machine they were using to do so turned out to transmit a faint electromagnetic signal that betrayed to the British the original text it was encoding.[261]

The NSA maintains standards grouped informally under the codename TEMPEST that detail both how to pick up such signals and how to shield machines to prevent them from leaking sensitive information to their surroundings.[262] The expensive and elaborate nature of the protection procedures that are in the public domain bears witness to the fact that the NSA must regard electromagnetic emanations as a very serious risk, and indeed all the evidence is that picking them up and analysing them is nowhere near as challenging as one might expect: private researchers who have carried out experiments in the field seem to have achieved a high degree of success relatively easily.

The Dutch computer scientist Wim van Eck showed in 1985 that it was feasible to pick up emanations from the cathode ray monitors that were in general use at the time and to recreate what was being displayed on the screen.[263] Even if today's monitors no longer broadcast their contents to the environment in the same way, Cambridge researcher Markus Kuhn demonstrated in 2003 that the cables supplying the image data to various types of laptop and desktop screens still gave out a recoverable signal.[264]

And in 2009, two Swiss students, Martin Vuagnoux and Sylvain Pasini, set out to discover whether they could use incidental emissions to recover what was being typed into a keyboard.[265] It would have been no surprise if this had turned out to be possible for a wireless keyboard, but their research concentrated on standard, old-fashioned keyboards connected to their computers with cables. The results were startling.

Your keyboard transmits a sequence of bits along the wire to represent each key you press, and Vuagnoux and Pasini discovered no fewer than four separate ways of recovering the bit sequences from the electromagnetic noise this generated. Even at a distance of 20m and with walls in between, they were able to identify the keys being pressed on one commonly used type of keyboard with an accuracy of 95%. In the light of how little information the Bletchley Park team needed to recover Enigma messages, it is obvious that correcting the remaining 5% would be child's play. The experiment showed that a spy or criminal who wished to discover what was being typed into a machine in his vicinity did not necessarily need to resort to sneaking key-logger malware on to it; pricking up his electromagnetic ears could be used to the same effect.

Keypads and USB sticks

There is a seemingly unending range of variations on the theme of systems inadvertently leaking confidential information to their environments as they are being physically operated. A case in point is when combination keypads are used to control access to buildings or other secure sites: buttons that are pressed on a regular basis are liable to attract dirt and to wear down more quickly than their neighbours, and unless the code is changed periodically this leads to a clearly visible distinction between the numbers that form part of the correct code and the numbers that do not. This means a trespasser only has to try out a few possible permutations of a handful of digits before he hits on the correct combination.

Migrants desperate to reach the United Kingdom used this technique in 2015 to breach a multi-million-dollar fencing system that essentially formed the international border at the Channel Tunnel complex in Northern France.[266] The media did not report the actual code that had been uncovered, but they did let on that the numbers two, four and zero were obviously worn. The breach is reported to have resulted in an old-fashioned padlock being added to the gate as an additional security measure. Presumably the secret combination on the keypad was changed at the same time.

Even simple technical means of breaching a target organisation can start to seem superfluous when you consider how easy it can be to persuade other people to do the job for you. A standard trick that has been known about for many years is to scatter USB sticks in and around a parking lot and to wait for the curious and helpful individuals who find them to plug them in to see what is on them as they arrive at work. In 2016, an experiment was carried out at an American university where the USB sticks contained a web page that downloaded an image from a server, which was then able to count the requests it received whenever a stick was plugged in.[267] Depending on the time of day and the outward appearance of the USB sticks, between one-third and one-half of people who picked them up went on to take the bait.

Social engineering

The U.S. military gives such phenomena their very own acronym: POBCAK, which stands for "Problem Occurs Between Chair and Keyboard." Social engineering is a complex topic that could fill several books on its own, but it is worth mentioning a few common features that make systems, organisations and individuals especially vulnerable to trickery that goes beyond the strictly technical.

Perhaps most obviously, people will almost certainly end up cutting corners and endangering the security of a system that they are finding difficult to use in the first place. In Chapter III, we looked at how websites employ cookie-based tokens to remember the identity of a user once he has logged in with the right password. If this mechanism is broken for some reason, the web server might start asking the user for his password every time he navigates from one page to another. If the website is an internal system running within an organisation, it will not take long before employees start reducing the lengths of their passwords so they can enter them more quickly and minimise the disruption to their work. Unless the website is then repaired promptly, it is a good bet that a significant proportion of users will eventually switch to using empty passwords if the system lets them.

And if a large organisation is not quick off the mark in issuing user identities to external contractors who arrive at their site, it is very likely that contractors will be lent the user names and passwords of the employees who have hired them. However unsafe and foolhardy this seems, few people will accept the secure alternative, which would be to pay for a contractor to twiddle his thumbs for a week while he waited for his credentials to come through.

The same phenomenon can be observed with the access badges that are required to enter a building: if obtaining them is too complicated, they will end up being passed around. In many companies, though, this is largely irrelevant to security, because an attacker is unlikely to need a badge to get on to the site in the first place. Unless there is an entry gate that is specifically designed only to allow one person through at a time, an intruder can just follow someone else through the door, which will very probably be politely held open for him. Few people are likely to confront tailgaters. Quite apart from general conflict avoidance, there is always the latent risk of challenging a colleague whom you should have recognised. This will be unpleasant in any workplace, but, in some organisations, a snub to the wrong person might mean a permanent career setback. Where this is the case, expediency will probably end up trumping security every single time.

Very political organisations are generally vulnerable to tricksters. In both the United States[268] and Germany[269], employees have been duped into transferring millions of U.S. dollars of their companies' funds into accounts belonging to fraudsters based in other countries. The scammers have typically been armed with plentiful information about the target firms, their current order books and their internal power structures. This has enabled them to build up a story based around the theme that the boss has asked for the money to be transferred and will be very disappointed and angry if his wishes are not fulfilled immediately.

There is no way of finding out anything about the cultures of the specific businesses that have fallen victim to this scam, but it seems obvious that it is much less likely to succeed in an atmosphere where everyone feels happy picking up the phone and checking with the boss what he really wants. In a culture where your superiors tend to put you down aggressively, on the other hand, you will be loath to confront them. You are more likely to accept instead what you probably perceive to be a small risk that you might be making a mistake. In the language of evolutionary theory, corporate cons select for antagonistic management.

Self-destructing peripherals and Stuxnet

A computer should be designed so that any software that runs on it, however malicious, is unable to harm its physical hardware. However much it has been ravaged by malware, a computer's owner can reasonably assume that it will always work normally again if he reinstalls from scratch its operating system and its BIOS, the firmware program that tells the hardware what to do when the computer is first switched on. In reality, though, this expectation has not always held true. In the early days of home computing, there were several types of gadget that could be programmed to self-destruct.

The vulnerabilities centred mostly around pieces of hardware being switched from one state to another too frequently or in an unforeseen fashion. The Commodore Amiga home computer that was popular in the late 1980s could be programmed to vibrate the heads on an attached disk drive so that they played music.[270] Getting it to perform this trick once too often had sadly predictable results; after all, it was not what the drive had been designed for.

And games running on some early Nintendo Game Boy models could permanently damage its LCD screen by switching it on and off at the wrong moment.[271] Official Nintendo software would not do this, but there were homebrew games available for the Game Boy just like the homebrew games we discussed for the Wii in Chapter II. In the Game Boy case, though, running homebrew was risky: if its programmer had been careless or malevolent, it could mean waving goodbye to your machine.

Today's computers may no longer allow programs to destroy their peripherals, but many of them are also connected to a lot more than mere disk drives and screens. Industrial control systems drive all sorts of expensive, critical and dangerous equipment, and cyberattacks that gain control over the software can often make the equipment behave in unintended and unpredictable ways. It is true that the highly specialised malware and hacks that focus on such systems are unlikely to provide their perpetrators with the same scope for making money as computer criminality focussing on everyday internet use. At the same time, however, attacks can have ramifications that extend far beyond the normal realm of bits and bytes.

Stuxnet, a rootkit worm based on no fewer than four Windows zero-day vulnerabilities, was first uncovered in 2010.[272] Although the version of it that was identified spread rapidly and indiscriminately among Windows machines, its payload only actually did anything when it happened to infect a machine that was running a certain type of Siemens industrial control software that controlled centrifuges used to produce the enriched uranium required to build a nuclear bomb.[273] Whenever this special state of affairs occurred, Stuxnet would silently command the centrifuges to spin first slightly faster than normal, then very slowly, and then at normal speed again before returning to the beginning of the cycle. Over time, a centrifuge subjected to this treatment tended to shake itself apart.

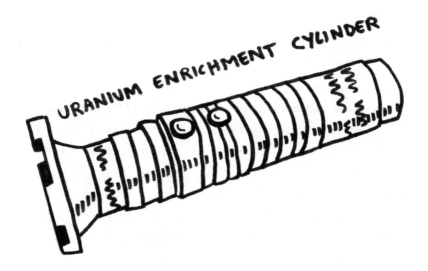

The worm is widely believed to have been created in a joint U.S.-Israeli effort, and what it achieved was genuinely beautiful. This is not an adjective that I would normally feel able to apply to a weapon, but getting the enemy's hardware to self-destruct without getting near it, without any loss of life or injury and without anybody knowing what happened must surely be one of the most elegant feats any military has ever accomplished.

Stuxnet succeeded against the background of the Iranians basing their nuclear programme on German industrial control software running on an American operating system. However ridiculous this choice seems with hindsight, though, the technical options in today's globalized world are so limited that Iranian engineers probably had no realistic alternative. After all, the task they had been given was to enrich uranium, and their political masters will have wanted them to get started quickly. Any pleas they might have made that they needed to build a new computer operating system first would inevitably have landed on deaf ears!

There will also have been a superficially valid argument for regarding the reliance on foreign software as irrelevant. Because the Iranian nuclear facility at Natanz was not directly connected to the internet, it should have remained unaffected by Stuxnet. There should have been no infection path for the worm to take. In the event, however, either an unwitting plant engineer or a double agent must have introduced the worm via a USB stick.[274]

Stuxnet will still have needed replication code to enable it to propagate through the rest of the target network. Initially, its authors must have struck a delicate balance between making it infectious enough to be effective and limiting its spread to prevent it from blowing its cover. The worm is thought to have wreaked havoc with the Iranian nuclear program from as early as November 2007.[275] Had it remained secret, it would probably have continued to thwart its victims' nuclear weapons activities for as long as they continued to pursue them.

Unfortunately, though, somebody appears to have felt that the worm was achieving too little. It is thought to have been modified, possibly to make it proliferate more aggressively. It then disseminated throughout the wider internet, which led to its discovery by Sergey Ulasen in June 2010.[276] Rumour has it that the guilty party was the Israeli secret service acting without the knowledge of their American counterparts.[277] As with any other malware, modifying Stuxnet was much easier than writing it had been.

The North Korean nuclear programme uses similar technology to the Iranian site at Natanz: both countries obtained their blueprints from rogue Pakistani scientist A.Q. Khan.[278] This means it would not have been surprising if the North Koreans had been vulnerable to Stuxnet as well, and indeed Reuters has reported that the NSA tried to target North Korean enrichment plants with a separate version of the worm.[279] Interestingly, though, if such an attempt was really made, it seems to have failed, presumably because nobody working in the hermit kingdom could be tricked into plugging an infected USB stick into the right network.

The North Korean government might well claim that the country remained unaffected because its scientists are more disciplined than their Iranian counterparts. In reality, however, the increased security probably has more to do with the fact that North Korean society is so much more restrictive than Iranian society. A North Korean nuclear scientist is perhaps unlikely to have a personal USB stick that is not under the strict control of his superiors, and planting a double agent in North Korea sounds pretty challenging as well.

Security professionals had already been well aware that more or less any industrial system that involved software was potentially vulnerable to malware, because the complexity of modern networks and the difficulty of keeping track of what all the technicians within a large organisation are doing sometimes meant that part of a network that had been believed to be completely separated from the outside world actually turned out to be connected to it via some unexpected route. And now, with the Stuxnet story, it became widely appreciated that even a system that was genuinely air-gapped, or physically segregated from the wider internet, was far from immune. A single careless individual is all that is needed to bridge the divide.

Cyberwar, electricity grids and nuclear power stations

Stuxnet represents the dawn of the era of cyberwar. In the serious international conflict of the future, each side is expected to try and use cyberattacks to cripple vital elements of its adversary's infrastructure, stretching from military hardware to civilian utilities such as water, telecommunications and electricity. This could happen either alongside or in lieu of old-fashioned hostilities.

The chaos that can ensue when even a small part of an electricity network goes down became only too clear in May 2017 when a contractor accidentally switched off the supply to a British Airways datacentre and then went on to reconnect it in an uncontrolled fashion.[280] The resulting lack of access to critical data forced the airline to cancel all flights from both major London airports for a full day. If an airline system were being written from scratch today, it would be designed to span multiple datacentres to make it immune to such a basic outage. However, the same toughness does not always extend to aging applications that were probably much less business-critical when they were first developed than they have since become.

Meanwhile, cyberwar theory had already become cyberwar reality in December 2015 with the first of a series of cyberattacks on the Ukrainian electricity supply grid. [281] The assault, which affected over 200,000 consumers, has widely been attributed to Russia. It should be clear in light of the discussion of the U.S. election hacking case in the previous chapter that the IP-address-based evidence that has been put forward to prove this has to be taken with a liberal pinch of salt. In this case, however, the ongoing military struggle between the Ukrainian government and Russian-backed separatists provides strong circumstantial support for the allegation.

The attack began with electricity company employees receiving spear-phishing mails that contained Word documents as attachments. Any time an addressee agreed to run the macros these documents contained, his computer was silently infected with malware that handed over control to the attackers. This provided them with a springboard from which they could slowly and methodically explore the company networks and work out how to reach the industrial systems they wanted to disrupt.

When they had collected enough information, the hackers broke the circuits at several substations as well as wiping both software and data from a number of the computers controlling the grid. They also turned off the lights in the control rooms and flooded the customer hotline with nuisance calls to make doubly sure that the operators would find it hard to build up an accurate picture of what was going on. Although the power was returned to customers' houses only a few hours after the attack, this was only achieved by manually bypassing computer-controlled components. The high-tech control systems had suffered much more long-lasting damage and were still not working several weeks later.

The sort of long antecedent phase observed in the Ukraine will probably turn out to be a typical feature of cyberwar attacks.

Gaining access to parts of a network that are intended to remain safe from outside intruders takes time. In July 2017, the FBI and the Department of Homeland Security issued a joint warning that at least a dozen US power stations had been infiltrated by hackers.[282] Their reassurance that the initial impact appeared to be "limited to administrative and business networks" offered scarce comfort: the systems that are easiest to penetrate do not necessarily constitute the final target.

Electricity grids are also at risk from Stuxnet-style physical destruction attacks. In 2007, the Idaho National Laboratory demonstrated that diesel-driven generators within the U.S. power grid could be sent a sequence of codes that persuaded them to self-destruct by shaking themselves apart.[283] The so-called Aurora vulnerability was especially worrying because diesel generators are typically used as a backup source of power in the event that the main supply fails. The 2011 Fukushima nuclear disaster occurred because a tsunami flooded the fuel tanks that fed the backup generators that were supposed to ensure that the reactors could continue to be cooled following an interruption in the external electricity supply.[284] It would be catastrophic if cyberwar actors disrupting an enemy's main electricity grid were able to destroy his fallback options at the same time.

The Fukushima incident demonstrated how quickly nuclear power stations metamorphose into uncontrollable monsters once their electricity supply has been removed. This leads us on to the spectre of an accident at a nuclear power station being actively engineered by terrorists or a hostile foreign government via a cyberattack. If it is easy to shut down an electricity substation, it is probably not impossible to shut down a nuclear power station as well. There are many instances of both types of installation still operational today that date from an age when cybersecurity was not yet a major concern.

Cutting off the electricity to a nuclear power plant is probably worryingly feasible, even if the response to the Ukrainian cyberattack demonstrated that, in the absence of a natural disaster like Fukushima, circuits broken purely by electronic means can soon be re-established by technicians working with old-fashioned cables. However, I hope I am not too misguided in believing that the nightmare scenario of external hackers causing a nuclear meltdown by directly manipulating the components within a reactor core remains firmly at the unlikely end of the scale, even if it is still nothing that can be ruled out categorically.

If we can believe what the nuclear industry tells us, which is clearly not a wholly trivial assumption, the central components within a reactor eschew computer-controlled electronics completely[285], while the second tier of data-acquisition and control software relies on operating systems like QNX that are deliberately stripped down so that what is left can be comprehensively verified as secure.[286] Furthermore, although the reactions that take place within a reactor core are extremely complex[287], the parameters with which those reactions can be influenced in real time are less numerous than for many software systems that deal purely with information; and the more constrained the range of possible inputs to a system, the more difficult it should be for a hacker to make it behave differently from how its architects intended. Theoretically at least, the heart of a nuclear reactor should not be a place to expect either software vulnerabilities or unintended access paths.

Nuclear weapons

Despite the fact that the security hall of fame of American nuclear missile systems still resounds with the absurd echo of the eight-zero launch code story told in Chapter III, any claims that somebody could use a cyberattack to fire a nuclear weapon are best taken with a pinch of salt.[288] A launch is likely to require manual actions by the military in any case, but even a purely computer-controlled missile system would encompass several distinct mechanisms. A hacker would need to bring all the relevant components under his control to trigger Armageddon; the risks with nuclear weapons are so self-evident that nobody in their right mind would design a system so that a single compromise sufficed.

On the other hand, a single compromise could conceivably be enough to disrupt the same systems and make them incapable of firing and delivering a missile with a functioning payload. For example, it is well within the realm of possibility that cyber-based interference by the United States was behind the one-time propensity of North Korean test missiles to blow themselves up shortly after lift-off.[289]

This is starting to sound like a generally positive scenario: World War Three fizzling out before it has even begun because when each side comes to launch its missiles it discovers they have been rendered inoperational by enemy hackers. Unfortunately, however, the early warning systems that are designed to alert a nuclear-armed nation to an incoming strike also have several features that would be expected to make them vulnerable to cyberattacks. They are complex, they rely on communication between multiple locations, and, terrifyingly, control of a single component could be sufficient to trigger an alert.

On several occasions in the past, false alarms in missile warning systems have led to nuclear-armed states believing they were under fire, and calm nerves and betting on the side of life have been all that has stood in the way of the destruction of civilisation. In November 1979, the United States Air Force concluded that the Soviet Union was attacking the country with around 250 ballistic missiles.[290] Preparations for a counterstrike were in full swing when it transpired that somebody had inadvertently loaded a training program on to the live system. And on the other side of the Iron Curtain in September 1983, a malfunctioning satellite reported that the United States had launched a handful of missiles at the Soviet Union.[291] The only thing that stopped the Russians from retaliating was that the officer on duty recognized that a genuine attack would have involved many more bombs. These are just two of a whole range of incidents that have made it into the public domain, and there is every reason to assume the existence of still more examples that have not.

A civilian false alarm could give rise to mass panic even if the military warning systems remained unaffected. The ease with which this could be engineered became clear in 2013 when hackers targeted television stations in two U.S. states, Michigan and Montana.[292] Regular programming was interrupted with a critical alert message that cautioned viewers that the bodies of the dead were rising from their graves and attacking the living. Any attempt to "approach or apprehend these bodies" was said to be extremely dangerous. Most viewers understood the zombie warning as the obvious joke as which it had been intended. However, the fact such a sensitive system had been compromised still had very serious implications. The hackers could easily have chosen to issue an alert about an impending nuclear strike instead.

Today, the assumed attempts of the nuclear states to interfere with one another's missile programs using cyberattacks add a new dimension of risk all of their own. Malware is no more immune to errors than any other software. Indeed, its uncontrolled spread and clandestine operation amplify the likelihood of blunders. If the United States really did use malware to hamstring North Korean missiles, what would have happened if the same code had reached missile systems in Pakistan that might reasonably be expected to be set up in a similar fashion given that Pakistan originally obtained much of its missiles know-how from North Korea in exchange for the warhead blueprints mentioned above?[293] A scenario could quite conceivably have come into being in which the Pakistanis reached unforeseen and mistaken conclusions about what was going on and who the enemy was.

The 1945 atomic bombs were miniature firecrackers in comparison to today's intercontinental ballistic missiles, which bear multiple warheads each of which is powerful enough to flatten an entire urban area. Several commentators have compared the relatively new spectre of cyberwar with the supposedly more familiar threat of nuclear war.[294] They have no idea. The lights going out may not be very pleasant, especially if it leads to food shortages, but I would still choose a power cut over a hydrogen bomb any day.

There are four ways of dealing with risks. You can accept them, reduce them, transfer them via insurance, or eliminate them. For nuclear weapons, only the last of these options makes any sense. Insurance is a contradiction in terms, and mere threat reduction is simply not a rational option: the consequences of a single slip-up would be so catastrophic that there is no level of residual hazard that can reasonably be tolerated.

There is also no basis for presuming that the actual level of residual hazard is particularly low in the first place. Today's systems are not necessarily any safer than the ones that were operational in the early eighties, even before cyberattacks are taken into account. The veil of secrecy with which those who build and maintain nuclear weapons are largely shielded from public accountability almost certainly ends up resulting in more rather than less danger, and the near misses described above may well represent but the tip of the iceberg.

States that own nuclear weapons typically cite deterrence as the rationale for retaining them, the idea being that nobody will launch an attack if he knows he would suffer one in retaliation.[295] However preposterous this proposition may seem in the age of the suicide bomber, the threat of a nuclear catastrophe is said to have acted as the guarantor of peace for over seventy years. But even if deterrence were guaranteed to work perfectly on a political level for an indefinite period of time, the risk of an accident would still represent a fatal flaw in the argument. That nothing serious has occurred up to now is no guarantee that it never will.

There is no such thing as a perfect system, even if we were in a position to make the ridiculously optimistic assumption that the safeguards protecting nuclear arsenals were as good as they possibly could be. In March 2014, nine U.S. Air Force commanders responsible for nuclear missiles were sacked for presiding over a culture of cheating on routine examinations which is said to have stemmed from a general expectation that officers achieve one hundred percent scores.[296] The story highlights perfectly the fundamental problem with nuclear weapons. On the one hand, only a total lack of errors can ever be acceptable. On the other hand, a total lack of errors is not something of which humans beings are realistically capable.

There is only one way of reducing the risk to zero, and that is to decommission the bombs. And even if you do believe in the need to retain a deterrent, that could surely be achieved with vastly fewer missiles than are currently in service, and hence with a greatly reduced level of danger. There are currently some 15,000 nuclear warheads in the world.[297] For each one in any given year, there is a quantifiable risk that some chain of events will lead to its detonation. The laws of statistics show that, if we wait for long enough, it is a mathematical certainty that a serious incident involving a nuclear weapon will occur at some point. It has to. With the current overkill, there is every reason to fear that the inevitable disaster may be just around the corner. We can only hope that mankind then manages to stop at a single blast, only pray that the accident does not trigger a political chain reaction that ends up destroying all life on the planet.

EternalBlue, WannaCry and HMS Queen Elizabeth

Nation states have a strong motivation to search for and hoard the zero-day vulnerabilities that offer the most effective means of writing malware, because malware plays such an important role both in spying and in cyberwar. In mid-2017, the world saw what happens when information about such software weaknesses is itself stolen by hackers and released into the public domain.

In Chapter II, we described how buffer overflow vulnerabilities work. EternalBlue, a buffer overflow vulnerability that allows an attacker to take over control of a Windows server, was first exposed in April 2017 by a hacker group called the Shadow Brokers[298] that Edward Snowden sees as circumstantially linked to the Russian government.[299] The Shadow Brokers had previously claimed to have stolen information about other vulnerabilities from the so-called Equation Group, which is widely associated with the American NSA.[300]

Microsoft clearly believed the same to be true of EternalBlue. When the vulnerability became public, the company went as far as to berate the NSA publicly for failing to disclose it in the first place and for then allowing it to be stolen.[301] Although somebody does seem to have tipped off Microsoft in advance of the Shadow Brokers tweet—Windows updates neutralising the weakness had been released around a month earlier in March 2017[302]—the firm's normal strategy would have been to patch the vulnerability without publishing any information about how it worked. Because a very substantial proportion of Windows users around the world do not keep their systems up to date, they remain susceptible to any vulnerabilities that have only been fixed in the latest versions. The last thing Microsoft wants is for details of the inner workings of newly patched flaws to enter the public domain so they can be exploited at will.

WannaCry, a ransomware worm that used EternalBlue to spread, hit in May 2017.[303] Much like the CryptoLocker trojan described in Chapter II, it encrypted the files on each victim's computer and then demanded a bitcoin ransom of around $300 to decode them again. What was different this time was the level of chaos the ransomware caused. It went way beyond the realm of inaccessible files and extortion. From Russian railways through Portuguese telecommunications giants to Chinese universities, there seemed to be no combination of geography and business sector that was immune.[304] Many organisations within the UK National Health Service fell victim to WannaCry, leaving hospitals and doctors' surgeries unable to access crucial information and forcing them to cancel operations.[305]

WannaCry had all the hallmarks of the cyberwar that the media had been telling everyone to expect. This led many commentators to try and attribute it to a state actor. The Washington Post claimed to be party to a leaked NSA report linking the ransomware to North Korea.[306] Anti-virus specialists Symantec did indeed discover that the WannaCry code shared a number of features with other malware that is believed to originate from a common set of hackers whom the security fraternity refer to as the Lazarus group.[307] (They have been given the name because they are felt to exhibit an ability to cheat mortality that puts them in the same category as their biblical namesake!) In turn, the Lazarus group has been identified with the Guardians of Peace group discussed in Chapter III, whose political behaviour clearly demonstrated their sympathies for the Kim dynasty.[308] In the absence of firm evidence, however, such attributions have a tendency to become circular.

The discussion of U.S. election hacking in the previous chapter showed that pointing fingers based on the software that was used to carry out an attack is flawed. Anyone can copy and reuse malware. However, this case was different. WannaCry had been used in a handful of targeted attacks earlier in 2017 before it became a large-scale infection, and these targeted attacks involved other strains of malware that have also been linked to the Lazarus group. The evidence that the Lazarus group was responsible is thus slightly stronger than in similar cases, although it still remains within the realms of possibility that the real culprit was somebody else trying to make themselves look like the

Lazarus group, and in any case the question remains unanswered as to who exactly is behind the Lazarus group in the first place.

From a purely technical vantage point, though, it seems almost unbelievable that WannaCry could really be the work of state-sponsored hackers. It bears all the hallmarks of an incompetent, inexperienced amateur. It simply comes nowhere close to the Stuxnet league. Even if one might expect the North Korean secret service to be less skilled than their American counterparts, they can surely not be this much worse. Looking at the manifold slipups the authors of WannaCry made, it is hard not to reach the conclusion that the Kim regime cannot have been involved, unless it was simply a crude attempt to raise funds and the real North Korean experts have better things to do with their time than write ransomware.

When WannaCry infects a new machine, it connects to one of a handful of Tor hidden services using the mechanisms described in the previous chapter. These hidden services have the job of tracking infections as well as of creating a new Bitcoin identity to accept each victim's ransom payment. The intention was that each infectee should receive a separate Bitcoin address to transfer his coins to. Because of a bug in the WannaCry system, however, only a handful of Bitcoin addresses were used.[309] Each one was quoted over and over again to different infected machines around the world. As well as making the system essentially inoperable by removing the means of knowing who had paid and who had not, this also put these addresses, which were soon amassing large quantities of bitcoins, firmly on to the radar of law enforcement. When the funds were spent in the summer of 2017, the world was watching.[310]

It also became clear just hours into the attack that the way the encryption was being carried out was itself insecure. A ransomware attack on a new machine involves paired asymmetric keys: the public key used to lock the files and the corresponding private key that could potentially be used to unlock them again later. As described for the CryptoLocker trojan in Chapter II, other strains of ransomware have generated and managed their keys on central command-and-control servers and only transmitted the public member of each pair to newly infected machines.

When WannaCry infected a new victim computer, however, it did the opposite: it created both keys on that computer before transmitting the private key to the server, and French researcher Adrien Guinet discovered that the random numbers used to generate the keys lingered in the victim machine's memory after the malware had completed its destructive deeds.[311] Provided an attacked computer had not yet been switched off, there was still a chance of recovering the private key and decoding the affected files. Two tools were subsequently released into the public domain to facilitate this process: Guinet's own program WannaKey, which only worked with the long-obsolete Windows XP operating system; and then WanaKiwi, which covered the still very much supported and more widely used Windows 7 as well.[312]

And very shortly after that, Marcus Hutchins, a 22-year-old IT security expert from South-West England who was to find himself arrested a few weeks later in Las Vegas on unrelated cybercrime charges[313], put a stop to the spread of WannaCry more or less by accident.[314] He saw that the malware attempted to access a random-looking DNS name that nobody was using at the time. Interested to see what messages WannaCry would send an IP address associated with the name, Hutchins decided to register it for himself. Nobody was more surprised that he was when it turned out that the worm, on finding that the domain was now populated, simply shut up shop and stopped spreading.

Hutchins had found a kill switch that, remarkably, seems to have been left in the malware code unintentionally. Predictably, WannaCry variants without the kill switch soon appeared; perhaps more tellingly, the kill switch domain was soon itself the target of an ultimately unsuccessful distributed denial-of-service attack.[315] The aim was to take the domain back offline again, which would have had the effect of resuscitating WannaCry.

On balance, then, the extent of the damage caused by WannaCry seems to have had little to do with the sophistication of its authors and much to do with the failure of its victims to follow standard IT best practice, coupled as always with society's ever-increasing reliance on computers to provide its essential services. Anyone running a current Windows version and updating it regularly was immune to the attack, but unfortunately that was far from everyone. Many British home computer users who had stopped using Windows XP when Microsoft announced they would no longer support the operating system in April 2014 were astonished to learn that their local hospitals had still not upgraded from it over three years later.[316]

A large part of the problem is certainly a collective failure to appreciate just how easy it is for malware to penetrate and ravish an inadequately protected computer system or network. When the British multi-billion-dollar aircraft carrier HMS Queen Elizabeth came into service in the summer of 2017, security commentators were astounded to glean from a news film that its computers appeared to be running the very same obsolete Windows XP system that had been shown to be so vulnerable to WannaCry just a few weeks previously.[317]

The then UK defence secretary Sir Michael Fallon tried to play down the risks, claiming that the computer software on the ship was "properly protected". Presumably his sense of security was based on the notion that the ship's systems were not connected to the internet, but, as we saw earlier in this chapter, a single USB stick would have sufficed to infect them, and they became especially likely targets once the world knew how vulnerable they were. Fallon's argument is a little bit like not worrying about going into hospital without a functioning immune system because barrier nursing in a sterile environment is capable of protecting patients from infections. It may well be, but, given the choice, I would still opt for my immune system every time.

NotPetya

A few weeks later in mid-June, the EternalBlue buffer overflow weakness was used once again as the basis of a second attack. The new scourge was an updated version of a program called Petya that had already been available for over a year as so-called ransomware–as–a–service: having downloaded the malware over the dark web and distributed it to your own targets, you then shared the proceeds with the authors, who also conveniently managed the infrastructure and the Bitcoin processing.[318] The original variety of Petya had already employed advanced infection techniques that allowed it to spread rapidly through local networks, and now the EternalBlue vulnerability had been added to its armoury to produce a new, virulent strain.[319] It represented a danger to any organisation with a single unpatched Windows machine through which it could squirm in.

However, it soon became clear that the new threat was not in fact ransomware at all.[320] As with the traditional version of Petya, each victim was presented with an installation code that he was to send to the operators once he had paid. Originally, this code had contained the information that enabled the criminals to recover the private key to send back to the victim's computer so he could be returned access to his files. But with this new version, which was given a variety of names including NotPetya and ExPetr, it transpired that the installation code was actually no more than a random string of letters and numbers that was of no use to anybody. It was certain that paying the ransom would not result in the malware authors unlocking your files again, because they had no means of doing so.

While WannaCry had not worked as ransomware because of a hapless blunder, though, there could be no doubt that the inoperability of NotPetya was a deliberate ploy. Overall, the NotPetya code was free of the many schoolboy errors that had peppered WannaCry's virtual DNA. Researchers analysing it were left with the impression of a much more professional and disciplined authorship.[321] NotPetya may well have been designed to ride the ransomware media hype wave that had followed in the wake of WannaCry, but its genuine purpose was much more sinister.

The initial infections were bundled together with updates for accounting software called MeDoc that is widely used in the Ukraine. Although it did emerge that MeDoc's security practices had been less than ideal and it is certainly possible that an insider could have planted the malware, the company seems to have been a victim rather than a perpetrator.[322] It later transpired that MeDoc had been breached some weeks earlier and used as a conduit to send its customers software that compromised their machines, and it is difficult to draw any other conclusion than that MeDoc was abused as an efficient means of distributing NotPetya to a large number of targets within the Ukraine while minimising collateral damage in other countries. Around 80% of infections worldwide were focussed on the single nation[323], with victims including the Ukrainian National Bank and the radiation monitoring installation at the Chernobyl disaster site.[324]

Against the background of the political conflict between Ukraine and Russia, there can be little serious doubt that NotPetya was an offensive cyberwar attack aimed from one nation state to another. At the same time, it may be that it has had an altogether welcome and probably unintended side effect. Following closely on the heels of the broken WannaCry ransomware, the epidemic of fake NotPetya ransomware seems to have been destined to etch into the popular consciousness that there is little point in meeting ransomware payment demands because once your files have been encrypted you have no realistic chance of ever seeing them again. This is bad news for business for genuine ransomware authors. It could well lead to a permanent shift in attitudes and behaviour, just as the 9/11 attacks put an end to the previously prevalent practice of hijacking aircraft for political or economic motives. Passengers who believe they have nothing to lose make poor hostages.

The Internet of Things and My Friend Cayla

It is not just businesses, governments and armies whose cyberattack vulnerability is increasing proportionally to their reliance on technology. In the home, too, there is an ever-broader spectrum of devices that are now being produced with internet connectivity as standard. In the world of the future, we are told, our standard of living will rocket as everything from our refrigerators to our cookers communicate in a network of appliances collaborating for our maximum convenience. The reach of the Internet of Things (IoT) seems unlimited. If you are trying to slow down at mealtimes as part of your strategy to lose weight, you can even buy a fork that records and analyses your every mouthful, uploading your eating patterns to your phone and, if you are so inclined, to the rest of the world.[325]

When complex software and IoT enablement are suddenly tacked on to types of appliances that have been faithfully performing their designated non-electronic tasks for decades, neither their designers nor their users are likely to have security concerns at the forefront of their minds. And a cyberattack that people have grown to expect when they use good old-fashioned computers and smartphones retains the potential to take its victims by surprise when it rears its ugly head in the context of an oven or freezer.

In October 2016, internet services ranging from the BBC and CNN to Twitter and Netflix became unavailable across Europe and North America.[326] The cause was the most intense distributed denial-of-service attack the world had ever seen. It focussed on Dyn, a company that operates a considerable proportion of DNS servers in the affected regions. Without the DNS infrastructure to translate domain names into IP addresses, users were left unable to access the internet. DNS had never been attacked so effectively before. Because it is designed to handle massive quantities of network traffic to begin with, the firepower required to bring it to its knees is enormous.

The botnet that had achieved it this time was made up largely of IoT devices like cameras and printers that had been infected with the Mirai malware strain. Mirai does nothing particularly spectacular.[327] Following a pattern that will be thoroughly familiar from Chapter III, it simply works its way through a list of default user names and passwords with which such gadgets are known to ship.

There are many ways in which IoT devices represent a botnet creator's dream. Quite apart from the fact that their typical owner may not even know how to change the user details with which they can be accessed, he is less likely to attempt to do so than he would be with a phone or computer because he will probably not be as alert to the security risks. IoT devices tend to lack the antivirus software that has become ubiquitous for normal computers. And once a device has been infected, its owner is typically in a poor position to detect any subtle sluggishness that might result from its illegal activities and may not particularly care if he does. Some people might not even be aware that the gadgets are connected to the internet in the first place.

Insecure IoT devices also expose ordinary consumers to the sort of physical cyberattacks that were previously the concern of factories and armies. Suddenly, potential problems everyday home users might face have grown to encompass malware causing toasters to overheat and catch fire, attacked refrigerators and freezers switching themselves off and spoiling their contents, and ransomware turning smart heating systems either off or up to their maximum temperatures until the unfortunate victim pays up.[328]

Such hacks largely remain the subject of speculation, research and non-offensive demonstrations. On the other hand, what is already a very real and present danger with IoT devices is the spectre of clandestine surveillance. The first smart toy doll, My Friend Cayla, which was designed to talk back to its toddler owners, has been widely criticised because anybody can link to it over Bluetooth, a wireless protocol that was originally developed to enable hardware like phones, headsets and game consoles to communicate over short distances.[329] There are no checks on who is accessing the doll; the only limitation is that only one device can be connected at once.[330] Most Bluetooth devices are manufactured to operate over a range of at least 10 metres, but, depending on environmental conditions, the true range can be considerably greater; it is quite possible that your neighbour could talk to your child over her doll without you realising.

As security researcher Tim Medin demonstrated in late 2015, if it was not already bad enough that he could get Cayla to reproduce any sound he wanted, including threatening or intimidating music and expletives, he could also listen in on whatever you and your child were saying.[331] This vulnerability led the German telecommunications agency to ban Cayla in February 2017 as an illegal surveillance device, going as far as to issue a dramatic pronouncement requiring parents of children who already had a doll to render it harmless.[332]

Baby monitors and Weeping Angel

Also in 2015, security company Rapid7 showed that a number of baby monitors on the market could easily be hacked by a variety of means.[333] Some sported software vulnerabilities. Others sent their information in an unencrypted form that could be siphoned off by eavesdroppers. Still more had default user names and passwords that were not only predictable as in the examples in Chapter III but that could not be changed by the monitor's owner even if he wanted to do so. Whichever weakness your particular model happened to be harbouring, you could have been unwittingly streaming both sound and images from your bedroom to anyone in the world who cared to watch.

Wherever covert surveillance opportunities raise their heads, the spooks are normally not far behind. In the spring of 2017, WikiLeaks published a massive treasure trove of internal CIA notes known as Vault7.[334] The many malware exploits correspond more or less to what one might expect; what is perhaps more surprising is the sense of dilettantism conveyed by the plethora of projects that seem to have been started but never finished, or at least not adequately documented. However, there was one technical revelation that did attract widespread attention, and that was the Weeping Angel malware product designed to compromise Samsung smart televisions so that they record whatever is being said in the room, even when they appear to be switched off.[335]

It is not quite clear from the documentation whether Weeping Angel was still a development project or was already in use, nor can we be certain how the malware was designed to get on to a television. The notes state that "Firmware version 1118+ eliminated the current USB installation method", which suggests that gaining physical access to the television was one infection strategy. However, it does not necessarily rule out the existence of other strategies. To take just one example, whenever a new firmware version is downloaded from Samsung, either automatically by the television or actively by its user, contacting the server will involve a DNS query. One might speculate that this would leave the television vulnerable to being redirected to a malware server using techniques like the QUANTUMDNS attack described at the beginning of this chapter.

Vehicles, key fobs and remote carjacking

Vehicles, too, are becoming increasingly susceptible to hacking as they become ever more dependent on electronics. In 2016, the German automobile club ADAC discovered a fatal flaw with so-called proximity key fobs, which unlock your car and often start the ignition as well based solely on the key fob being next to or inside the vehicle. Because the communication did not require the car owner to press a button, his key fob could be tricked into activating without his knowledge just like the contactless cards we discussed in Chapter III. And however far apart the key fob and the car were, an attacker who managed to get within a couple of metres of both objects could use additional hardware to amplify the signal between the two ends and open the car.[336]

It did not matter how cutting–edge the encryption mechanism was that was being used to encode the messages, because a car thief did not need to read what was being sent. He merely had to pass it on. A suggested remedy that was in any case only said to work some of the time was to keep your key fob in a tin can. The TEMPEST programme described earlier in the chapter had originally come into being as the preserve of armies and secret services; now related techniques had become the concern of ordinary car owners.

Even if you had an old-fashioned remote key system that caused you the supposed inconvenience of having to touch it when you wanted to get into your vehicle, you were still far from immune. A correctly designed encryption procedure would have been based on the use of a unique private encryption key stored only within the physical key device; it would have worked analogously to the system described for European bankcards in Chapter III. Again in 2016, however, researchers based in the UK and Germany claimed that the access mechanisms of millions of Volkswagen group cars produced over the previous twenty years actually used encryption keys selected from a tiny common pool.[337] The paper stopped short of publishing the keys that had been reverse-engineered, but an attacker in their possession would have been able to clone any affected remote control unit simply based on eavesdropping on a single exchange of traffic between it and the car it was supposed to be protecting.

2016 may well go down in history as the year when automotive security came on to the radar in earnest. The year saw a revelation far more frightening than the mere facilitation of car theft. It transpired that an attacker who had connected an appropriate gadget to the diagnostic port of a Chrysler Jeep Cherokee could make it do terrifying things while it was being driven.[338] These included turning the steering wheel, applying the parking brake or setting the cruise control speed. Some commentators saw the fact that the attack scenario required physical access to the interior of the vehicle as evidence of its infeasibility, but this argument hardly seems valid in light of the above discussion about key fobs: it seems improbable that there is no make of vehicle for which the two procedures could be combined.

One might contend that criminals already had at their disposal a number of ways of committing murder with a vehicle, many of which are considerably less easily trackable than sending it electronic instructions. It is indeed the case that such wantonly violent cyberattacks are probably not as interesting to most criminals as their less dramatic financial counterparts.

As fully automated, self-driving vehicles appear on the horizon ahead, though, it does seem certain that the years to come will bring all sorts of novel hacks targeting them. For example, once all cars drive themselves, emergency vehicles will presumably ditch their blue lights and sirens and send out a signal ordering everyone else out of the way. And unless the encryption supporting this procedure is absolutely watertight, it is probably only a matter of time until somebody works out how to spoof the signal; with this knowledge would come the power to command everyone else off the road and to use the highway at speed as a solitary driver. Moving a process online always carries risks as well as benefits.

OUTLOOK

It should be obvious by this point that it is impossible to use computer technology in general and the internet in particular without bearing some risk of falling victim to cyberattacks and hacking. This need not lead to paranoia on the part of the private user or small business owner, any more than you would incarcerate yourself voluntarily in a high-security compound to eliminate risks such as being burgled or having a car accident.

Backing up your files periodically is a good idea anyway and will reduce your vulnerability to ransomware. If you also use rare passwords that are not dictionary words and that you change regularly, if you keep your anti-virus software, operating system and browser up to date, follow the recommendations of your firewall and stay alert when you access websites and open E-mail attachments, you are taking reasonable precautions, just as everyday locks on doors and windows are sufficient to secure a typical home.

On the other hand, what is genuinely scandalous and cries out for urgent attention is the failure of many large corporations, utility infrastructure companies and militaries to follow even these simple practices, often on the basis of the catch-all excuse that total security is not attainable anyway. It is simply not good enough that ordinary householders upgrade their Windows software when it reaches its end-of-life only for a ransomware attack some three years later to reveal that neither their local hospital nor their navy had been so prudent.

There is a second general issue for society to consider. The risks that inevitably accompany connectivity are only acceptable if they are counterbalanced by some sort of benefit. The ability to bank or shop online has changed lives for the better to such an extent that nobody would seriously suggest returning to the pre-internet era merely to expunge the scourge of cybercrime. But many Internet of Things gadgets seem to espouse connectivity as a goal in itself. In the worst case, their owners may end up suffering the consequences of cyberattacks that could have been painlessly avoided simply by staying offline in the first place.

The internet was originally designed for a narrow range of mainly academic communication tasks.[339] The wave of crime it is now facilitating is a symptom of its unanticipated meteoric success. Of the areas of technology covered in *Cybertwists*, only one—encryption—has reached sufficient maturity that it can be used in a way that provides watertight security. It is no coincidence that encryption is also exceptional in that it well predates the internet.

Although wherever technology goes, cyberattacks and hacking are bound to follow shortly behind it, the criminals' head start will be gradually reduced over the coming decades. There will surely come a time when the current fragility of network communication, authentication and software is regarded as a historical detail resulting from unplanned innovation that left the technical experts and infrastructure managers unable to keep up.

If you have enjoyed reading *Cybertwists*, please take a moment to spread the word to other readers by leaving a positive review on Amazon. Reviews are one of the main criteria that Amazon uses to decide which books to suggest to potential customers.

REFERENCES

1 BBC News, "'Top Mafia boss' caught in Italy", 11 April 2006, *See* http://news.bbc.co.uk/2/hi/europe/4898930.stm

2 La Repubblica, "Mercadante chiama in causa Schifani 'Il cassiere di Binnu lo fece votare'", 05 December 2008, *See* http://ricerca.repubblica.it/repubblica/archivio/repubblica/2008/12/05/mercadante-chiama-in-causa-schifani-il-cassiere.html

3 Suetonius, edited by Carey, W., "Svetoni Tranqvilii Vita Divi Avgvsti", *See* http://thelatinlibrary.com/suetonius/suet.aug.html#88

4 Suetonius, edited by Shuckburgh, E.S., "Svetoni Tranqvilii Vita Divi Ivli", *See* http://thelatinlibrary.com/suetonius/suet.caesar.html#56

5 Palazzolo, S., "Segni Particolari", 2007, *See* http://www.ausili.net/bernardoprovenzano/content.asp?prov=4

6 La Repubblica, "'Voglio sangue e onore'. Ecco il giuramento (criptato) degli affiliati alla 'ndrangheta", 09 January 2014, *See* http://www.repubblica.it/cronaca/2014/01/09/news/ndrangheta_giuramento_criptato-75456087/

7 Electrospaces.net, "The Washington-Moscow Hotline", 28 October 2012, *See* https://electrospaces.blogspot.de/2012/10/the-washington-moscow-hot-line.html

8 National Security Agency, Cryptographic Almanac 50th Anniversary Series, "VENONA: An Overview", January-February 2002, *See* https://www.nsa.gov/news-features/declassified-documents/crypto-almanac-50th/assets/files/VENONA_An_Overview.pdf

9 Nova Online, "The February 9, 1944 cable: Klaus Fuchs and Harry Gold", updated January 2002, *See* http://www.pbs.org/wgbh/nova/venona/inte_19440209.html

10 Gewerkschaft Securitas in Berlin, "Chiffrierapparat", German Patent 416219, 23 February 1918, *See* http://cryptomuseum.com/crypto/enigma/patents/files/DE416219.pdf

11 Deutsche Wehrmacht, "Schlüsselanleitung zur Schlüsselmaschine Enigma vom 13. 1. 40", April 1940, *See* http://www.ilord.com/enigma-manual1940-german.pdf

12 Bletchley Park Trust, "Our Story", *See* https://www.bletchleypark.org.uk/our-story

13 Helgason, G., & Erskine, R., "Allied Breaking of Naval Enigma", *See* https://uboat.net/technical/enigma_breaking.htm

14 Ellsbury, G., "The History of Hut Eight", updated 19 December 2014, *See* http://www.ellsbury.com/hut8/hut8-022.htm

15 Large, C., "Some Human Factors in Codebreaking", North Atlantic Treaty Organisation, RTO HFM Symposium on 'The Role of Humans in Intelligent and Automated Systems', 7-9 October 2002, *See* https://fas.org/irp/eprint/large.pdf

16 Erskine, R., "Breaking Naval Enigma (Dolphin and Shark)", updated 28 January 2016, *See* http://cryptocellar.org/bgac/HMTR-2066-2.pdf

17 Bauer, F. L., "Die Komödie der Irrungen im Wettstreit der Kryptologen", Bayerische Akademie der Wissenschaften, Mathematisch-naturwissenschaftliche Klasse, Abhandlungen – Neue Folge, Heft 176, 14 December 2007, *See* http://docplayer.org/43630240-Die-komoedie-der-irrungen-im-wettstreit-der-kryptologen.html

18 The Telegraph, "John Herivel", 21 January 2011, *See* http://www.telegraph.co.uk/news/obituaries/military-obituaries/special-forces-obituaries/8275117/John-Herivel.html

19 Deutsch, H. C., "The Historical Impact of Revealing the Ultra Secret", National Security Agency, Approved for Release on 26 October 2006, *See* https://www.nsa.gov/news-features/declassified-documents/cryptologic-spectrum/assets/files/ultra_secret.pdf

20 Ehrsam, W. F., Meyer, C.H.W., Powers, R.L., Smith, J.L., & Tuchman, W.L., "Product block cipher system for data security", U.S. Patent 3,962,539, 8 June 1976, *See* https://www.google.com/patents/US3962539

21 National Institute of Standards and Technology, "Announcing the Advanced Encryption Standard (AES)", 26 November 2001, *See* https://csrc.nist.gov/csrc/media/publications/fips/197/final/documents/fips-197.pdf

22 Institute of Electrical and Electronics Engineers, "802.11-2016 - IEEE Standard for Information technology--Telecommunications and information exchange between systems Local and metropolitan area networks--Specific requirements - Part 11: Wireless LAN Medium Access Control (MAC) and Physical Layer (PHY) Specifications", 14 December 2016, *See* http://ieeexplore.ieee.org/document/7786995/

23 Vanhoef, M., & Piessens, F., "Key Reinstallation Attacks: Forcing Nonce Reuse in WPA2", ACM Conference on Computer and Communications Security 2017, *See* https://papers.mathyvanhoef.com/ccs2017.pdf

24 Rivest, R.L., Shamir, A., & Adleman, L., "A method for obtaining digital signatures and public-key cryptosystems", Communications of the ACM, Volume 21 Issue 2, February 1978, *See* https://dl.acm.org/citation.cfm?id=359342

25 Sullivan, N., "A (relatively easy to understand) primer on elliptic curve cryptography", Condé Nast, 24 October 2013, *See* https://arstechnica.com/information-technology/2013/10/a-relatively-easy-to-understand-primer-on-elliptic-curve-cryptography/

26 Kaliski, B., "PKCS #1: RSA Encryption Version 1.5", The Internet Society, March 1998, *See* https://tools.ietf.org/html/rfc2313

27 Langley, A., "Protecting data for the long term with forward secrecy", Google, 22 November 2011, *See* https://security.googleblog.com/2011/11/protecting-data-for-long-term-with.html

28 Greenberg, A., "Leaked NSA Doc Says It Can Collect And Keep Your Encrypted Data As Long As It Takes To Crack It", Forbes, 20 June 2013, *See* https://www.forbes.com/sites/andygreenberg/2013/06/20/leaked-nsa-doc-says-it-can-collect-and-keep-your-encrypted-data-as-long-as-it-takes-to-crack-it

29 Diffie, W., & Hellman, M.E., "New Directions in Cryptography", IEEE Transactions in Information Theory, Vol .IT-22, No. 6, November 1976, *See* https://ee.stanford.edu/%7Ehellman/publications/24.pdf

30 Barker, E., Chen, L., Roginsky, A., & Smid, M., "Recommendation for Pair-Wise Key Establishment Schemes Using Discrete Logarithm Cryptography", NIST Special Publication 800-56A Revision 2, May 2013, *See* http://nvlpubs.nist.gov/nistpubs/SpecialPublications/NIST.SP.800-56Ar2.pdf

31 Robertson, N., Cruickshank, P., & Lister, T., "Documents reveal al Qaeda's plans for seizing cruise ships, carnage in Europe", Cable News Network, 1 May 2012, *See* http://edition.cnn.com/2012/04/30/world/al-qaeda-documents-future/

32 Wilson, W.R., "World War II: Navajo Code Talkers", American History, February 1997, *See* http://www.historynet.com/world-war-ii-navajo-code-talkers.htm

33 Korte, T., "How Effective was Navajo Code?", Native American & Indigenous People, *See* http://www.thepeoplespaths.net/articles/navcode.htm

34 BBC News, "Mafia boss in prison Bible probe", 11 January 2008, *See* http://news.bbc.co.uk/2/hi/europe/7184091.stm

35 Moore, M., "FBI called in to crack Mafia boss's Bible code", The Telegraph, 08 September 2006, *See* http://www.telegraph.co.uk/news/1528376/FBI-called-in-to-crack-Mafia-bosss-Bible-code.html

36 China Internet Network Information Center, "Standards of encryption algorithms", 04 December 2013, *See* https://cnnic.com.cn/ScientificResearch/LeadingEdge/soea/intro/201312/t20131204_43348.htm

37 Moriai, S., Kato, A., & Kanda, M., "Addition of Camellia Cipher Suites to Transport Layer Security (TLS)", The Internet Society, July 2005, *See* https://tools.ietf.org/html/rfc4132

38 Lee, H.J., Lee, S.J., Yoon, J.H., Cheon, D.H., & Lee, J.I., "The SEED Encryption Algorithm", The Internet Society, December 2005, *See* https://tools.ietf.org/html/rfc4269

39 Bundesamt für Sicherheit in der Informationstechnik, "Kryptographische Verfahren: Empfehlungen und Schlüssellängen", 8 February 2017, *See* https://www.bsi.bund.de/SharedDocs/Downloads/DE/BSI/Publikationen/TechnischeRichtlinien/TR02102/BSI-TR-02102.pdf?__blob=publicationFile

40 Moore, G.E., "Cramming more components onto integrated circuits", McGraw-Hill, Electronics volume 38 number 8, 19 April 1965, *See* https://cis.upenn.edu/~cis501/papers/mooreslaw-reprint.pdf

41 Grover, L.K., "A fast quantum mechanical algorithm for database search", 28th Annual ACM Symposium on the Theory of Computing (STOC), May 1996, updated 19 November 1996, *See* https://arxiv.org/abs/quant-ph/9605043

42 Shor, P.W., "Polynomial-Time Algorithms for Prime Factorization and Discrete Logarithms on a Quantum Computer", IEEE Computer Society Press, Proceedings of the 35th Annual Symposium on Foundations of Computer Science, November 20-22, 1994, updated 25 January 1996, *See* https://arxiv.org/abs/quant-ph/9508027v2

43 Tosi, G., Mohiyaddin, F.A., Schmitt, V., Tenberg, S., Rahman, R., Klimeck, G., & Morello, A., "Silicon quantum processor with robust long-distance qubit couplings", Macmillan, Nature Communications 8, 06 September 2017, *See* https://www.nature.com/articles/s41467-017-00378-x

44 Schneier, B., "More Details on the NSA Switching to Quantum-Resistant Cryptography", 02 February 2016, *See* https://www.schneier.com/blog/archives/2016/02/more_details_on_2.html

45 Greenwald, G., "Revealed: how US and UK spy agencies defeat internet privacy and security", The Guardian, 05 September 2013, *See* https://www.theguardian.com/world/2013/sep/05/nsa-gchq-encryption-codes-security

46 Menn, J., "Exclusive: Secret contract tied NSA and security industry pioneer", Reuters, 20 December 2013, *See* http://www.reuters.com/article/us-usa-security-rsa-idUSBRE9BJ1C220131220

47 Schoenmakers, B., & Sidorenko, A., "Cryptanalysis of the Dual Elliptic Curve Pseudorandom Generator", International Association for Cryptologic Research, Cryptology ePrint Archive, Repot 2006/190, 29 May 2006, *See* https://eprint.iacr.org/2006/190.pdf

48 Schneier, B., "Did NSA Put a Secret Backdoor in New Encryption Standard?", Wired, 15 November 2007, *See* https://www.wired.com/2007/11/securitymatters-1115/

49 Green, M., "RSA warns developers not to use RSA products", 20 September 2013, *See* https://blog.cryptographyengineering.com/2013/09/20/rsa-warns-developers-against-its-own/

50 Perlroth, N., Larson, J., & Shane, S., "N.S.A. Able to Foil Basic Safeguards of Privacy on Web", New York Times, 05 September 2013, *See* http://www.nytimes.com/2013/09/06/us/nsa-foils-much-internet-encryption.html

51 SECROM, "What is the NSA's Suite A & B?", *See* https://secrom.com/content/what-nsas-suite-b

52 Mason, R., "UK spy agencies need more powers, says Cameron", The Guardian, 12 January 2015, *See* https://www.theguardian.com/uk-news/2015/jan/12/uk-spy-agencies-need-more-powers-says-cameron-paris-attacks

53 Grossman, L., "Inside Apple CEO Tim Cook's Fight With the FBI", Time, 17 March 2016, *See* http://time.com/4262480/tim-cook-apple-fbi-2/

54 Koops, B., "Overview per country", Crypto Law Survey, Version 27.0, February 2013, *See* http://www.cryptolaw.org/cls2.htm#nk

55 Code of Federal Regulations, "International Traffic in Arms Regulations", updated 01 April 1992, *See* https://epic.org/crypto/export_controls/itar.html

56 WhatsApp, "WhatsApp Encryption Overview: Technical white paper", 05 April 2016, updated 06 July 2017, *See* https://www.whatsapp.com/security/WhatsApp-Security-Whitepaper.pdf

57 Canetti, R., Dwork, C., Naor, M., & Ostrovsky, R., "Deniable Encryption", Springer, Advances in Cryptology – Annual International Cryptology Conference CRYPTO 1997, 17-21 August 1997, *See* https://link.springer.com/chapter/10.1007%2FBFb0052229

58 F-Secure, "Form: Threat description", *See* https://www.f-secure.com/v-descs/form.shtml

59 Haines, J.R., "Weaponizing Ebola?", Foreign Policy Research Institute, 27 October 2014, *See* https://www.fpri.org/article/2014/10/weaponizing-ebola/

60 Hosmer, C., „Polymorphic & Metamorphic Malware", WetStone, Black Hat Conference 2008, *See* https://www.blackhat.com/presentations/bh-usa-08/Hosmer/BH_US_08_Hosmer_Polymorphic_Malware.pdf

61 Barkly, "Polymorphic Malware: How to Spot and Stop this Shapeshifting Menace", May 2017, *See* https://blog.barkly.com/what-is-polymorphic-malware

62 Kirk, J., "Greek spying case uncovers first phone switch rootkit", Washington Post, 13 July 2007, *See* http://www.washingtonpost.com/wp-dyn/content/article/2007/07/13/AR2007071300602.html

63 Symantec, "VBS.LoveLetter.Var", updated 12 March 2002, *See* http://www.symantec.com/security_response/writeup.jsp?docid=2000-121815-2258-99

64 Curtis, S., "Cyber black market 'more profitable than drug trade'", The Telegraph, 26 March 2014, *See* http://www.telegraph.co.uk/technology/internet-security/10724704/Cyber-black-market-more-profitable-than-drug-trade.html

65 Jarvis, K., "CryptoLocker Ransomware", Secureworks, 18 December 2013, *See* https://www.secureworks.com/research/cryptolocker-ransomware

66 Ward, M., "Cryptolocker victims to get files back for free", BBC News, 06 August 2014, *See* http://www.bbc.com/news/technology-28661463

67 Krebs, B., "'Operation Tovar' Targets 'Gameover' ZeuS Botnet, CryptoLocker Scourge", 02 June 2014, *See* https://krebsonsecurity.com/2014/06/operation-tovar-targets-gameover-zeus-botnet-cryptolocker-scourge/

68 Krebs, B., "New Site Recovers Files Locked by Cryptolocker Ransomware", 06 August 2014, *See* https://krebsonsecurity.com/tag/decryptcryptolocker-com/

69 Tynan, D., "HummingBad Android malware: who did it, why, and is your device infected?", The Guardian, 07 July 2016, *See* https://www.theguardian.com/technology/2016/jul/06/what-is-hummingbad-malware-android-devices-checkpoint

70 Symantec, "Trojan.Zbot", updated 16 August 2016, *See* https://www.symantec.com/security_response/writeup.jsp?docid=2010-011016-3514-99&tabid=2

71 United States Department of Justice, Office of Public Affairs, "U.S. Leads Multi-National Action Against 'Gameover Zeus' Botnet and 'Cryptolocker' Ransomware, Charges Botnet Administrator", 02 June 2014, *See* https://www.justice.gov/opa/pr/us-leads-multi-national-action-against-gameover-zeus-botnet-and-cryptolocker-ransomware

72 Russinovich, M., "Sony, Rootkits and Digital Rights Management Gone Too Far", Microsoft, 31 October 2005, *See* https://blogs.technet.microsoft.com/markrussinovich/2005/10/31/sony-rootkits-and-digital-rights-management-gone-too-far/

73 Rosenblatt, S., "Lenovo's Superfish security snafu blows up in its face", CNET, 20 February 2015, *See* https://www.cnet.com/news/superfish-torments-lenovo-owners-with-more-than-adware/

74 United States Computer Emergency Readiness Team, "Lenovo Computers Vulnerable to HTTPS Spoofing", Released 20 February 2015, updated 04 March 2015, *See* https://www.us-cert.gov/ncas/current-activity/2015/02/20/Lenovo-Computers-Vulnerable-HTTPS-Spoofing

75 F-Secure, "Cruncher: Threat description", *See* https://www.f-secure.com/v-descs/cruncher.shtml

76 Ballano, M., "Is there an Internet-of-Things vigilante out there?", Symantec, 01 October 2015, *See* https://www.symantec.com/connect/blogs/there-internet-things-vigilante-out-there

77 The White Team, "Official Linux.Wifatch Source Repository", updated 27 January 2016, *See* https://gitlab.com/rav7teif/linux.wifatch

78 Hackett, R., "Microsoft Ups Rewards for Windows Bugs", Fortune, 27 July 2017, *See* http://fortune.com/2017/07/27/microsoft-windows-security-bug-bounty/

79 eEye Digital Security, "ANALYSIS: .ida 'Code Red' Worm", 17 July 2001, *See* https://web.archive.org/web/20110722192419/http://www.eeye.com/Resources/Security-Center/Research/Security-Advisories/AL20010717

80 Curry, J., "The man next door is starting a war", BCS, September 2011, *See* http://www.bcs.org/content/conWebDoc/41572

81 Team Twiizers, "Twilight Hack", Wiibrew, updated 02 June 2017, *See* http://www.wiibrew.org/wiki/Twilight_Hack

82 OpenSSL Software Foundation, "OpenSSL: Cryptography and SSL/TLS Toolkit", updated 02 November 2017, *See* https://www.openssl.org/

83 Cox, M. J., 09 April 2014, *See* https://plus.google.com/+MarkJCox/posts/TmCbp3BhJma

84 Synopsys, "The Heartbleed Bug", updated 29 April 2014, *See* http://heartbleed.com/

85 Netcraft, "Half a million widely trusted websites vulnerable to Heartbleed bug", 08 April 2014, *See* https://news.netcraft.com/archives/2014/04/08/half-a-million-widely-trusted-websites-vulnerable-to-heartbleed-bug.html

86 LibreOffice, "CVE-2014-0160", 07 April 2014, *See* http://www.libreoffice.org/about-us/security/advisories/cve-2014-0160/

87 Kerner, S.M., "Heartbleed SSL Flaw's True Cost Will Take Time to Tally", eWeek, 19 April 2014, *See* http://www.eweek.com/security/heartbleed-ssl-flaw-s-true-cost-will-take-time-to-tally

88 Finkle, J., & Kurane, S., "U.S. hospital breach biggest yet to exploit Heartbleed bug: expert", Reuters, 20 August 2014, *See* https://www.reuters.com/article/us-community-health-cybersecurity/u-s-hospital-breach-biggest-yet-to-exploit-heartbleed-bug-expert-idUSKBN0GK0H420140820

89 GMA News, "Report: CIA site hacked, defaced", 18 June 2011, *See* http://www.gmanetwork.com/news/scitech/content/223774/report-cia-site-hacked-defaced/story/

90 Pagliery, J., "Meet the guy who just broke TweetDeck", Cable News Network, 11 June 2014, *See* http://money.cnn.com/2014/06/11/technology/security/tweetdeck-hacked/index.html

91 Blue, V., "TweetDeck wasn't actually hacked, and everyone was silly", CBS Interactive, 12 June 2014, updated 13 June 2014, *See* http://www.zdnet.com/article/tweetdeck-wasnt-actually-hacked-and-everyone-was-silly/

92 Morrison, K., "Tweetdeck Hack Exposes Javascript Vulnerability", Adweek, 12 June 2014, *See* http://www.adweek.com/digital/tweetdeck-hack-exposes-javascript-vulnerability/

93 Open Web Application Security Project, "HTTPOnly", updated 24 August 2017, *See* https://www.owasp.org/index.php/HttpOnly

94 Fontana, J., "LinkedIn will pay $1.25 million to settle suit over password breach", CBS Interactive, 23 February 2015, *See* http://www.zdnet.com/article/linkedin-will-pay-1-25-million-to-settle-suit-over-password-breach/

95 Lennon, M., "LinkedIn: Breach Cost Up to $1M, Says $2-3 Million in Security Upgrades Coming", SecurityWeek, 03 August 2012, *See* http://www.securityweek.com/linkedin-breach-cost-1m-says-2-3-million-security-upgrades-coming

96 TalkTalk PLC, "Statement by TalkTalk PLC on Cyber Attack – Thursday October 22th 2015", *See* https://www.talktalkgroup.com/articles/talktalkgroup/TalkTalk-Group--moved-articles-/2015/Statement-by-TalkTalk-PLC-on-Cyber-Attack---Thursday-October-22th-2015

97 Bisson, D., "The TalkTalk Breach: Timeline of a Hack", Tripwire, 03 November 2015, updated 25 November 2015, *See* https://www.tripwire.com/state-of-security/security-data-protection/cyber-security/the-talktalk-breach-timeline-of-a-hack/

98 Farrell, S., "TalkTalk counts costs of cyber-attack", The Guardian, 02 February 2016, *See* https://www.theguardian.com/business/2016/feb/02/talktalk-cyberattack-costs-customers-leave

99 BBC News, "TalkTalk fined £400,000 for theft of customer details", 05 October 2016, *See* http://www.bbc.com/news/business-37565367

100 Moscaritolo, A., "NASA sites hacked via SQL injection", SC Media, 07 December 2009, *See* https://www.scmagazine.com/nasa-sites-hacked-via-sql-injection/article/557172/

101 Paganini, P., "Anonymous Hacker breached WTO database and Leaked data of internal staff" [sic], 04 May 2015, *See* http://securityaffairs.co/wordpress/36528/hacking/anonymous-breached-wto-db.html

102 Kirk, J., "SQL injection flaw in Wall Street Journal database led to breach", IDG Communications, 23 July 2014, *See* https://www.pcworld.com/article/2457240/sql-injection-flaw-in-wall-street-journal-database-led-to-breach.html

103 The Code Curmudgeon, ,"SQLi Hall of Shame", *See* http://codecurmudgeon.com/wp/sql-injection-hall-of-shame/

104 Official Journal of the European Union, "Regulation (EU) 2016/679 of the European Parliament and of the Council of 27 April 2016", 04 May 2016, *See* http://ec.europa.eu/justice/data-protection/reform/files/regulation_oj_en.pdf

105 Mulholland, H., "Phone hacking: David Cameron bows to calls for public inquiries", The Guardian, 06 July 2011, *See* https://www.theguardian.com/media/2011/jul/06/david-cameron-phone-hacking-inquiry

106 BBC News, "Who, What, Why: Can phone hackers still access messages?", 06 July 2011, *See* http://www.bbc.com/news/magazine-14044499

107 Tobias, M.W., "It's Too Easy To Hack Voice Mail", Forbes, 25 July 2011, *See* https://www.forbes.com/sites/marcwebertobias/2011/07/25/its-too-easy-to-hack-voice-mail

108 Sony Pictures Entertainment, 08 December 2014, *See* https://oag.ca.gov/system/files/12%2008%2014%20letter_0.pdf

109 United States Computer Emergency Readiness Team, "Alert (TA14-353A): Targeted Destructive Malware", 19 December 2014, updated 30 September 2016, *See* https://www.us-cert.gov/ncas/alerts/TA14-353A

110 Robb, D., "Sony Hack: A Timeline", Deadline, 22 December 2014, *See* http://deadline.com/2014/12/sony-hack-timeline-any-pascal-the-interview-north-korea-1201325501/

111 British Board of Film Classification, "The Interview", 27 January 2015, *See* http://www.bbfc.co.uk/releases/interview-film

112 Federal Bureau of Investigation, "Update on Sony Investigation", 19 December 2014, *See* https://www.fbi.gov/news/pressrel/press-releases/update-on-sony-investigation

113 Associated Press in Seoul, "North Korea: Sony hack a righteous deed but we didn't do it", The Guardian, 07 December 2014, *See* https://www.theguardian.com/world/2014/dec/07/north-korea-sony-hack-a-righteous-deed-but-we-didnt-do-it

114 Vaas, L., "LinkedIn settles class action suit over 2012 unsalted password leak", Sophos, 25 February 2015, *See* https://nakedsecurity.sophos.com/2015/02/25/linkedin-settles-class-action-suit-over-2012-unsalted-password-leak/

115 National Institute of Standards and Technology, "NIST Releases SHA-3 Cryptographic Hash Standard", 05 August 2015, updated 27 November 2017, *See* https://www.nist.gov/news-events/news/2015/08/nist-releases-sha-3-cryptographic-hash-standard

116 Merkle, R.C., "Secrecy, Authentication and Public Key Systems", Stanford Electronic Laboratories, Technical Report No. 1979-1, *See* http://www.merkle.com/papers/Thesis1979.pdf

117 Villanueva, J.C., "How Many Atoms Are There in the Universe?", Universe Today, 30 July 2009, updated 24 December 2015, *See* https://www.universetoday.com/36302/atoms-in-the-universe/

118 Kuliukas, K., "How Rainbow Tables work", 11 December 2006, *See* http://kestas.kuliukas.com/RainbowTables/

119 Percival, C., & Josefsson, S., "The scrypt Password-Based Key Derivation Function", IETF Trust, August 2016, *See* https://tools.ietf.org/html/rfc7914

120 Van Goethem, T., Joosen, W., & Nikiforakis, N., "The Clock is Still Ticking: Timing Attacks in the Modern Web", 22nd ACM Conference on Computer and Communications Security, 12-16 October 2015, *See* https://tom.vg/papers/timing-attacks_ccs2015.pdf

121 Johnson, B., "Sarah Palin vs the hacker", The Telegraph, 27 May 2010, *See* http://www.telegraph.co.uk/news/worldnews/sarah-palin/7750050/Sarah-Palin-vs-the-hacker.html

122 McNamara, P., "Palin e-mail snoop sentenced to a year in custody", IDG Communications, 12 November 2010, updated 30 January 2012, *See* https://www.networkworld.com/article/2227724/security/palin-e-mail-snoop-sentenced-to-a-year-in-custody.html

123 Perlroth, N., "Yahoo Says Hackers Stole Data on 500 Million Users in 2014", The New York Times, 22 September 2016, *See* https://www.nytimes.com/2016/09/23/technology/yahoo-hackers.html

124 Rushe, D., & agencies, "Yahoo says all of its 3bn accounts were affected by 2013 hacking", The Guardian, 03 October 2017, *See* https://www.theguardian.com/technology/2017/oct/03/yahoo-says-all-of-its-3bn-accounts-were-affected-by-2013-hacking

125 Yahoo!, "Yahoo Security Notice December 14, 2016", *See* https://help.yahoo.com/kb/SLN27925.html

126 Chitu, A., "Google Drops Support for Security Questions", 11 December 2014, *See* https://googlesystem.blogspot.de/2014/12/google-drops-support-for-security.html

127 The Telegraph, "Gary McKinnon: timeline of the computer hacker's case", 31 July 2009, *See* http://www.telegraph.co.uk/news/worldnews/northamerica/usa/5945693/Gary-McKinnon-timeline-of-the-computer-hackers-case.html

128 The Telegraph, "Gary McKinnon profile: Autistic 'hacker' who started writing computer programs at 14", 23 January 2009, *See* http://www.telegraph.co.uk/news/worldnews/northamerica/usa/4320901/Gary-McKinnon-profile-Autistic-hacker-who-started-writing-computer-programs-at-14.html

129 Casciani, D., "Gary McKinnon extradition to US blocked by Theresa May", BBC News, 16 October 2012, *See* http://www.bbc.com/news/uk-19957138

130 Warren, P., "Gary was unlucky. He's not even a good hacker", The Independent, 17 October 2012, *See* http://www.independent.co.uk/voices/comment/gary-was-unlucky-hes-not-even-a-good-hacker-8215802.html

131 The White House, "National Security Action Memorandum No. 160", 06 June 1962, *See* https://www.jfklibrary.org/Asset-Viewer/DOwYUab4b0mVeDyLvL58jQ.aspx

132 Blair, B.G., "Keeping Presidents in the Nuclear Dark (Episode #1: The Case of the Missing 'Permissive Action Links')", Center for Defense Information, 11 February 2004, *See* https://web.archive.org/web/20120511191600/http://www.cdi.org/blair/permissive-action-links.cfm

133 Lamothe, D., "Air Force Swears: Our Nuke Launch Code Was Never '00000000'", Foreign Policy, 21 January 2014, *See* https://foreignpolicy.com/2014/01/21/air-force-swears-our-nuke-launch-code-was-never-00000000/

134 Allison, G., "No, America doesn't control Britain's nuclear weapons", UK Defence Journal, 20 July 2017, *See* https://ukdefencejournal.org.uk/no-america-doesnt-control-britains-nuclear-weapons/

135 BBC, "British nukes protected by bicycle lock keys", 15 November 2007, *See* http://www.bbc.co.uk/pressoffice/pressreleases/stories/2007/11_november/15/newsnight.shtml

136 GNUCITIZEN, "Default key algorithm in Thomson and BT Home Hub routers", 14 April 2008, *See* http://www.gnucitizen.org/blog/default-key-algorithm-in-thomson-and-bt-home-hub-routers/

137 Kaps, R., "Voreingestellte WPA-Passphrase bei EasyBox-Routern berechenbar", Heise Online, 16 March 2012, *See* https://www.heise.de/newsticker/meldung/Voreingestellte-WPA-Passphrase-bei-EasyBox-Routern-berechenbar-1473896.html

138 Lee, C-F., Chang, C-H., & Chou, M-K., "Key recognition method and wireless communication system", U.S. Patent 7,894,379, 22 February 2011, *See* https://www.google.com/patents/US7894379

139 German, E., "The History of Fingerprints", updated 30 October 2017, *See* http://onin.com/fp/fphistory.html

140 Knapton, S., "Why your fingerprints may not be unique", The Telegraph, 23 April 2014, *See* http://www.telegraph.co.uk/science/2016/03/14/why-your-fingerprints-may-not-be-unique/

141 Bundesamt für Sicherheit in der Informationstechnik, "Study: 'Evaluation of Fingerprint Recognition Technologies –BioFinger'", 06 August 2004, *See* https://www.bsi.bund.de/SharedDocs/Downloads/EN/BSI/Publications/Studies/BioFinger/BioFinger_pdf.pdf

142 Kent, J., "Malaysia car thieves steal finger", BBC News, 31 March 2005, *See* http://news.bbc.co.uk/2/hi/asia-pacific/4396831.stm

143 Chaos Computer Club, "Fingerabdruck an der Supermarkt-Kasse genauso unsicher wie Biometrie im Reisepass", 27 November 2007, *See* https://www.ccc.de/de/updates/2007/umsonst-im-supermarkt

144 Sammons, B., "Breakthrough 3D fingerprint authentication with Snapdragon Sense ID", Qualcomm, 02 March 2015, *See* https://www.qualcomm.com/news/onq/2015/03/02/breakthrough-3d-fingerprint-authentication-snapdragon-sense-id

145 Morley, K., "British supermarket offers 'finger vein' payment in worldwide first", The Telegraph, 20 September 2017, *See* http://www.telegraph.co.uk/news/2017/09/20/british-supermarket-offers-payment-fingerprint-worldwide-first/

146 Gelb, A., Mukherjee, A., & Diofasi, A., "Iris Recognition: Better than Fingerprints and Falling in Price", Center for Global Development, 01 August 2016, *See* https://www.cgdev.org/blog/iris-recognition-better-and-falling-price

147 Prospector PJ, "Biometric identification: the eyes have it", Royal Pharmaceutical Society, 09 December 2009, *See* http://www.pharmaceutical-journal.com/opinion/blogs/biometric-identification-the-eyes-have-it/10988922.blog

148 International Civil Aviation Organization, "Machine Readable Travel Documents", Seventh Edition, 2015, *See* https://www.icao.int/publications/pages/publication.aspx?docnum=9303

149 Zamost, S., "Exclusive: Man in disguise boards international flight", Cable News Network, 05 November 2010, *See* http://edition.cnn.com/2010/WORLD/americas/11/04/canada.disguised.passenger/index.html

150 Krempl, S., "31C3: CCC-Tüftler hackt Merkels Iris und von der Leyens Fingerabdruck", Heise Online, 28 December 2014, *See* https://www.heise.de/security/meldung/31C3-CCC-Tueftler-hackt-Merkels-Iris-und-von-der-Leyens-Fingerabdruck-2506929.html

151 Jin, Z., Lai, Y-L, Hwang, J.Y., Kim, S., & Teoh, A.B.J., "Ranking Based Locality Sensitive Hashing Enabled Cancelable Biometrics: Index-of-Max Hashing", IEEE Transactions on Information Forensics and Security, Volume 13, Issue: 2, 15 September 2017, *See* http://ieeexplore.ieee.org/document/8038818/

152 Krebs, B., "All About Skimmers", updated 24 June 2016, *See* https://krebsonsecurity.com/all-about-skimmers/

153 Seibel, K., "So knackten Betrüger die Konten der Telekom-Kunden", Die Welt, 21 October 2015, *See* https://www.welt.de/finanzen/verbraucher/article147897210/So-knackten-Betrueger-die-Konten-der-Telekom-Kunden.html

154 RSA, "RSA SecurID Hardware Tokens", *See* https://www.rsa.com/en-us/products/rsa-securid-suite/rsa-securid-access/securid-hardware-tokens.html

155 Jackson, W., "RSA confirms its tokens used in Lockheed hack", GCN, 07 June 2011, *See* https://gcn.com/articles/2011/06/07/rsa-confirms-tokens-used-to-hack-lockheed.aspx

156 Goodin, D., "RSA won't talk? Assume SecurID is broken", The Register, 24 March 2011, *See* https://www.theregister.co.uk/2011/03/24/rsa_securid_news_blackout/

157 Jones. S., & Bechis, U., "EMV Goes Global: The End of an Era for the Magnetic Stripe Payment Card", European Payments Council, 29 October 2012, *See* https://www.europeanpaymentscouncil.eu/news-insights/insight/emv-goes-global-end-era-magnetic-stripe-payment-card

158 Advanced Card Systems, "EMV Specification", 17 December 2013, *See* http://downloads.acs.com.hk/technology/491-08-emv.pdf

159 Focus Online, "mTAN und Chip-TAN – beide Standard, aber nicht gleich sicher", *See* http://www.focus.de/finanzen/banken/tid-34577/betrug-mit-mobilen-transaktionsnummern-welches-online-banking-ist-jetzt-noch-sicher-mtan-und-chiptan-beide-standard-aber-nicht-gleich-sicher_aid_1152951.html

160 Drimer, S., Murdoch, S.J., & Anderson, R., "Optimised to Fail: Card Readers for Online Banking", Springer, International Conference on Financial Cryptography and Data Security, 23-26 February 2009, *See* http://sec.cs.ucl.ac.uk/users/smurdoch/papers/fc09optimised.pdf

161 Roland, M., & Langer, J., "Cloning Credit Cards: A combined pre-play and downgrade attack on EMV Contactless", 7th USENIX Workshop on Offensive Technologies, 13 August 2013, *See* https://www.usenix.org/system/files/conference/woot13/woot13-roland.pdf

162 The Chromium Projects, "Root Certificate Policy", *See* https://www.chromium.org/Home/chromium-security/root-ca-policy

163 Fielding, R., & Reschke, J., "Hypertext Transfer Protocol (HTTP/1.1): Message Syntax and Routing", IETF Trust, June 2014, *See* https://tools.ietf.org/html/rfc7230

164 Markoff, J., "Larger Prey Are Targets of Phishing", The New York Times, 16 April 2008, *See* http://www.nytimes.com/2008/04/16/technology/16whale.html

165 The Linux Foundation, "Let's Encrypt: How It Works", *See* https://letsencrypt.org/how-it-works/

166 Ottow, C., "StartEncrypt considered harmful today", Computest, 30 June 2016, *See* https://www.computest.nl/blog/startencrypt-considered-harmful-today/

167 Cooper, D., Santesson, S., Farrell, S., Boeyen, S., Housley, R., & Polk, W., "Internet X.509 Public Key Infrastructure Certificate and Certificate Revocation List (CRL) Profile", IETF Trust, May 2008, *See* https://tools.ietf.org/html/rfc5280

168 Santesson, S., Myers, M., Ankney, R., Malpani, A., Galperin, S., & Adams, C., "X.509 Internet Public Key Infrastructure Online Certificate Status Protocol – OCSP", IETF Trust, June 2013, *See* https://tools.ietf.org/html/rfc6960

169 Microsoft, "Microsoft Security Bulletin MS01-017 – Critical: Erroneous VeriSign-Issued Digital Certificates Pose Spoofing Hazard", 22 March 2001, updated 23 June 2003, *See* https://technet.microsoft.com/en-us/library/security/ms01-017.aspx

170 Nightingale, J., "DigiNotar Removal Follow Up", Mozilla, 02 September 2011, *See* https://blog.mozilla.org/security/2011/09/02/diginotar-removal-follow-up/

171 The Internet Society, "The Internet Engineering Task Force (IETF)", *See* http://ietf.org/

172 Stephens, A., "IEEE 802.11 Wireless Local Area Networks", IEEE 802.11, *See* http://www.ieee802.org/11/

173 Rekhter, Y., Li, T., & Hares, S., "A Border Gateway Protocol 4 (BGP-4)", The Internet Society, January 2006, *See* https://tools.ietf.org/html/rfc4271

174 Postel, J., "Internet Protocol", Information Sciences Institute, September 1981, *See* https://tools.ietf.org/html/rfc791

175 Ziff Davis, "Definition of: Fraggle attack", *See* https://www.pcmag.com/encyclopedia/term/43462/fraggle-attack

176 Rouse, M., "Definition: ping of death", TechTarget, updated May 2006, *See* http://searchsecurity.techtarget.com/definition/ping-of-death

177 Symantec, "Glossary: Smurf DoS attack", *See*
https://www.symantec.com/security_response/glossary/define.jsp%3Fletter%3Ds%26word%3Dsmurf-dos-attack

178 BBC News, "Anonymous Wikileaks supporters explain web attacks", 10 December 2010, *See*
http://www.bbc.com/news/technology-11971259

179 Postel, J., "Transmission Control Protocol", Information Sciences Institute, September 1981, *See*
https://tools.ietf.org/html/rfc793

180 Phrack, "Loki2 (the implementation)", 01 September 1997, *See*
http://phrack.org/issues/51/6.html

181 Postel, J., "Internet Control Message Protocol", Information Sciences Institute, September 1981,
See https://tools.ietf.org/html/rfc792

182 Bryant, M., "DNS (and ICMP) Tunneling or How to Get Free Wifi at the Airport/Café", 12
March 2013, *See* https://thehackerblog.com/dns-and-icmp-tunneling/index.html

183 Mockapetris, P., "Domain names – Implementation and Specification", Information Sciences
Institute, November 1987, *See* https://tools.ietf.org/html/rfc1035

184 Totti-k3rb3ros, "Routers 2Wire vulnerables a ataques Cross-site request forgery (XSRF) y
Drive-by-pharming", 05 April 2008, *See* http://totti-k3rb3ros.blogspot.de/2008/04/blog-post_05.html

185 Constantin, L., "Attack hijacks DNS settings on home routers in Brazil", IDG Communications,
03 September 2014, *See* https://www.pcworld.com/article/2602040/attack-hijacks-dns-settings-on-home-routers-in-brazil.html

186 Olney, M., Mullen, P., & Miklavcic, K., "Dan Kaminsky's 2008 DNS Vulnerability", Sourcefire,
25 July 2008, *See* https://www.ietf.org/mail-archive/web/dnsop/current/pdf2jgx6rzxN4.pdf

187 Davies, K., "DNS Cache Poisoning Vulnerability: Explanation and Remedies", Internet
Corporation for Assigned Names & Numbers, October 2008, *See*
https://www.iana.org/about/presentations/davies-viareggio-entropyvuln-081002.pdf

188 Arends, R., Austein, R., Larson, M., Massey, D., & Rose, S., "DNS Security Introduction and
Requirements", The Internet Society, March 2005, *See* https://tools.ietf.org/html/rfc4033

189 The Internet Society, "DNSSEC Statistics", *See*
https://www.internetsociety.org/deploy360/dnssec/statistics/

190 Microsoft Support, "How to Disable Client-Side DNS Caching in Windows XP and Windows
Server 2003", updated 07 January 2017, *See* https://support.microsoft.com/en-us/help/318803/how-to-disable-client-side-dns-caching-in-windows-xp-and-windows-serve

191 Schneier, B., "The Storm Worm", 04 October 2007, updated 24 October 2007, *See*
https://www.schneier.com/blog/archives/2007/10/the_storm_worm.html

192 BBC, "I live outside the UK. Can I use BBC iPlayer?", *See*
https://www.bbc.co.uk/iplayer/help/outsideuk

193 Revoir, P., "BBC iPlayer 'watched by more than 60 million people outside the UK for free'",
The Guardian, 21 July 2015, *See* https://www.theguardian.com/media/2015/jul/21/bbc-iplayer-uk-vpn-proxy-server

194 Office for National Statistics, "Population Estimates for UK, England and Wales, Scotland and
Northern Ireland: mid-2015", 23 June 2016, *See*
https://www.ons.gov.uk/peoplepopulationandcommunity/populationandmigration/populationestimates/bulletins/annualmidyearpopulationestimates/mid2015

195 Orphanides, K.G., "BBC blocks international iPlayer viewers ahead of US launch", Wired, 20
October 2015, updated 20 October 2015, *See* http://www.wired.co.uk/article/bbc-iplayer-vpn-access

196 Stevens, D.R., "Best BBC iPlayer VPN 2017 – What to Do if Your BBC VPN is Not
Working", Secure Thoughts, 16 April 2017, updated 01 October 2017, *See*
https://securethoughts.com/best-bbc-iplayer-vpn/

197 Bletchley Park Trust, "Low Level Codes and Ciphers", *See* https://bletchleypark.org.uk/our-story/the-challenge/low-level-codes-and-ciphers

198 Schmeh, K., "Interview with Bart Wessel: The traffic analysis methods developed in WW2 are still valid today", Konradin Medien, 30 September 2016, *See* http://scienceblogs.de/klausis-krypto-kolumne/2016/09/30/interview-with-bart-wessel-the-traffic-analysis-methods-developed-in-ww2-are-still-valid-today/

199 Martin, A.J., "Bletchley Park remembers 'forgotten genius' Gordon Welchman", The Register, 27 September 2015, *See* http://www.theregister.co.uk/2015/09/27/gordan_welchman_bletchley_park_remembers/

200 Reed, M.G., Syverson, P.F., & Goldschlag, D.M., "Onion routing network for securely moving data through communication networks", U.S. Patent 6,266,704, 24 July 2001, *See* https://www.google.com/patents/US6266704

201 Dingledine, R., & Mathewson, N., "Tor Protocol Specification", The Tor Project, 07 March 2003, updated 20 September 2017, *See* https://gitweb.torproject.org/torspec.git/tree/tor-spec.txt

202 The Tor Project, "Tor: Sponsors", *See* https://www.torproject.org/about/sponsors.html.en

203 Reed, M., "Iran cracks down on web dissident technology", The Tor Project, 22 March 2011, *See* https://lists.torproject.org/pipermail/tor-talk/2011-March/019913.html

204 Neary, L., "Real 'Sybil' Admits Multiple Personalities Were Fake", National Public Radio, 20 October 2011, *See* http://www.npr.org/2011/10/20/141514464/real-sybil-admits-multiple-personalities-were-fake

205 Dingledine, R., Mathewson, N., Murdoch, S., & Syverson, P., "Tor: The Second-Generation Onion Router (2014 DRAFT v1)", *See* http://sec.cs.ucl.ac.uk/users/smurdoch/papers/tor14design.pdf

206 The Tor Project, "What are Entry Guards?", *See* https://www.torproject.org/docs/faq.html.en#EntryGuards

207 Leyden, J., "The 'one tiny slip' that put LulzSec chief Sabu in the FBI's pocket", The Register, 07 March 2012, *See* https://www.theregister.co.uk/2012/03/07/lulzsec_takedown_analysis/

208 The Tor Project, "Want Tor to really work?", *See* https://www.torproject.org/download/download.html.en

209 Perry, M., Clark, E., Murdoch, S., & Koppen, G., "The Design and Implementation of the Tor Browser [DRAFT]", The Tor Project, 10 March 2017, *See* https://www.torproject.org/projects/torbrowser/design/

210 Chen, W., "Here's that FBI Firefox Exploit for You (CVE-2013-1690)", Rapid7, 07 August 2013, *See* https://blog.rapid7.com/2013/08/07/heres-that-fbi-firefox-exploit-for-you-cve-2013-1690/

211 Vitáris, B., "Firefox Zero-Day Can Be Used to Deanonymize Tor Users", DeepDotWeb, 11 December 2016, *See* https://www.deepdotweb.com/2016/12/11/firefox-zero-day-can-used-deanonymize-tor-users/

212 Appelbaum, J., Gibson, A., Goetz, J., Kabisch, V., Kampf, L., & Ryge, L., "NSA targets the privacy-conscious", ARD, 03 July 2014, *See* http://daserste.ndr.de/panorama/aktuell/nsa230_page-1.html

213 Cavna, M., "'NOBODY KNOWS YOU'RE A DOG': As iconic Internet cartoon turns 20, creator Peter Steiner knows the joke rings as relevant as ever", The Washington Post, 31 July 2013, *See* https://www.washingtonpost.com/blogs/comic-riffs/post/nobody-knows-youre-a-dog-as-iconic-internet-cartoon-turns-20-creator-peter-steiner-knows-the-joke-rings-as-relevant-as-ever/2013/07/31/73372600-f98d-11e2-8e84-c56731a202fb_blog.html

214 Department of Homeland Security and Federal Bureau of Investigation, "GRIZZLY STEPPE – Russian Malicious Cyber Activity", 29 December 2016, *See* https://www.us-cert.gov/sites/default/files/publications/JAR_16-20296A_GRIZZLY%20STEPPE-2016-1229.pdf

215 RT America, "McAfee breaks down inconsistencies in FBI's Grizzly Steppe report", 05 January 2017, *See* https://www.youtube.com/watch?v=C2jD4SF9gFE

216 Lee, R.M., "Critiques of the DHS/FBI's GRIZZLY STEPPE Report", 30 December 2016, *See* http://www.robertmlee.org/critiques-of-the-dhsfbis-grizzly-steppe-report/

217 Office of the Director of National Intelligence, "Background to 'Assessing Russian Activities and Intentions in Recent US Elections': The Analytic Process and Cyber Incident Attribution", 06 January 2017, *See* https://www.dni.gov/files/documents/ICA_2017_01.pdf

218 Alperovitch, D., "Bears in the Midst: Intrusion into the Democratic National Committee", CrowdStrike, 15 June 2016, *See* https://www.crowdstrike.com/blog/bears-midst-intrusion-democratic-national-committee/

219 Department of Homeland Security, "Enhanced Analysis of GRIZZLY STEPPE Activity", 10 February 2017, *See* https://www.us-cert.gov/sites/default/files/publications/AR-17-20045_Enhanced_Analysis_of_GRIZZLY_STEPPE_Activity.pdf

220 The Tor Project, "Tor Browser: add DuckDuckGo hidden service into default search engines list", 11 May 2014, updated 13 January 2016, *See* https://trac.torproject.org/projects/tor/ticket/11884

221 The Tor Project, "Tor security advisory: 'relay early' traffic confirmation attack", 30 July 2014, *See* https://blog.torproject.org/tor-security-advisory-relay-early-traffic-confirmation-attack

222 Sanatinia, A, & Noubir, G., "HOnions: Towards Detection and Identification of Misbehaving Tor HSDirs", Security & Privacy Week 2016, Darmstadt, Germany, 18-22 July 2016, *See* https://www.securityweek2016.tu darmstadt.de/fileadmin/user_upload/Group_securityweek2016/pets2016/10_honions-sanatinia.pdf

223 Nakamoto, S., "Bitcoin: A Peer-to-Peer Electronic Cash System", 31 October 2008, *See* https://bitcoin.org/bitcoin.pdf

224 Sihvart, M., "Blockchain – security control for government registers", e-estonia, August 2017, *See* https://e-estonia.com/blockchain-security-control-for-government-registers/

225 O'Dwyer, K.J., & Malone, D., "Bitcoin Mining and its Energy Footprint", The Institution of Engineering and Technology, 25th IET Irish Signals & Systems Conference 2014 and 2014 China-Ireland International Conference on Information and Communities Technologies, 26-27 June 2014, *See* https://www.researchgate.net/publication/271467748_Bitcoin_Mining_and_its_Energy_Footprint

226 Coin ATM Radar, "Bitcoin ATM map", *See* https://coinatmradar.com/

227 Coindesk, "Bitcoin (USD) Price", *See* https://www.coindesk.com/price/

228 Gough, N., "Bitcoin Value Sinks After Chinese Exchange Move", The New York Times, 18 December 2013, *See* http://www.nytimes.com/2013/12/19/business/international/china-bitcoin-exchange-ends-renminbi-deposits.html

229 Apostolaki, E., Zohar, A., & Vanbever, L., "Hijacking Bitcoin: Routing Attacks on Cryptocurrencies", 2017 IEEE Symposium on Security and Privacy, 24 March 2017, *See* https://arxiv.org/pdf/1605.07524v2.pdf

230 Wood, G., "Ethereum: A Secure Decentralised Generalised Transaction Ledger: EIP-150 Revision", January 2014, *See* http://gavwood.com/paper.pdf

231 Ben-Sasson, E., Chiesa, A., Garman, C., Green, M., Miers, I., Tromer, E., & Virza, M., "Zerocash: Decentralized Anonymous Payments from Bitcoin", 18 May 2014, *See* http://zerocash-project.org/media/pdf/zerocash-extended-20140518.pdf

232 CoinMarketCap, "Cryptocurrency Market Capitalizations", *See* https://coinmarketcap.com/all/views/all/

233 Robinson, M., "The eBay for drugs: 'Silk Road' website allows UK drug users to buy cocaine and heroin by mail order from all over the world", Mail Online, 19 November 2012, *See* http://www.dailymail.co.uk/news/article-2235199/The-eBay-drugs-Silk-Road-website-allows-drug-users-buy-heroin-cannabis-mail-order-world.html

234 BBC News, "FBI arrests Silk Road drugs site suspect", 02 October 2013, *See* http://www.bbc.com/news/technology-24373759

235 Lee, D., "Silk Road: How FBI closed in on suspect Ross Ulbricht", BBC News, 02 October 2013, *See* http://www.bbc.com/news/technology-24371894

236 Hern, A., "Five stupid things Dread Pirate Roberts did to get arrested", The Guardian, 03 October 2013, *See* https://www.theguardian.com/technology/2013/oct/03/five-stupid-things-dread-pirate-roberts-did-to-get-arrested

237 Hamilton, G., "Lavish life of dead Canadian multimillionaire — and accused cybercriminal — revealed", National Post, 20 July 2017, *See* http://nationalpost.com/news/canada/u-s-authorities-identify-dead-canadian-as-creator-of-dark-web-site-alphabay

238 Murdoch, L., "Death penalty call for accused Australian child sex predator Peter Scully in Philippines", The Sydney Morning Herald, 20 September 2016, *See* http://www.smh.com.au/world/death-penalty-call-for-accused-australian-child-sex-predator-peter-scully-in-philippines-20160920-grk65r.html

239 The Tor Project, "Abuse FAQ", *See* https://www.torproject.org/docs/faq-abuse.html.en

240 The Tor Project, "Tor FAQ", *See* https://www.torproject.org/docs/faq.html.en#BlockContent

241 Sophos, "Facebook users worldwide (minus some mobile phones) now getting secure web browsing by default", 02 August 2013, *See* https://nakedsecurity.sophos.com/2013/08/02/facebook-users-worldwide-minus-some-mobile-phones-now-getting-secure-web-browsing-by-default/

242 Frickel, C, "Spionage-Apps manipulieren Facebook-Einträge", Focus Online, 15 March 2012, *See* http://www.focus.de/digital/internet/j-spionage-apps-manipulieren-facebook-eintraege_aid_724385.html

243 Infosec Institute, "From Turbine to Quantum: Implants in the Arsenal of the NSA", 24 March 2014, *See* http://resources.infosecinstitute.com/turbine-quantum-implants-arsenal-nsa/

244 Larson, J., Angwin, J., Moltke, H., & Poitras, L., "A Trail of Evidence Leading to AT&T's Partnership with the NSA", ProPublica, 15 August 2015, *See* https://www.propublica.org/article/a-trail-of-evidence-leading-to-atts-partnership-with-the-nsa

245 Gallagher, R., & Greenwald, G., "How the NSA Plans to Infect 'Millions' of Computers with Malware", The Intercept, 12 March 2014, *See* https://theintercept.com/2014/03/12/nsa-plans-infect-millions-computers-malware/

246 Weston, G., Greenwald, G., & Gallagher, R., "CSEC used airport Wi-Fi to track Canadian travellers: Edward Snowden documents", CBC News, 30 January 2014, *See* http://www.cbc.ca/news/politics/csec-used-airport-wi-fi-to-track-canadian-travellers-edward-snowden-documents-1.2517881

247 Microsoft, "How and why to use random hardware addresses", updated 20 November 2017, *See* https://support.microsoft.com/en-us/help/4027925/windows-how-and-why-to-use-random-hardware-addresses

248 Rekhter, Y., Moskowitz, B., Karrenberg, D., de Groot, G.J., & Lear, E., "Address Allocation for Private Internets", The Internet Society, February 1996, *See* https://tools.ietf.org/html/rfc1918

249 Flynn, L.J., "Drumming Up More Addresses on the Internet", The New York Times, 14 February 2011, *See* http://www.nytimes.com/2011/02/15/technology/15internet.html

250 Nortel Networks Inc., et al. v. Debtors, Delaware Bankruptcy Court 1:09-bk-10138, plan confirmed 24 January 2017, *See* http://domainincite.com/docs/nortel-ipv4-sale.pdf

251 "Internet Census 2012", *See* http://internetcensus2012.github.io/InternetCensus2012/paper.html

252 Deering, S., & Hinden, R., "Internet Protocol, Version 6 (IPv6): Specification", The Internet Society, December 1998, *See* https://tools.ietf.org/html/rfc2460

253 Hinden, R., & Deering, S., "IP Version 6 Addressing Architecture", The Internet Society, July 1998, *See* https://tools.ietf.org/html/rfc2373

254 Narten, T., Draves, R., & Krishnan, S., "Privacy Extensions for Stateless Address Autoconfiguration in IPv6", IETF Trust, September 2007, *See* https://tools.ietf.org/html/rfc4941

255 Bennett, C.H., & Brassard, G., "Quantum Cryptography: Public Key Distribution and Coin Tossing", IEEE International Conference on Computers, Signals & Signal Processing, 10-12 December 1984, *See* https://ars.els-cdn.com/content/image/1-s2.0-S0304397514004241-mmc1.pdf

256 Marks, P, "Quantum cryptography to protect Swiss election", New Scientist, 15 October 2007, *See* https://www.newscientist.com/article/dn12786-quantum-cryptography-to-protect-swiss-election/

257 Allison, P.R., "The next stage in quantum key distribution", TechTarget, December 2015, *See* http://www.computerweekly.com/feature/The-next-stage-in-quantum-key-distribution

258 Brassard, G., Lütkenhaus, N., Mor. T., & Sanders, B., "Security Aspects of Practical Quantum Cryptography", American Physical Society, Physical review letters 85, 12 November 1999, updated 01 February 2008, *See* https://www.researchgate.net/publication/12330710_Limitations_on_Practical_Quantum_Cryptography

259 Lydersen, L., Wiechers, C., Wittmann, C., Elser, D., Skaar, J., & Makarov, V., "Hacking commercial quantum cryptography systems by tailored bright illumination", Nature, 29 August 2010, *See* https://www.nature.com/articles/nphoton.2010.214

260 Schneier, B., „COTTONMOUTH-I: NSA Exploit of the Day", 05 March 2014, *See* https://www.schneier.com/blog/archives/2014/03/cottonmouth-i_n.html

261 Kuhn, M.G., & Anderson, R.J., "Soft Tempest: Hidden Data Transmission Using Electromagnetic Emanations", Springer, International Workshop on Information Hiding, 14-17 April 1998, *See* https://www.cl.cam.ac.uk/~mgk25/ih98-tempest.pdf

262 SANS Institute, "An Introduction to TEMPEST", *See* https://www.sans.org/reading-room/whitepapers/privacy/introduction-tempest-981

263 van Eck, W., "Electromagnetic radiation from video display units: An eavesdropping risk?", Elsevier, Computers & Security Volume 4 Issue 4, December 1985, *See* http://www.sciencedirect.com/science/article/pii/016740488590046X

264 Kuhn, M.G., "Compromising emanations: eavesdropping risks of computer displays", University of Cambridge, December 2003, *See* http://www.cl.cam.ac.uk/techreports/UCAM-CL-TR-577.pdf

265 Vuagnoux, M., & Pasini, S., "Compromising Electromagnetic Emanations of Wired and Wireless Keyboards", 18th USENIX Security Symposium, 10-14 August 2009, *See* https://www.usenix.org/legacy/event/sec09/tech/full_papers/vuagnoux.pdf

266 Barrett, D., & Samuel, H., "Calais migrants find the door to Britain wide open", The Telegraph, 07 August 2015, *See* http://www.telegraph.co.uk/news/uknews/immigration/11791237/calais-migrants-open-secret-channel-tunnel-door-to-britain.html

267 Tischer, M, Durumeric, Z., Foster, S., Duan, S., Mori, A., Bursztein, E., & Bailey, M., "Users Really Do Plug in USB Drives They Find", IEEE Symposium on Security and Privacy, 23-26 May 2016, *See* https://www.elie.net/static/files/users-really-do-plug-in-usb-drives-they-find/users-really-do-plug-in-usb-drives-they-find-paper.pdf

268 Bisson, D., "Business Email Compromise Scams Have Cost Victims $3B, Reports FBI", Tripwire, 17 June 2016, *See* https://www.tripwire.com/state-of-security/latest-security-news/business-email-compromise-scams-have-cost-victims-3b-report-feds/

269 Handel, S., "Buchhalterin der Hofpfisterei überweist 1,9 Millionen Euro an Trickbetrüger", Süddeutsche Zeitung, 14 July 2017, *See* http://www.sueddeutsche.de/muenchen/prozess-buchhalterin-der-hofpfisterei-ueberweist-millionen-euro-an-trickbetrueger-1.3586564

270 Lemon Retro Store Forum, "'Singing' 1541 floppy drive?", 16 March 2011, updated 23 March 2011, *See* http://www.lemon64.com/forum/viewtopic.php?t=37208&sid=e28fe8b23eb1ae844c4234ed215330d8

271 BGB Homepage, "Pan Docs", updated October 2001, *See* http://bgb.bircd.org/pandocs.htm#lcdcontrolregister

272 Prince, B., "Sophisticated Stuxnet Worm Uses 4 Microsoft Zero-Day Bugs", eWeek, 14 September 2010, *See* http://www.eweek.com/security/sophisticated-stuxnet-worm-uses-4-microsoft-zero-day-bugs

273 Nakashima, E., & Warrick, J., "Stuxnet was work of U.S. and Israeli experts, officials say", The Washington Post, 01 June 2012, *See* https://www.washingtonpost.com/world/national-security/stuxnet-was-work-of-us-and-israeli-experts-officials-say/2012/06/01/gJQAlnEy6U_story.html?utm_term=.40a9408ee6c8

274 Terdiman, D., "Stuxnet delivered to Iranian nuclear plant on thumb drive", CNET, 12 April 2012, *See* https://www.cnet.com/news/stuxnet-delivered-to-iranian-nuclear-plant-on-thumb-drive/

275 Finkle, J., "Researchers say Stuxnet was deployed against Iran in 2007", Reuters, 26 February 2013, *See* https://www.reuters.com/article/us-cyberwar-stuxnet/researchers-say-stuxnet-was-deployed-against-iran-in-2007-idUSBRE91P0PP20130226

276 Kaspersky, E., "The Man Who Found Stuxnet – Sergey Ulasen in the Spotlight", 2 November 2011, *See* https://eugene.kaspersky.com/2011/11/02/the-man-who-found-stuxnet-sergey-ulasen-in-the-spotlight/

277 Sanger, D. E., "Obama Order Sped Up Wave of Cyberattacks Against Iran", The New York Times, 01 June 2012, *See* http://www.nytimes.com/2012/06/01/world/middleeast/obama-ordered-wave-of-cyberattacks-against-iran.html

278 Rashid, A., & La Guardia, A., "I've sold nuclear secrets to Libya, Iran and N Korea", The Telegraph, 03 February 2004, *See* http://www.telegraph.co.uk/news/worldnews/asia/pakistan/1453353/Ive-sold-nuclear-secrets-to-Libya-Iran-and-N-Korea.html

279 Menn, J., "Exclusive: U.S. tried Stuxnet-style campaign against North Korea but failed – sources", Reuters, 29 May 2015, *See* https://www.reuters.com/article/us-usa-northkorea-stuxnet/exclusive-u-s-tried-stuxnet-style-campaign-against-north-korea-but-failed-sources-idUSKBN0OE2DM20150529

280 Topham, G., "For BA, a £100m compensation bill could be just the start", The Guardian, 03 June 2017, *See* https://www.theguardian.com/business/2017/jun/03/ba-compendsation-bill-could-be-just-start-it-failure-iag

281 Zetter, K., "Inside the Cunning, Unprecedented Hack of Ukraine's Power Grid", Wired, 03 March 2016, *See* https://www.wired.com/2016/03/inside-cunning-unprecedented-hack-ukraines-power-grid/

282 Riley, M., Dlouhy, J.A., & Gruley, B., "Russians Are Suspects in Nuclear Site Hackings, Sources Say", Bloomberg, 07 July 2017, *See* https://www.bloomberg.com/news/articles/2017-07-07/russians-are-said-to-be-suspects-in-hacks-involving-nuclear-site

283 Zeller, M., "Common Questions and Answers Addressing the Aurora Vulnerability", Schweitzer Engineering Laboratories, DistribuTECH Conference, 01-03 February 2011, *See* https://cdn.selinc.com/assets/Literature/Publications/Technical%20Papers/6467_CommonQuestions_MZ_20101209_Web.pdf

284 World Nuclear Association, "Fukushima Accident", updated October 2017, *See* http://www.world-nuclear.org/information-library/safety-and-security/safety-of-plants/fukushima-accident.aspx

285 Conca, J., "Is Hacking Nuclear Power Plants Something We Should Be Afraid Of?", Forbes, 07 July 2017, *See* https://www.forbes.com/sites/jamesconca/2017/07/07/is-hacking-nuclear-power-plants-something-we-should-be-afraid-of

286 Himmelsbach, V., "Nuclear plant powers up on real-time OS", ITBUSINESS.CA, 04 October 2006, *See* https://www.itbusiness.ca/news/nuclear-plant-powers-up-on-real-time-os

287 Chandler, D., "Benoit Forget: Unraveling complexities of nuclear reactors", Massachusetts Institute of Technology, 03 October 2016, *See* http://news.mit.edu/2016/benoit-forget-complexities-nuclear-reactors-1003

288 Cirincione, J., "What happens when our nuclear arsenal is hacked?", San Francisco Chronicle, 17 June 2015, *See* http://www.sfchronicle.com/opinion/openforum/article/What-happens-when-our-nuclear-arsenal-is-hacked-6333739.php

289 Broad, W.J., & Sanger, D.E., "U.S. Strategy to Hobble North Korea Was Hidden in Plain Sight", The New York Times, 04 March 2017, *See* https://www.nytimes.com/2017/03/04/world/asia/left-of-launch-missile-defense.html

290 The National Security Archive, "The 3 A.M. Phone Call", 01 March 2012, *See* http://nsarchive2.gwu.edu/nukevault/ebb371/

291 Askenov, P., "Stanislav Petrov: The man who may have saved the world", BBC News, 26 September 2013, *See* http://www.bbc.com/news/world-europe-24280831

292 Zuckerman, L., "That 'zombie apocalypse' warning in Montana? It was fake", Reuters, 12 February 2013, *See* http://www.reuters.com/article/us-usa-zombie-montana/that-zombie-apocalypse-warning-in-montana-it-was-fake-idUSBRE91B1IA20130212

293 Khan, S., "Pakistan's indirect role in North Korea's nuclear program", Deutsche Welle, 14 September 2017, *See* http://www.dw.com/en/pakistans-indirect-role-in-north-koreas-nuclear-program/a-40507693

294 Gutteridge, N., "ISIS to unleash TENS OF MILLIONS of jihadi hackers on West in blitz worse than NUCLEAR WAR", Daily Express, 17 December 2015, *See* http://www.express.co.uk/news/world/627486/Islamic-State-ISIS-jihadis-hackers-cyber-war-US-Britain-president-hopeful-John-McAfee

295 Merrick, R., "Theresa May would fire UK's nuclear weapons as a 'first strike', says Defence Secretary Michael Fallon", The Independent, 24 April 2017, *See* http://www.independent.co.uk/news/uk/politics/theresa-may-nuclear-weapons-first-strike-michael-fallon-general-election-jeremy-corbyn-trident-a7698621.html

296 Cooper, H., "Air Force Fires 9 Officers in Scandal Over Cheating on Proficiency Tests", The New York Times, 27 March 2014, *See* https://www.nytimes.com/2014/03/28/us/air-force-fires-9-officers-accused-in-cheating-scandal.html

297 Kristensen, H.M., & Norris, R.S., "Status of World Nuclear Forces", Federation of American Scientists, 2017, *See* https://fas.org/issues/nuclear-weapons/status-world-nuclear-forces/

298 Goodin, D., "NSA-leaking Shadow Brokers just dumped its most damaging release yet", Condé Nast, 14 April 2017, *See* https://arstechnica.com/information-technology/2017/04/nsa-leaking-shadow-brokers-just-dumped-its-most-damaging-release-yet/

299 Fox-Brewster, T., "Edward Snowden: Russia Is Chief Suspect In NSA Hack", Forbes, 16 August 2016, *See* https://www.forbes.com/sites/thomasbrewster/2016/08/16/edward-snowden-russia-nsa-hacked

300 Risk Based Security, "The Shadow Brokers: Lifting the Shadows of the NSA's Equation Group?", 15 August 2016, *See* https://www.riskbasedsecurity.com/2016/08/the-shadow-brokers-lifting-the-shadows-of-the-nsas-equation-group/

301 Smith, B., "The need for urgent collective action to keep people safe online: Lessons from last week's cyberattack", Microsoft, 14 May 2017, *See* https://blogs.microsoft.com/on-the-issues/2017/05/14/need-urgent-collective-action-keep-people-safe-online-lessons-last-weeks-cyberattack/

302 Goodin, D., "Mysterious Microsoft patch killed 0-days released by NSA-leaking Shadow Brokers", Condé Nast, 15 April 2017, *See* https://arstechnica.com/information-technology/2017/04/purported-shadow-brokers-0days-were-in-fact-killed-by-mysterious-patch/

303 Samani, R., Beek, C., & McFarland, C., "An Analysis of the WannaCry Ransomware Outbreak", McAfee, 12 May 2017, *See* https://securingtomorrow.mcafee.com/executive-perspectives/analysis-wannacry-ransomware-outbreak/

304 BBC News, "Massive ransomware infection hits computers in 99 countries", 13 May 2017, *See* http://www.bbc.com/news/technology-39901382

305 Sawer, P., Mendick, R., Walter, S., & Harley, N., "NHS cyber chaos hits thousands of patients", The Telegraph, 13 May 2017, *See* http://www.telegraph.co.uk/news/2017/05/13/nhs-cyber-chaos-hits-thousands-patients/

306 Nakashima, E., "The NSA has linked the WannaCry computer worm to North Korea", 14 June 2017, The Washington Post, *See* https://www.washingtonpost.com/world/national-security/the-nsa-has-linked-the-wannacry-computer-worm-to-north-korea/2017/06/14/101395a2-508e-11e7-be25-3a519335381c_story.html?utm_term=.2082f8974a50

307 Symantec, "WannaCry: Ransomware attacks show strong links to Lazarus group", 22 May 2017, *See* https://www.symantec.com/connect/blogs/wannacry-ransomware-attacks-show-strong-links-lazarus-group

308 Pearce, M., "Their code was used to hack Sony and create 'WannaCry.' Meet the 'Lazarus Group,' the armed robbers of the Internet", Los Angeles Times, 18 May 2017, *See* http://www.latimes.com/nation/la-fg-lazarus-group-20170518-story.html

309 Symantec, "Ransom.Wannacry", 12 May 2017, updated 24 May 2017, *See* https://www.symantec.com/security_response/writeup.jsp?docid=2017-051310-3522-99

310 Gibbs, S., "WannaCry: hackers withdraw £108,000 of bitcoin ransom", The Guardian, 03 August 2017, *See* https://www.theguardian.com/technology/2017/aug/03/wannacry-hackers-withdraw-108000-pounds-bitcoin-ransom

311 Greenberg, A., "A WannaCry Flaw Could Help Some Victims Get Files Back", Wired, 18 May 2017, *See* https://www.wired.com/2017/05/wannacry-flaw-help-windows-xp-victims-get-files-back/

312 Goodin, D., "More people infected by recent WCry worm can unlock PCs without paying ransom", Condé Nast, 19 May 2017, *See* https://arstechnica.com/information-technology/2017/05/more-people-infected-by-recent-wcry-worm-can-unlock-pcs-without-paying-ransom/

313 McGoogan, C., Field. M., & Ward, V., "WannaCry hero Marcus Hutchins could face 40 years in US prison", The Telegraph, 04 August 2017, *See* http://www.telegraph.co.uk/technology/2017/08/03/fbi-arrests-wannacry-hero-marcus-hutchins-las-vegas-reports/

314 Malware Tech, "How to Accidentally Stop a Global Cyber Attacks" [sic], 13 May 2017, *See* https://www.malwaretech.com/2017/05/how-to-accidentally-stop-a-global-cyber-attacks.html

315 Gibbs, S., "WannaCry hackers still trying to revive attack says accidental hero", The Guardian, 22 May 2017, *See* https://www.theguardian.com/technology/2017/may/22/wannacry-hackers-ransomware-attack-kill-switch-windows-xp-7-nhs-accidental-hero-marcus-hutchins

316 Smith, A., Smith, S., Bailey, N., & Cahill, P, "Why 'WannaCry' Malware Caused Chaos for National Health Service in U.K.", NBC News, 17 May 2017, *See* https://www.nbcnews.com/news/world/why-wannacry-malware-caused-chaos-national-health-service-u-k-n760126

317 Boyle, D., & Farmer, B., "HMS Queen Elizabeth is 'running outdated Windows XP', raising cyber attack fears", The Telegraph, 27 June 2017, *See* http://www.telegraph.co.uk/news/2017/06/27/hms-queen-elizabeth-running-outdated-windows-xp-software-raising/

318 Abrams, L., "Petya and Mischa Ransomware Affiliate System Publicly Released", Bleeping Computer, 26 July 2016, *See* https://www.bleepingcomputer.com/news/security/petya-and-mischa-ransomware-affiliate-system-publicly-released/

319 Symantec, "Petya ransomware outbreak: Here's what you need to know", 24 October 2017, *See* https://www.symantec.com/connect/blogs/petya-ransomware-outbreak-here-s-what-you-need-know

320 Ivanov, A., & Mamedov, O., "ExPetr/Petya/NotPetya is a Wiper, Not Ransomware", Kaspersky Lab, 28 June 2017, *See* https://securelist.com/expetrpetyanotpetya-is-a-wiper-not-ransomware/78902/

321 Hern, A., "Ransomware attack 'not designed to make money', researchers claim", The Guardian, 28 June 2017, *See* https://www.theguardian.com/technology/2017/jun/28/notpetya-ransomware-attack-ukraine-russia

322 Goodin, D., "Backdoor built in to widely used tax app seeded last week's NotPetya outbreak", Condé Nast, 05 July 2017, *See* https://arstechnica.com/information-technology/2017/07/heavily-armed-police-raid-company-that-seeded-last-weeks-notpetya-outbreak/

323 Wakefield, J., "Tax software blamed for cyber-attack spread", BBC News, 28 June 2017, *See* http://www.bbc.com/news/technology-40428967

324 Dearden, L., "Ukraine cyber attack: Chaos as national bank, state power provider and airport hit by hackers", The Independent, 27 June 2017, *See* http://www.independent.co.uk/news/world/europe/ukraine-cyber-attack-hackers-national-bank-state-power-company-airport-rozenko-pavlo-cabinet-a7810471.html

325 Lépine, J., "HAPIfork", HAPILABS, *See* https://www.hapi.com/product/hapifork

326 Woolf, N., "DDoS attack that disrupted internet was largest of its kind in history, experts say", The Guardian, 26 October 2016, *See* https://www.theguardian.com/technology/2016/oct/26/ddos-attack-dyn-mirai-botnet

327 Symantec, "Mirai: what you need to know about the botnet behind recent major DDoS attacks", 27 October 2016, *See* https://www.symantec.com/connect/blogs/mirai-what-you-need-know-about-botnet-behind-recent-major-ddos-attacks

328 Franceschi-Bicchierai, L., "Hackers Make the First-Ever Ransomware for Smart Thermostats", Vice Media, 07 August 2016, *See* https://motherboard.vice.com/en_us/article/aekj9j/internet-of-things-ransomware-smart-thermostat

329 Bluetooth, "Our History", *See* https://www.bluetooth.com/about-us/our-history

330 My Friend Cayla, "Frequently Asked Questions", 2014, *See* http://myfriendcayla.co.uk/help

331 BBC News, "What did she say?! Talking doll Cayla is hacked", 30 January 2015, *See* http://www.bbc.com/news/av/technology-31059893/what-did-she-say-talking-doll-cayla-is-hacked

332 Bundesnetzagentur, "Bundesnetzagentur zieht Kinderpuppe 'Cayla' aus dem Verkehr", 17 February 2017, *See* https://www.bundesnetzagentur.de/SharedDocs/Pressemitteilungen/DE/2017/14012017_cayla.html

333 Stanislav, M., & Beardsley, T., "HACKING IoT: A Case Study on Baby Monitor Exposures and Vulnerabilities", Rapid7, updated 29 September 2015, *See* https://www.rapid7.com/docs/Hacking-IoT-A-Case-Study-on-Baby-Monitor-Exposures-and-Vulnerabilities.pdf

334 Shane, S., Rosenberg, M., & Lehren, A.W., "WikiLeaks Releases Trove of Alleged C.I.A. Hacking Documents", The New York Times, 07 March 2017, *See* https://www.nytimes.com/2017/03/07/world/europe/wikileaks-cia-hacking.html

335 Smith, R., "WikiLeaks Vault 7: How to stop the CIA from hacking your TV with Weeping Angel", Daily Express, 08 March 2017, *See* http://www.express.co.uk/life-style/science-technology/776500/wikileaks-vault-7-cia-samsung-smart-tv-hack-weeping-angel-how-to-stop

336 ADAC, "Fahrzeuge mit Keyless leichter zu klauen", updated 16 October 2017, *See* https://www.adac.de/infotestrat/technik-und-zubehoer/fahrerassistenzsysteme/keyless/default.aspx

337 Garcia, F.D., Oswald, D., Kasper, T., & Pavlidès, P, "Lock It and Still Lose It—On the (In)Security of Automotive Remote Keyless Entry Systems", 25th USENIX Security Symposium, 10-12 August 2016, *See* https://www.usenix.org/system/files/conference/usenixsecurity16/sec16_paper_garcia.pdf

338 Greenberg, A., "The Jeep Hackers Are Back to Prove Car Hacking Can Get Much Worse", Wired, 01 August 2016, *See* https://www.wired.com/2016/08/jeep-hackers-return-high-speed-steering-acceleration-hacks/

339 Leiner, B.M., Cerf, V.G., Clark, D.D., Kahn, R.E., Kleinrock, L., Lynch, D.C., Postel, J., Roberts, L.G., & Wolff, S., "Brief History of the Internet", 1997, *See* https://www.internetsociety.org/internet/history-internet/brief-history-internet/

INDEX